Teaching Happiness and Well-Being in Schools

ONE WEEK LOAN

Also available from Continuum

Promoting Children's Well-Being – Edited by Andrew Burrell and Jeni Wragg
Future Directions – Diane Carrington and Helen Whitten
Emotional Intelligence and Enterprise Handbook – Cheryl Buggy
Winning the H Factor – Alistair Smith with Sir John Jones and Joanna Kurlbaum

Teaching Happiness and Well-Being in Schools

Learning to ride elephants

Ian Morris

network
continuum

Continuum International Publishing Group

The Tower Building   80 Maiden Lane, Suite 704
11 York Road   New York, NY 10038
London, SE1 7NX

www.continuumbooks.com

British Library Cataloguing-in-Publication Data
A catalogue record for this book is available from the British Library.

ISBN: 9780826443038 (paperback)

Library of Congress Cataloguing-in-Publication Data
Requested by publisher

Typeset by YHT Ltd, London
Printed and bound in Great Britain by Bell & Bain Ltd, Glasgow

Dedication

For Georgie and Olivia, the most
important people in my life and for
my parents, who taught me how
to find important things in the first place.

Contents

Foreword by Richard Layard

This is a remarkable book and it reflects a remarkable change that is happening in our culture. Throughout human history people have wanted to be happy and happiness has been a central theme in literature. But in education? Not really.

The reason is partly that education is about systematic knowledge, and systematic knowledge about happiness has been a late developer. For 300 years modern science has increased our understanding and mastery of the external natural world – and this has led to the astonishing economic growth we have experienced. Material wealth-creation is easy to measure and it has taken centre stage in our civilization and in much of our education.

But it remains to understand and master ourselves. Fortunately in the last 30 years psychology has turned to this vital task. That is what has made this book possible, and it also provides the foundation for a new culture in which the quality of our subjective experience becomes the test of our progress as a society.

Of course much of this new knowledge supports (from the strongpoint of empirical science) the wisdom of the ages. So this book draws on the wisdom of the Bible, of the Buddha and of the Greeks as well as modern science. And it puts them together in a delightful way – including hundreds of practical hints for the conduct of lessons.

The book is based on the author's own experience of teaching these lessons at Wellington College. When Anthony Seldon became head of the school, he took the enormously brave decision to introduce these lessons, with Ian Morris in charge. Gloomsters predicted a backlash. But in fact it has been a huge success, both with students and their parents.

For this is what young people want. They want to be happy, not in a selfish way (since selfishness produces misery) but because being happy is the true mark of human flourishing. The government has now begun to realize this and made the teaching of well-being an integral part of the national curriculum in England and Wales. For teachers of that curriculum, this book will be a god-send.

I hope it will be widely used around the world and contribute greatly to the spread of human happiness.

London, January 2009.

1 Learning to train elephant riders: teaching techniques for happiness and well-being

Chapter preview

- Why learning to ride elephants?
- Full catastrophe teaching
- Teaching well-being: the process
- Some ideas for teaching happiness and well-being
- Teachers and well-being
- Whole-school well-being

I'd like to begin by asking you to imagine that you are about go for a journey on the back of a magnificent, big-eared, African elephant. Having climbed onto his back, you are sitting astride him, your legs resting against his thick, wrinkly skin and your hands upon his shoulders. You don't know the elephant, but the guide assures you that he is good natured and that he likes humans. You set off: just you, alone on top of your elephant, following on behind a procession of other elephant riders. Pretty soon you get used to the elephant's lumbering rhythm: the movement of his shoulders, the swaying of his head and trunk, the bellows-like swell and shrink of his flanks as he breathes beneath you. You lift your head from your elephant's neck and begin to notice the other riders – some seem steadier than you, others seem less secure, some are ecstatically happy, others are nervous and seem to cling on to their animal for dear life. You're happy with your first attempt at elephant riding.

Then you begin to think about your destination and suddenly realize that you don't know where you are going. You try to look to the head of the procession, but amidst the clouds of dust kicked up by giant feet and the swaying, colourfully clothed compatriots ahead, you realize that the guide you had assumed to be at the front, might not be there after all. You start to get concerned. You look around nervously, but nobody else seems to share your fears: the lady behind you smiles and waves. Your mind rushes on to thinking about how to stop the elephant to get off. The guides all spoke Swahili to the elephants. You don't speak Swahili. You don't even have reins to make him change direction. It dawns on you that this elephant is out of your control. All the while, he plods along ten paces behind the elephant in front, keeping perfect step, following the route set out for him. It eventually strikes you that the elephant knows exactly where it is going: all you have to do is relax and let him carry you there.

Why learning to ride elephants?

The metaphor of riding elephants comes from Jonathan Haidt's book *The Happiness Hypothesis* and it is a metaphor which helps to illustrate the purpose of teaching happiness and well-being. Haidt explains in his analogy that the key to successful animal riding is a harmonious relationship between the animal and its rider. In order to guide an elephant to where you want to go, you have to be able not only to know your destination, but also to understand the elephant and all of the little aspects of elephant behaviour which might lead to your journey going wrong. You also have to be able to trust that, in certain circumstances, the elephant knows best and allow yourself to be guided by him.

For Haidt, the elephant and its rider is a metaphor for being human. The rider, the small component attempting to control everything, represents the conscious, thinking self. The elephant, the vast, powerful set of forces which the rider is attempting to control, represents everything else: all of the myriad unnoticed processes of the brain and all of the extraordinary panoply of events which take place in the body:

> Our minds are loose confederations of parts, but we identify with and pay too much attention to one part: conscious verbal thinking . . . Because we can see only one little corner of the mind's vast operation, we are surprised when urges, wishes, and temptations emerge, seemingly from nowhere . . . We sometimes fall into the view that we are fighting with our unconscious, our id, or our animal self, but really we are the whole thing. We are the rider, and we are the elephant.[1]

Teaching happiness and well-being is about trying to help children to bring the elephant and rider into one harmonious whole, as Haidt describes above. Our mistake is often to believe that the rider, the conscious thinking self, holds all the answers, is the master in all situations and always knows best. The aim of teaching happiness and well-being is to teach the rider, not only about himself, but also about the elephant that he rides. Many people go through life experiencing an antagonistic relationship between, metaphorically speaking, the elephant and the rider and this antagonism is the source of psychological and physiological problems. If we can provide young people with an elephant rider's manual, in other words, if we can teach them how they function as humans and then teach them how to be not just functioning humans, but excellent ones, we might be able to help them to avoid many of the pitfalls that arise either from a rider that tries to exert too much control, or from a runaway elephant.

Full catastrophe teaching

'. . . education needs to be more than just the accumulation of knowledge, whether scientific, technical, historical, or whatever. It should really be education in how to be.'[2]

Traditionally, much of the type of material that this book covers has been found either in a minuscule proportion of the curriculum, in the work of the pastoral tutor or guidance counsellor, or has come incidentally as the result of good teachers who role-model the skills of elephant riding. It has had to compete, as the above quotation from Matthieu Ricard indicates, with the acquisition of skills and qualifications for the workplace or for university entrance, rather than the skills of being human that are needed once students get there.

Where it has come as part of the curriculum, it often follows a disaster model of education: in other words, the worst-case scenario is presented to the students along with the different ways of avoiding it. For example, drug and substance misuse education often focuses on the worst case scenario: addiction to drugs such as heroin or crack cocaine, usually coupled with crime, homelessness, prostitution or death. Similarly, sex education will focus on teenage pregnancy and the transmission of sexually transmitted infections (with gruesome pictures). Whilst it is important for young people to be aware of the risks that lie in the world around them, the ultimate dangers should not be the *focus* of education, because they simply will not affect the majority of students.[3]

Apart from this, full catastrophe teaching doesn't have a useful philosophy behind it, as it simply teaches young people that the world is a dangerous place which will do them harm and this is not the world that they will come to experience. Because of the focus on preparing children for the worst-case scenario, we can neglect to educate them in how to achieve the best-case scenario; we neglect to systematically teach them the skills of how to be successful as human beings – how to create and sustain meaningful relationships, how to find and develop what they are good at, how to care for the body and the mind. We have to turn the disaster model on its head and teach children what it means to flourish – teach them how to be competent elephant riders, how to be excellent human beings; not try at all costs to safeguard the elephant so much that the rider becomes bored and frustrated, or to allow the elephant complete free rein to do as it pleases.

Teaching well-being: the process

Teaching well-being is not quite like other academic disciplines: whilst the skills acquired through academic study are in constant use, it is possible for the concepts learned to exist in the mind alone, divorced from application and experience, where they can eventually cease to exist through lack of use (can you remember everything you crammed for your finals?). Well-being is different, as it relates directly to experiences that students will have in their everyday lives. It is possible to teach all *about* well-being to our students, but that would be to miss the point. The teaching of well-being must have *experience* as its primary aim: we should be teaching the students *how* to be well, how to *do* well-being. In order for this stuff to work, we have to get the students to experience it. If you are teaching about the benefits of exercise, you have to get the students to do some exercise so that they can see those benefits for themselves. If you are teaching cognitive skills (such as those on resilience), you have to get the students practising them and applying them in real-life situations: it is no good just talking about it or handing over a worksheet.

Teaching well-being involves students in a very simple three-stage, cyclical process:

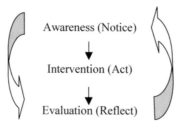

Awareness (Notice)

↓

Intervention (Act)

↓

Evaluation (Reflect)

The process starts with awareness, or noticing: asking the students to simply notice things about themselves and about the world around them, including other people. The sources of this noticing will be very broad and will range from becoming aware of changes in the mind or the body brought on by positive or negative states such as flow or sadness, to noticing body language in others or things in the natural or man-made world. This is the primary skill in well-being: it is the alert system which tells us that things are going well or things are not going well, it is the audit or the stock-take we need to do to realize we have to make changes in our lives. In many cases, students will have to be taught what to look out for; they will need to be shown when their body is telling them something is wrong, or when the body language of others tells them they have made a social mistake. Noticing is a skill that has to be learned and it arises from stillness and patience: if we are constantly bombarded by sensory noise, or we do not stop from one thing to the next, we will not notice things about ourselves or others.

The second stage is the intervention, or action which will enable the students to flourish; these are the practical things, after noticing, that the students need to learn to do to keep themselves healthy and happy: they are the doctor diagnosing and prescribing. The interventions and the evidence that supports their use form the backbone of the rest of the book.

The third and final stage in the process is evaluation and reflection: how well did the intervention work? Students must get into the habit of tuning in to the effects of interventions such as practising gratitude, getting into flow or doing exercise: how does it affect the mind and body? How does it affect relationships? How does it affect progress? It is this part of the process where the students must act as 'self-scientists' and evaluate the effectiveness of the treatment they prescribed for themselves in stage two. Students must be willing to accept both that an intervention didn't work, and that it did: especially if it's an intervention (such as watching less television) which they might not in the first instance enjoy prescribing for themselves. Journals are an essential part of this process: students must be encouraged to reflect meaningfully on the effectiveness of interventions.

At the end of this process, students should be able to have the following internal dialogue:

> 'I know when something helpful/unhelpful is happening in my life. I know this because . . .'
> (Noticing)
>
> 'When X is happening in my life, I know that I have to do Y.'
> (Acting)
>
> 'I know how successful Y is because . . .'
> (Reflecting)

Some ideas for teaching happiness and well-being

Teaching well-being is in many ways just like the teaching of other subjects, but with one important difference. The subject is *directly* about the students and about being human, rather than being about ideas by and large at some sort of remove from them, which then have to be translated back into something relevant. The aim of the subject is to allow students to experience something that they can then put into practice in their own lives. There are a variety of strategies that can be employed in devising a well-being curriculum,[4] but the guiding principle should be that the students first *experience* the ideas at first hand and then *reflect* on their usefulness for them.

Experiencing techniques

There is the hackneyed but true saying about getting someone to *do* something being the best form of teaching, and experiencing is a vital strategy for the teaching of well-being. Unless students have an opportunity to *feel* how the subject can affect them, it is of lesser value and all they are left with is an intellectual grasp rather than one that is embedded in the core of their being.

The lab

The idea behind this teaching technique is to ask students to play the role of 'scientist' and test out the theories that you suggest to them using the simple process of observation, hypothesis, testing and reflection. Let's take the example of teaching mindfulness as a way of dealing with stress. The students need to connect with the concept of stress. I often use clips of Basil Fawlty losing his temper, and there are plenty of great examples in film. The aim is to create a resonance: do the students recognize this behaviour? The next step is to prescribe a cure. Ask the students for ideas and perhaps suggest meditation if it does not arise from their examples. Do some meditation and ask the students to think about whether this might help to relieve stress. Ask them to test the hypothesis that meditation lowers the symptoms of stress by practising it between lessons for homework and writing up their findings.

The students evaluate the usefulness of various well-being techniques and in this way equip themselves with techniques appropriate to them. This technique has to be open to the possibility that the students will reject the technique that you teach them, which is unusual for us as teachers as very often we require the students to accept *everything* that we teach them. This technique must also be open to evaluative discussion afterwards, where students discuss usefulness with each other and also discuss hurdles they encountered and how they overcame them. It is unusual for students to be set homework and then find in class the week afterwards that their teacher does not punish them for not doing it. I recently asked a well-being class to keep a gratitude journal for a week: half the class had not managed it. They were surprised when I wasn't annoyed and the penny dropped when I explained that *they* are experimenting with the usefulness of these techniques: if it doesn't work, don't use it.

If it is hoped that students will adopt the skills of well-being, they should be given every opportunity to practise and experiment with them. Just reading through a worksheet once on the benefits of altruism will have little effect: getting the students to practise a random act of kindness and write about the effect it had will raise their chances of using that skill more frequently.

Game playing

Game playing is a great way of bringing a difficult concept to life through experience and it is of course something that comes naturally to us as humans. Game playing provides an opportunity for experiential learning which can help students to understand a concept in a different and fuller way than just by using the intellect: it can make a concept a lot more visceral. There are some excellent books available with some very good ideas for games in them which can be used either as ice-breakers or warm-ups, or have more specific value for well-being lessons.[5]

Making

Want to show students how their emotional brain works? Why not get them building brains out of brightly coloured modelling clay? Want to teach them about gratitude? Get them to write thank you letters. Want to teach them about flow? Get some musical instruments into the classroom and get them to make a noise. This advice is not just for the younger children: we may think that those surly 16 year olds just want to sit and watch videos, but they love playing just as much as 6 year olds. Every 'making' exercise is valuable because it offers students an opportunity to become immersed in a simple task which has important implications for their own under-standing of being human. The lesson will stick with them for longer too. I still refer to the image of a brain I made out of a bagel, some sweets and a piece of broccoli in a lesson taught by a colleague, to remind me of the organs involved in emotional decision making.

Re-enacting experiments

Much of our understanding of human well-being comes from experiments conducted in the world of the psychologist's lab and some of these experiments lend themselves nicely to being re-enacted with students. With a bit of preparation and the use of 'confederates' (students whom you use as stooges), very important lessons can be learned by students about themselves and how they are prone to act in certain situations. They can be a great way of highlighting to students some of the hurdles that we have to overcome in order to enjoy well-being fully.[6]

Drama and role-play techniques

The use of drama and role play has been popular in teaching for years for obvious reasons. One of the key problems that drama techniques face is that of authenticity and when using drama, it is important to set certain standards of preparation and performance to avoid the inevitable descent into painful attempts at humour and entertainment.

When taken seriously, one of the best techniques to use is called Forum Theatre. This was developed by an Argentinean theatre practitioner called Augusto Boal in order to put oppressed Latin American people back in touch with the issues that governed their lives. The basic idea is to create a short piece of theatre; a story which is acted out by a cast. The piece ends on some kind of cliff-hanger decision and the audience is then invited, via a compère called the 'joker', to decide what should happen next in the story, or in fact to make changes to the earlier parts of the story that might impact the outcome. Audience members are invited to take the place of cast members and the story is re-enacted to see if a different outcome is possible. Obviously this is something of an undertaking, but elements of this technique can be used in short lessons. 'What happened next?' is a particularly useful technique for the classroom and invites dialogue and discussion of key ideas that you may have been exploring. For example, a group could stage a conflict and the audience could be invited to suggest solutions to that conflict based upon techniques that you have taught them.

Role play is extremely important for getting students to develop empathy; one of the most important skills that we can teach our young people. The more it is used, the better it gets and if groups are particularly proficient, they can be used to teach children in lower years.

Reflective techniques

As mentioned above, reflection is a vital component of a life lived well and students should be taught to reflect, but not to dwell, as soon as possible. How many times do we find ourselves wondering why students (and indeed colleagues) don't stop and think before they do X, Y or Z? Reflection is a skill that helps to insert that all important punctuation between events.

Reflection should be distinguished from rumination. If we reflect upon an event, we study it and draw lessons from it with a view to making changes or resolutions. Rumination is dwelling: it is rarely productive and usually leaves situations unchanged. Reflection leads to the skill of meta-cognition: thinking about thinking. Many of the advances that a person makes in their life come from reflecting on who they are and how they can change that for the better in the light of learning something about how humans function.

Keeping a journal

Keeping a journal between well-being lessons is vital. Each well-being lesson should end by setting a 'reflective exercise' where students are encouraged to write about their experiments with particular well-being techniques using 'the lab' method, or perhaps to make notes on things that they notice about themselves, about others and about situations. For example, if you are teaching about the benefits of altruism, ask the students to practise a random act of kindness between lessons and write about how it felt afterwards compared with some other form of pleasurable activity such as eating chocolate. If you are teaching about emotions the following week, ask students to notice their emotional states, what causes them, what physical symptoms accompany them and how they move out of that state.

But why do they have to write? Research conducted by James Pennebaker[7] has suggested that writing about the events in our lives, particularly bad ones, can make us healthier. But it's not just any old writing; it's writing that makes sense of the event that counts – simply venting spleen or letting off steam is not helpful as it encourages us to rehearse the negative event rather than the more constructive approach of trying to find explanations that enable us to prevent those events from happening again. In processing our thoughts by turning them into written language, it can help us to structure our ideas and learn important lessons from them. Of course, there will be some children whose faces fill with dread at the prospect of writing, but you may find that by giving them an exercise that is about them and that will not be graded, they overcome that fear and grow to enjoy the exercise.

Sharing

An exercise related to the keeping of a journal is that of sharing ideas through anonymous feedback. Students' learning is often moved on most when they are exposed to what their peers are capable of. By asking students to share some of the reflections from their journals and by getting other students in the group to read them out anonymously, you can often visibly see eyebrows raise and heads nod as peers absorb ideas that are often not shared. For example, I observed a lesson with 14 to 15 year olds once, where the students had been asked to write about the experience of striking up a conversation with someone they didn't know well at school. They emailed their observations to the teacher who then printed them off anonymously and handed them round at random. When it came to the more astute observations, you could see how much the others in the group were learning from realizing that one of their peers saw the world in this way. It was very moving. The anonymity also guarantees safety for individuals and doesn't put anyone on the spot.

Discussion

All good lessons are based upon the gently guided, but free flow of ideas through dialogue. What is important to well-being is that the students are given the opportunity to discuss their experiences of implementing these techniques into their lives and that they are allowed to be constructively critical of them. The subject stands or falls by whether or not students feel as if they are being indoctrinated or preached at.

Discussion can be led in myriad ways: you can work it in pairs, small groups or whole class. You can provide fixed structure through questions that have to be answered. You can use Edward de Bono's thinking hats method, which restricts the type of discussion in order to solve thinking problems fully.

Stimuli

Complex ideas are often best brought to life by a short clip from a film or from a TV programme, a piece of music, a piece of art or an excerpt from a book. There are some unrivalled characters in comedy who exemplify much of what we try to teach in well-being, not least of which is John Cleese's portrayal of Basil Fawlty in 'Fawlty Towers'. Every topic that is covered in well-being classes will have some kind of resonant clip available to it in the world of film: just keep your eyes peeled and remember to have some kind of recorder ready. Alternatively, most broadcast material seems to appear on YouTube or GoogleVideo sooner or later as do some more inventive approaches to film making.

Anything that is visual and engaging can be used to tease out the kind of ideas that a well-being course ought to explore and very often the students are the best source of ideas for things that can be used to enlighten a particular topic.

Scenarios

A very effective way of enabling students to discuss 'real-life' situations is the use of scenarios: give them a very short situation and ask them to speculate upon why the characters did what they did and, also, what they would do in that situation and why.

Biographical learning

Learning from others is a very important human skill and young people seem unusually prone to not heeding the advice of others and to repeating other people's mistakes. This is part of being human and part of growing up, but if learning from others can be made an integral part of someone's outlook on life, and indeed of their character, some of those silly mistakes might be avoided.

As the aphorism goes, there is nothing new under the sun and you can be sure that for anything that you want to teach as far as well-being goes, there will be examples of it and you don't have to be an avid reader of biography to stumble across them (although it can help). Sunday supplements often have fascinating articles about individuals who exemplify something we wish to teach: in April 2006, for example, the *Observer Magazine* ran an article on Jean-Christophe Lafaille, one of the world's greatest climbers, who died pushing himself to the absolute limit of what is possible. I have used his story to teach about the idea of challenging ourselves but also of retaining balance. 'Celebrities' provide some great examples of how to live or how not to live. Amy Winehouse is a good current (at the time of writing) example of someone tortured by substance misuse; her music reflects many of her troubles too and could be used to stimulate interesting discussion.[8]

Testing

I have left this to last as it is a thorny issue. Modern education is dominated by testing and students are rightly tired of it. Well-being classes should be a haven away from the pressures of preparation for testing where students can learn strategies for coping with pressures heaped upon them in other areas of their educational lives.

However, it is helpful to have some kind of measure that the students have made progress in their well-being classes, particularly if senior leaders are unwilling to allocate resources without empirical verification of the worth of something new, even if other areas of the curriculum do not have to justify their existence.

We should remember to ask ourselves why we are testing in the first place though. If it is being used to help the students to move towards leading more fulfilling lives, then it is worthwhile. If it is being used to justify our place in the school, I think that there are ethical problems with taking the students' time up to pursue what is essentially an ego-driven endeavour.

There are a number of tools for testing of 'happiness' out there, some of which are free to use on the internet,[9] others of which are widely available[10] and still others which require training and have a cost and a licence attached to them.[11] Most of these tests are what's known as 'self-reporting' measures, where the outcome of the test is essentially a subjective picture of what we think about ourselves at the time of the test. Others provide a more objective picture but may be more time-consuming to administer.

The best tests out there are those that give the students a better insight into themselves as personalities. In this respect, the VIA strengths test[12] is hard to beat as it gives students an understanding of what they are good at in terms of virtues and what they value, rather than being good at accomplishing certain tasks (e.g. playing scales on a violin). This is an insight that we rarely get.

In terms of summative (and also formative) assessment of the course, one approach could be a non-graded interview/Socratic dialogue where each student is given a particular well-being-related problem to solve and they have to apply what they have learned throughout their lessons to that problem. Because it is a dialogue between a student and their teacher, those who have clearly absorbed the materials and put them into practice can be congratulated and those who may not have been quite so sponge-like can be given some non-judgemental advice and hopefully helped to see that this stuff is relevant to them. The dialogue would take the form of a tutorial, rather than a check up and it is imperative that no grade is awarded, although a report could be written. Well-being should be exempt from the obsessive desire to quantify and grade that permeates education.

Teachers and well-being

'Teachers who are stressed, or demoralised, make poor role models for young people.'[13]

I was lucky enough to have had a lot of very good teachers at school. The best one, though, taught me English. I can't remember him ever losing his temper, or even getting frustrated. He turned readily to humour and a razor sharp wit that would cut through even the worst miscreant's behaviour: never through humiliation but simply by showing his challenger that continued misbehaviour was pointless. In fact, despite the fact that my English class had some real characters in it, I don't recall them ever being difficult, especially given what we did to some supply teachers. This teacher was fascinating: a master of accents when telling stories, provider of occasional snippets from his own life; but never so many that we thought him narcissistic and setter of great work that inspired us to do our very best. Praise came when it was merited; guidance and assistance was the alternative. There was never any ego, never any clash of personalities, just dialogue and enjoyment of the subject. His classroom was a place where creativity was encouraged and when trying to interpret a difficult text we always had room to voice our ideas and were gently guided towards something meaningful if we were a little bit off the beaten track.

This particular teacher was a very important role model for me. Not only did I learn the joys of interpreting text from him, but also a million and one little things about life which became lodged in my character. The best teachers are those who not only impart skill in a particular academic discipline, but also successfully and intelligently model the skills of being human.

Teachers leave a huge impression on the people that they teach and children are fascinated by them. They look not only to the leadership of their teachers in academic matters, but also to their leadership in social ones too. How many times have you seen students mimicking teachers that they either love or despise? How quickly do students notice the strange little peccadilloes that we have as teachers, the peculiar character traits that set us apart from our colleagues in the way we pronounce certain words, explain certain concepts, or even hold our posture at the board? That children will go to such lengths to imitate their teachers to win approval from their peers is a sure sign that, as teachers, we have an enormous influence over our students. When it comes to the teaching of happiness and well-being, perhaps more than any other subject, we have to be conscious of our status as role models.

Whilst there may be new content to teaching well-being that has developed over the last few years, some of the most important content has been happening in schools for years, where dedicated and excellent teachers show young people how to be skilled elephant riders: for example, how to excel at what they are good at or how to overcome adversity without incurring physical or psychological damage and hurt. It has been said that no matter what our discipline, we are all teachers of English: well, no matter what our discipline, we are all teachers of well-being too.

When I think back to the teachers that I most admire, they are the ones who resolved conflict patiently and with care; they are the ones who never raised their voices in anger at students; they are the ones who never humiliated students in a vain attempt to preserve their ego in front of the rest of the class; they are the ones who did interesting things outside school and they are the ones who took care of themselves and didn't drown in alcohol to get over a hard day at the chalk-face. Teaching is a testing profession, but as people responsible for teaching well-being, we must respond to those tests in a way that exhibits the behaviour we desire our young people to emulate.

If we are aspiring to use educational opportunities to inculcate important skills of well-being in our students, we must model those skills ourselves: this means, that for a school to take the teaching of well-being seriously, it must make sure that its teachers are given the opportunity to learn the skills of well-being through continuing professional development. An inspiring example of this in practice is Geelong Grammar School in Australia. In January 2008, almost all of the teaching staff and a good number of the school's support staff were trained for a week in the skills of resilience and Positive Psychology (resilience is explained in Chapter 6). The school then spent several months looking at how to incorporate the skills that the staff had acquired into every aspect of school life, from the entire curriculum to the letters it sends home to parents. Staff at the school have described this investment in the skills of the teaching and support staff as transformative. Where Geelong have really taken the lead is in realizing that there is little point in having happiness or well-being on the curriculum if it forms only a small slice of the experience the students have at school. Why teach students the skills of well-being if the work is going to be undone in other areas of their lives? Everywhere that every member of a school community turns, in every interaction, every system and every structure, they should see well-being reflected back at them. It is with this that we turn to the idea of whole-school well-being.

Whole-school well-being

Whilst few in the teaching profession would disagree with the premise that the improvement of well-being should be a function of education, I think that we should go further than that and argue that well-being should be the *primary* function of education and that all schools should be geared to the maximization of the flourishing of the students and staff that comprise them.

In a culture that is, at the time of writing, dominated by measurable outcomes, it is easy to lose sight of what the real function of areas of life such as health care and education really is. Education is about finding, drawing out and building upon the strengths of individuals and enabling them to excel. There are ways of measuring this, such as examinations, or winning places at universities, but these measures are incidental to what is being measured: excellence. In places, especially where the call to raise standards has been heeded too literally, the measure has become the driver and this is wrong. Exams are not going to go away and they serve an important function, but we should be bold and place well-being at the centre of education, not hidden away once a fortnight in a classroom.

With well-being at the core, there are six satellite principles which can help guide a school towards enabling everyone who belongs to the community to flourish. The diagram below helps to illustrate this:

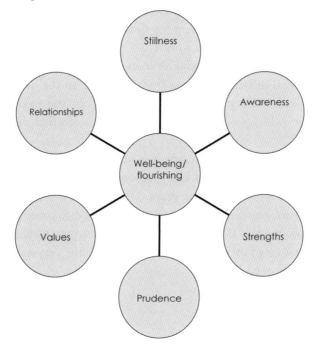

Stillness

Stillness is probably the most important feature to introduce into school communities. Schools are busy, hectic places and it is very easy to get swept along by that; to feel the need to *appear* busy; to rush from task to task and to feel guilty every time you stop. Teachers very often find that between the hours of 9 a.m. and 3.30 p.m. their blood pressure is higher than during the rest of the day. They may feel that they don't have time to stop. Chapter 10 looks at stillness and meditation in detail, but for the moment it is sufficient to point out three main benefits to be had from its practice:

1. Reduced stress.
2. Increased immune function.
3. Increased creativity.

There is an alarming and oft-quoted statistic that a male teacher who retires at 60, on average has a life-expectancy of 20 years, but a male teacher who retires aged 65 on average has a life-expectancy of 20 months. This statistic is probably apocryphal; however, the belief prevails that teaching is an unusually stressful occupation. Not only this, but one which causes illness. How often do teachers fall ill on the first day of the holiday? It doesn't need to be so. Schools must build periods of stillness into the day. Just practising deep breathing for three breaths begins a virtuous cycle of calm, which brings its own benefits with it.

Stillness is also important for taking time to reflect, for both students and staff. Far too often we find ourselves running from one thing to the next, without being fully present in each activity: constantly worrying about the next one or fretting about the last one (which went badly because you were worried about the way this one would go).

The first step on creating an atmosphere of sustainable well-being in schools is to introduce periods of stillness into every school day, something which has been happening in Quaker schools for many years. This doesn't have to be meditation, but it should at the very least be a structured time where everyone is expected to do nothing apart from be still. If we can introduce this into the lives of our colleagues and our students, it may provide a powerful antidote to the very modern problem of the unhealthily fast-paced life.

Awareness

Once we have taken the time to stop, we can become aware of things which we might not have previously noticed. Awareness is foundational to the successful functioning of individuals and of relationships because instead of, metaphorically speaking, rushing along with our head down and fixing our attention on nothing beyond the end of our nose, we stop, look up and take time to appreciate what lies within and around us. A person who is aware and who cultivates awareness not only understands who they are, but also takes the time to appreciate and understand who others are. You know instantly when you meet with a person who practises awareness: they listen to you and accept you fully. Schools do not always encourage the practice of awareness because so many demands are placed upon us and it is very easy to become fixated on the completion of 'tasks' to the exclusion of all else. This can be costly because by focusing solely on the task in hand, we can lose sight of other things of greater importance.

The practice of awareness is related to one of Tal ben Shahar's foundations of happiness: giving ourselves and others the permission to be human. As this book goes on to explain, there is often a great deal more to being human than meets the eye, simply because many of the processes which occur to keep us alive happen beyond the control of the conscious mind. This can sometimes leave us at the mercy of things we would much sooner have complete control over: those angry outbursts we regret;

being tired when we need to be alert; feeling uncontrollable desire; doing and saying things to preserve the ego and so on. As ben Shahar argues, we should live in accordance with the natural laws that drive us and if we don't, it's rather like trying to ignore the law of gravity: we do so at our own peril and we may very well imperil others.[14] If we become aware of how the human organism functions both physically and psychologically, we can make allowances for people when they get it wrong, which they inevitably do.

There is a flipside to this. Whilst we should be gentle to, and understanding of, those who need it, this does not mean that we should exercise indifference or laxity and allow people to sink to lowest common denominator levels of human behaviour. Humans are flawed: we have our foibles and we make mistakes, but humans also possess the remarkable skills of self-consciousness and reflection. We can step outside ourselves to examine what we have done in the past and make decisions about what we will do in the future; we are not trapped in an endless present moment like almost all other species. Humans also have extraordinary capacities such as compassion, kindness, ingenuity, creativity, courage and perseverance and we can place all of those capacities in historical context and learn lessons from them. We have to be aware of the great and diverse array of talents that we have as humans and we should encourage and expect ourselves and others to develop and display those talents. Therefore, awareness should not only be based upon the permission to be human, but also the expectation of humanity.

Values

Values, covered in more detail in Chapter 8, are essential to a sense of well-being because they tie in with our understanding of our self and of our purpose in life and they inform our behaviours. If we do not have a carefully mapped out set of values, we are like a small boat being thrown about on a choppy sea. Values anchor us to meaning and they help to give purpose to our lives. If I am a person without values, how can I progress as a human? I have nothing to test my dreams of the future against. I have nothing to measure my strengths and competencies against. A valueless life is an incomplete life.

It is not just individuals who must hold values, but communities too. The holding of values has been a feature of human communities for thousands of years. Values regulate behaviour and act as a compass with which people can orientate themselves.

But values cannot be imposed, as Moses discovered with the story of the Golden Calf in Exodus, where the Hebrews whom he had led to safety with the help of God rejected their new supernatural saviour and went back to worshipping idols as they had always done. The failing in that story was not of the sinful mass of pagans that Moses had dragged across the Red Sea: they were simply adhering to the values that had been passed on to them for centuries and to which they had allegiance. Moses failed because he unilaterally attempted to kill off well-loved gods and impose rules that the community of intelligent adults had not agreed to. Moses was, I think, acting on very poor advice.

Values must be agreed by communities. Schools should regularly re-visit their values and negotiate them with students, all staff, parents and governors.

If a school community decides to espouse certain values or virtues, then those values must be woven through the fabric of everyday life and opportunities to adhere to those values must be given. For example, the Cheney School in Oxfordshire recently took a stand on fair trade and sent a small group of students to India to source fair trade school shirts, rather than relying on shirts originating from sweat shops. If a school expects 'helping others' from its students, those students should have 'helping others' modelled to them by adults and peers, and opportunities for helping others should be provided: how can one know the gratification brought by altruism unless one has experienced it?

Values are also an important lesson in philosophy and philosophical thinking. A community might aspire to the value of 'tolerance of everyone's views' but only upon philosophical inspection will they find this value unsustainable. As Chapter 4 will show, philosophy can be a life-saver.

Relationships

Human life is about three basic relationships. Our relationship with ourselves, our relationship with others and our relationship with the outside world. To lead a happy life, we need to get these three relationships right and I would argue that in schools, the major agent of stress is people being unskilful in relationships.

I have often wanted to spend a day following the naughtiest child in a school around. Not because I have a morbid fascination with deviant behaviour, nor because I feel the need to pick up some hints and tips, but because I would like to see the treatment those children get from the teachers they interact with during a given day. My hunch is that most of those 'naughtiest children' are treated pretty badly by a number of adults. My hunch is that the moment they walk into a classroom, they are a marked child who gets treated quite differently to the other children. They probably get treated with suspicion and prejudice quite a lot. They probably get shouted at quite a lot too. And we wonder why it is that they play up. Faced with these miscreants and exhausted in the staffroom afterward, teachers suddenly become pretty right wing when referring to those children and start to talk about separating them out for special treatment in separate behavioural units. Those children are branded 'unteachable'. To be sure, some of them are. There are children who, in a classroom of 30, when faced with a curriculum they can't access, become problematic. This should not be a mystery or a surprise to us.

And this is precisely the moment that teachers start to feel like failures. Teaching is a funny profession: at once deeply, wholly social and extremely lonely and highly pressured. The drive for results and achievement, unskilful management by teachers not trained to manage other adults and resources stretched to bursting all contribute to teachers feeling undermined and de-skilled. In many schools, teachers do not treat each other with respect because the pressure-cooker-like atmosphere in the school, created by poor management, leads to suspicion, defensiveness and a lack of support for teachers who are struggling.

Schools are all about relationships. Human learning takes place in the context of a relationship: either with one's self, with another or with the environment. If (and with a tinge of sadness, I hesitate to use this expression) there is not *love* somewhere in that relationship, the learning will be defective in some way.

Teachers and students alike should all be taught about attachment theory, emotional function and management, the role of the brain in creating emotion and in learning, the role of the ego in causing problems in relationships, the importance of removing stress to enable learning; they should be taught how to empathize, they should be taught the importance of altruism and kindness, the importance of reciprocity in relationships. Schools must provide opportunities for all of these things to be taught and practised by students and teachers alike and, above all, love should not be a dirty word in education.

The topic of relationships is covered in Chapter 8.

Prudence

This word may seem a little bit outdated; like the word your grandmother might use when giving you financial advice. I have lifted it straight from Aristotle's *Nicomachean Ethics* and he used the Greek equivalent of this word to mean 'practical wisdom' or, in other words, anything which we *do* that is aimed at enabling us to flourish.

Human life is partially about striking balances between competing desires and interests, and very often in school life we feel as if we are compromising between the vast range of commitments that we have. If we get this balancing act wrong, we become unwell. If we rush around without time to take stock, we become stressed and our immune system stops fighting off illness as effectively as it might. If we do not have a range of facets to our relationships and make them only about achieving professional objectives, we will find life dull and unfulfilling. If we do not have interests outside the classroom (beware saying 'teaching is a way of life': it is not) do not be surprised if you feel hemmed in by your career, or that your life seems a little monochrome.

Practical wisdom involves taking a helicopter-eye view of your own life and recognizing areas that need a little attention. It takes as its first premise the idea that aspects of your life can be changed and encourages us to contemplate what we ought to change to make things go better. Schools that focus solely on the academic output of their students and staff are missing the point. Strong academic output is just one indicator of a healthy community that encourages and supports its members. We've all heard the scare stories of the league table and results-obsessed schools, which turn into pressure cookers for teachers and students alike, where people leave with great results, but are emotionally scarred in the process. Oliver James quotes this example in his book *Affluenza*:

> I became anxious and depressed from the age of thirteen. I was always worrying about other people's opinions: whether they liked me or thought I was attractive. If I do something less than perfectly I will think about it for quite a long time. It's petty, but in my mock GCSEs I got two As and the rest A*s. One of the As was in maths and I cried for so long. It was my best subject and I didn't get the top grade.[15]

Any environment which encourages an unbalanced outlook such as this is unhealthy. Similarly, schools with a high sporting profile which encourage their athletes to become obsessive about body shape and strength are allowing for disproportionate obsessions and laying the foundations for an unhealthy lifestyle.

Schools should be encouraging *everyone* who belongs to the community to learn about what it means to be fully human: to improve relationships, to develop a range of interests and abilities, to live healthily and to be able to manage adversity and stress.

Strengths

Education is *all* about our strengths: about finding out what we are good at and building our levels of skill in those areas and stretching ourselves out into new areas that are as yet uncharted. At least, it should be. Very often, teachers and students find themselves scared of getting out of their 'comfort zone': they rely on old habits and old ways of doing things which are tried, tested and safe, but which don't help them to make progress. Either that or they stretch themselves so far and so thinly, without support and guidance, that they become overwhelmed, de-skilled and de-motivated.

It seems obvious to state that we are at our best and happiest when we are absorbed in doing something and playing to our strengths by doing so – so why does education sometimes neglect to provide opportunities either to allow people to play to their strengths, or not equip them with the necessary skills they are expected to have when they do something new? We seem to treat strengths, in terms of both abilities and character strengths, as fixed and unchangeable: as if we are permanently equipped with them at birth. This is simply not true. Strengths are built over time by continued practice and we can acquire new strengths at any time of life. Communities should also be structured around celebrating strengths, not highlighting weaknesses and we should take time to find out what our colleagues and students are *really* good at: what do they love to spend every waking moment doing and how can we mirror the experience they have doing that whilst they are in school?

The development of strengths is dealt with in detail in Chapter 7.

With an idea of what the teaching of happiness and well-being might look like and with a description of the setting in which we might find it, it is time to look at what sort of material might be taught.

2   Happiness

Case study: Lawrence and the fox

I didn't expect to find happiness in a builder's van at 7a.m., with a cup of tea and a roll-up, parked next to a small lake of cow-pat on a farm in Wiltshire, with a bloke called Lawrence, but I did. It was early February in 2000 and I had graduated from university seven months earlier with a degree in Theology. Because I had dallied and dithered with career decisions, I had to wait for 12 months before I could start teacher training, so I decided to live at home for a year and do whatever work I could find. After a couple of months serving behind a bar, I ended up working as a labourer for a fencing company, which is how I found myself sitting in the cab of a Transit van with another man so early in the morning.

My two favourite times of year are early autumn and early spring. There is a cold crispness about everything and the world seems as if it has been brought into sharper focus. This particular morning there was a thick hoar-frost on the ground and a bright white winter mist. It was very cold. Lawrence and I were keeping ourselves warm in the van, sipping our tea and pulling on our cigarettes before we started work for the day.

I liked Lawrence. He was about ten years older than me and had spent his life doing this kind of work. He was physically lean, sinewy and very strong indeed. He was someone for whom school had been a difficult place and when he left aged 16 he had few qualifications and a lot of bad advice. He took drugs of various sorts recreationally every weekend and this affected his mood, which could be unpredictable. He was on the vulnerable side, but also robust and a man of great integrity. He was also gentle and a very fine teacher. We spent three months working in difficult conditions together to build a fence that was over a kilometre long, so we saw the best and worst of each other.

Normally we just sat in the van, looked outside and didn't say very much, but today we were talking about how beautiful the day was. There was a lull in the conversation. We sipped our tea, drew on our cigarettes and in that moment of silence, a fox skipped across the brittle whitened grass about 50 yards in front of us. She was deep russet orange with a bright white underbelly. As she came in front of the van, she stopped and looked right at us. We both held our breath and stayed still and silent. In that moment the three of us were locked together in attention the one to the other. The fox nonchalantly turned and trotted off across the field and into the mist.

Just thinking about that moment, which Lawrence and I swore never to forget, I am moved almost to tears. For several seconds both Lawrence and I were overwhelmed by a scene of deep natural beauty and peace and what made it a moment of greater meaning for us both was that we had appreciated it together. This moment of my life, which will be similar to moments that you will have had, is important to illustrate the meaning of happiness and well-being as I intend to use them throughout this book.

Lawrence was not totally happy. He took drugs to mask his feelings of unhappiness and his infrequent bursts of anger revealed a person who was at the mercy of turbulence and yet in that moment he was overwhelmed by the sight of the fox and was unusually open about the way that it had moved him. What Lawrence and I felt in that moment was conditional: if the fox had not been there, if it had been raining rather than crisp and frosty, if one of us had been ill or hungover we probably would not have been moved in the way that we were. Despite a feeling of profound 'happiness' that morning, Lawrence would have felt the need later that day or that week to take drugs to feel better: the moment was fleeting for him. True happiness and well-being are not conditional; they are states that are present regardless of what happens around us. The mistake that we often make is to confuse happiness with *pleasure*. Pleasures are conditional states that come and go. True happiness and well-being in this sense are like the proverbial house built on rock – steadfast and capable of withstanding assault; whereas pleasures are like their counterpart founded on sand – shifting and subject to the mercy of changing conditions.

The nature of happiness

In the Western world there are misconceptions of what happiness is. We come to believe that true happiness lies in the meeting of certain conditions: 'I will be happy if . . . I own that car/I get that promotion/I meet that person', or we are given to believe that happiness lies in the transformation of social or political circumstances: 'We will all be happy if such and such a government is elected or removed/if such and such a policy is changed/when the Messiah comes.' We are also given to believe that happiness results from an absence of certain things – drug addiction, promiscuity, teenage parenthood, poverty and so on – and much personal and health education, especially in the UK focuses on flagging up the huge hazards of life to students and telling them how to avoid them. I would argue that at a fundamental level, these ideas of happiness are mistaken and that it is a mistake to encourage young people to follow in these footsteps too.

We can all call to mind stories of people who even when confronted with extraordinary adversity seem to retain an aura of happiness and contentment. Regardless of the fact that they have suffered some huge physical or emotional injury they engage in life without succumbing to depression. These people are living proof of the idea that external conditions should not *necessarily* hold the key to our happiness, well-being or lack thereof. If we make our happiness or well-being conditional on external circumstances, we become like an unanchored boat in a harbour, bashing its way around at the mercy of the sea.

The language of literature on happiness, much of it from those heaving shelves of 'self-help' books, is quite misleading. We often see books with titles such as *The Secrets of Happiness* or *The 10 Steps to Happiness* or *The Easy Way to Lasting Happiness*. These book titles play to our wishful thinking that happiness is just within reach of a little bit of esoteric knowledge or is attainable if only we did certain things. But the truth of finding real happiness, as research is showing more and more, involves changing bad thinking habits that we probably picked up in childhood and which we cling on to out of a desire to preserve our fragile egos. The journey to lasting happiness is precisely that: it is a journey, not a destination. One of the Buddha's oft-quoted pithy sayings is 'people often ask me "what is the way to happiness?" and I reply "happiness is the way"'.

The secret to happiness and well-being lies within and in our own self-awareness and attitude to the world that surrounds us. Happiness begins with us and remains with us and in our own efforts, and of course it can only ever be so, as the external world is unpredictable: as Seneca wrote in his letter to Marcia, 'the only thing that you own is the capacity to control your own mind'. Matthieu Ricard, the Buddhist monk, expands upon that idea a little more in his dialogue with his father, the French philosopher Jean-François Revel, when he defines suffering:

> Suffering arises when the self, the 'me' that we cherish and protect, is threatened, or doesn't get what it wants. The most intense physical sufferings can be experienced in very different ways depending upon our state of mind. Moreover, ordinary goals in life, like power, possessions, the pleasures of the senses and fame, can

procure temporary satisfaction but are never permanently satisfying. One day or another, they're bound to turn into sources of unhappiness. They can never bring lasting fulfilment, or an inner peace untouched by outer circumstances. Pursuing such worldly goals all our lives, we have no more chance of attaining true happiness than a fisherman has of catching fish by throwing his nets into a dry riverbed.[16]

Happiness in the ancient world

A great deal of the writing on happiness and well-being, be it ancient or modern, focuses us on the states of mind that we must cultivate to bring it about. The two richest seams in ancient writings appear to come from the Buddhist tradition and the thinking of classical philosophers such as Aristotle, Seneca and Epicurus. Buddhism, with its focus on mindfulness, aims to teach us to take control of our minds and extend feelings of loving kindness to all beings. The ancient philosophers similarly focus on training, but this time in training the character. For Aristotle, who has inspired much of the work on happiness and well-being, happiness, or *eudaimonia*, consisted of a long process of learning how to be fully human, learning how to flourish. This understanding of happiness both as a state of mind and as a process can often appear radically different to the hedonistic focus on pleasure that our consumer culture would have us believe in, as Richard Schoch points out:

> Deaf to the wisdom of the ages, we deny ourselves the chance of finding a happiness that is meaningful. We've settled, nowadays, for a much weaker, much thinner, happiness: mere enjoyment of pleasure, mere avoidance of pain and suffering. Somewhere between Plato and Prozac, happiness stopped being a lofty achievement and became an entitlement.[17]

Happiness and Positive Psychology

In the last few years, there has been an explosion in publishing on this topic and much of it coincides with the growth of Positive Psychology – the modern academic discipline sparked into life by Martin Seligman in America in the mid-1990s. Seligman, upon assuming presidency of the American Psychological Association, announced that psychology had been obsessed with human misery for too long instead of looking at what makes humans flourish.

Positive Psychology has since yielded some fascinating pieces of research that show that there are certain key things we can do to increase the amount of happiness that we feel. Perhaps primary amongst these are Seligman's research on 'learned optimism' and Carol Dweck's research on 'mindset'. Both of these theories indicate that a significant barrier to happiness and fulfilment is the belief that there are conditions in your life that cannot be changed. This of course stands to reason: if we believe that we possess certain traits that we have inherited from our parents either genetically or behaviourally and if we believe that we can do nothing about those traits, our view of life instantly becomes more fatalistic and helpless: imagine two students who have just received a bad mark on a piece of work. The student who thinks 'Oops, I made a mistake on that piece, but if I take the comments into account, I'll do better next time' is much less likely to suffer from depression than the student who thinks 'I'm such a failure, I'm rubbish at this subject, and the teacher clearly hates me'. Seligman calls the latter view pessimism and Dweck calls it the 'fixed mindset'. Chapters 6 and 7 respectively look at the work of Seligman and Dweck and explore how their theories can be taught.

Martin Seligman has also come up with what has become quite a famous 'happiness formula'. The formula, where H = Happiness, S = Set point, C = Circumstances of your life and V = Voluntary activities, is as follows:

$$H = S + C + V$$

One of my best friends is the head of a physics department and nearly choked on his tea at the suggestion that this is a proper formula. It is really more of a recipe. Nevertheless, this formula arises out of years of detailed study and thousands upon thousands of research results. The basic idea is that happiness consists of a 'set point', in other words a component part of happiness relies upon your temperament, which is to an extent fixed at birth. Estimates of how much your temperament is set vary from 25–50 per cent and Seligman works on the figure of 50 per cent. How do they know this? The best way to find out how much of a person's character is set by their genetic make-up and how much by the circumstances of their lives is to study people who have identical DNA, but who have grown up in different places and been reared by different parents. One of the most fascinating studies done in the last century was that of identical twins who were separated at birth as it yields just these results. Jonathan Haidt relates an extraordinary story about a set of identical twin sisters:

> Raised outside London, [Daphne and Barbara] both left school at the age of fourteen, went to work in local government, met their future husbands at the age of sixteen at local town hall dances, suffered miscarriages at the same time, and then each gave birth to two boys and a girl. They feared many of the same things (blood and heights) and exhibited unusual habits (each drank her coffee cold; each developed the habit of pushing up her nose with the palm of the hand, a gesture they both called "squidging"). None of this may surprise you until you learn that separate families had adopted Daphne and Barbara as infants; neither knew of the

other's existence until they were reunited at the age of forty. When they finally did meet, they were wearing almost identical clothing.'[18]

Of course, if temperament is to varying degrees fixed by our DNA, we seem to have a contradiction with our earlier point about choosing our attitude to the world, which is made all the more ironic when we discover that Seligman is a self-confessed grouch. It is only contradictory if we fail to acknowledge the small role played by the circumstances of our lives such as poverty, ill-health or gender (only 10 per cent) and the significant role (40 per cent) played by voluntary activities: the things that we *choose* to do.

Why do the circumstances play such a small role? Surely the amount of money we earn, how good-looking we are, what job we do, where we live, what car we drive and so on are the crucial and fundamental guarantors of our happiness? Not so for two reasons: *habituation* and *the hedonic treadmill*. Studies done into people who lose limbs or become paralyzed and people who have won the lottery tend to show that within a comparatively short period of time, they become used to these changes of circumstance – a phenomenon known as habituation. I'm sure that you have experienced this about six months after Christmas when that lovely present you had longed for throughout the summer and autumn found itself unused at the bottom of the wardrobe? Humans get used to and adapt to changes in their circumstances very quickly and old patterns of behaviour re-emerge fairly soon.

The hedonic treadmill is the feeling we get after becoming habituated to a change in circumstances. It is the feeling of keeping up with the Joneses: we buy a 40-inch flat-screen TV, they buy a 45-inch flat-screen TV, suddenly that new 50-inch flat-screen TV seems so much more appealing than our minuscule and now obsolete 40-inch screen. As Jesus of Nazareth cleverly said in his Sermon on the Mount: 'Do not store up for yourselves treasures on earth, where moth and rust may consume them and where thieves may break in and steal them.' He might have added 'because you'll just get used to them and want something else to keep you amused or make you feel complete five minutes later'. This is discussed in greater depth in Chapter 9.

So, we are given a head-start or a hindrance by our genetic make-up and the beautiful objects we are tempted to acquire add nothing of significant value to our happiness. This brings us to the 'V': the voluntary contributions. What seems to be the advice on what we should do to improve our sense of happiness and fulfilment? Unsurprisingly, nothing our grandmother wouldn't have told us:

1. Practise mindfulness meditation (she might not have told you that).
2. Take care of the body: get sleep, exercise and eat healthily.
3. Work at establishing and maintaining positive and meaningful relationships with others.
4. Practise gratitude: actively be thankful for the people and things in your life.

5. Learn optimism and the 'growth mindset'.

6. Be altruistic: don't just help old ladies across the road, develop feelings of kindness to all.

7. Do what you're good at, in terms of both abilities (e.g. fixing cars) and your character strengths (e.g. standing up for justice) and develop new strengths.

8. Find the meaning and purpose of your life and do things which positively contribute to achieving this.

The rest of this book explains these ideas in more detail, including some of the research that has led to these findings. It also gives some ideas on how we might go about teaching this to others. But before that, a quick word on why we should be teaching this.

Why teach happiness?

One of the reasons that there has been controversy about the teaching of happiness and well-being in schools is quite simply that, for many, education is all about cold, hard, transferable skills and knowledge that gets us ready to go out to work; it's not about teaching children to be happy. My headmaster plays a fun game with people and audiences: he asks them two questions and gives them only 30 seconds to think about their answer. The first question is 'What do you most want for your children?' and the second is 'What is the point of education?' The answers to the first question usually revolve around ideas such as 'happiness', 'fulfilment', 'meaning and purpose'; the answers to the second question usually revolve around ideas such as 'discipline', 'knowledge', 'skills'. It seems strange that the answers should be so different doesn't it?

I think that this feeling of antipathy (and outright animosity from some) to the teaching of happiness and well-being arises from misconceptions about the nature of happiness. If we believe that happiness comes down to character traits, genetic dispositions and the conditions of our lives, then we will believe that there is no place for teaching it in schools, because *it cannot be taught*. If, on the other hand, we believe that happiness comes down to an attitude of mind that can be practised and certain actions that we can choose to perform, then we will see a place for it in education as we will believe that people *can be taught to be happy*.

I think also, that there can exist forms of Puritanism and elitism in education, where people are of the opinion that if kids aren't learning Greek or astrophysics through hard graft, then they aren't learning. I'm never entirely sure about this attitude, but I get the feeling that it usually stems from the bruised ego of the person who says it and that their endeavours to ensure the 'academic rigour' of education usually stem from a desire to project an image of intellectualism that may have been unfulfilled when they themselves were students. But we can all be armchair psychoanalysts can't we?

Education must not be afraid of teaching happiness and well-being to children, as it plays to these modern, Western prejudices that happiness is dictated to us by external circumstances and that happiness consists in pleasure, which, according to our cultural heritage, is inherently sinful. It also plays into a very narrow view of what it means to educate and what it means to be an educator. Happiness, in its proper sense has nothing to do with pleasure and instead has everything to do with character development and consistent, mindful attention to who we are and to our relationship to the world. If education and particularly education in England is not to get bogged down by constant change and political whimsy on the one hand and the desire for measures and exams on the other, it must seize the initiative and get back to being focused on what the purpose of education really is: that is, quite simply, to do what we would most want for our children; to help them to be fulfilled and truly happy. After all, surely that is their entitlement?

Putting it into practice: teaching about happiness

Before students get into the business of fine tuning the factors in their lives which will enable them to flourish, they need to get a good idea of where they are first, and this involves them evaluating the circumstances of their lives. Here are some ideas and resources for enabling them to do this.

- **Validated questionnaires**: visit www.authentichappiness.org. There are a number of questionnaires designed by psychologists which help to provide a detailed profile of how happy you perceive yourself to be. It is free to register and anyone can take these tests.
- **Reflection**: ask students to recall and write about a time when they felt truly happy. Ask for feedback from the group and see if patterns emerge from what they say.
- **The ingredients**: ask students to speculate upon what the ingredients of a happy life might be. Also see if they can work out what are 'happiness red herrings': things that we are given to believe will make us happy, but in fact don't.

Ingredients of the happy life: close relationships/friendship, accomplishment, optimism, education, health, altruism, meaning and purpose.

Happiness red herrings: e.g. lots of money, appearance/beauty, fame, living in a warm climate, having lots of possessions.

This should lead to discussion of the difference between pleasures and gratifications and that true happiness is usually to be found in things which cost nothing, or which involve personal engagement and effort.

- **Plan to flourish**: ask students to imagine themselves flourishing. What would it mean for them to be the best that they can be? What do they need to do to achieve this? How long will it take? What obstacles do they need to remove/overcome?
- **Lessons from others**: ask students to find out about the happiest person they know. What are the ingredients in their life that make them so happy? If possible, students should interview that person and write about what they discover.
- **Films**: everyone has their favourite film clip which examines the nature of true happiness. Here are three examples.

It's a Wonderful Life: a great example, particularly in the closing scenes, of a man realizing that all the ingredients he needs to be happy are right there in front of him.

Charlie and the Chocolate Factory (the Tim Burton version): clear examples not only of what makes you happy – relationships, love and support despite hardship in the case of Charlie – and what makes you unhappy – material goods and bad role models in the case of Augustus Gloop, Violet Beauregard, Veruca Salt and Mike Teevee.

Shrek: this explores the simple idea that true beauty has nothing to do with appearance and that happiness lies in engaging in challenges and struggles.

3

Learning to unite elephant and rider: caring for the human body

Chapter preview

- The human machine and harmony
- The elephant beneath us: the subconscious mind
- Keeping the body healthy: exercise and sleep
- Harmony with the outside world: the human body and the environment
- Choosing harmony: decision making and executive function
- Decision making and risk
- More than a machine: learning, love and attachment theory

The human machine and harmony

Nobody forgets their first car. Mine was a 1973 VW Beetle in British racing green and it cost me £900. I had dreamed of the day I would finally own my own car from a very young age and the moment when I handed over the cash and took hold of my first set of car keys in January 2000 was almost mystical. Up until that moment I had always driven my parents' cars, which were modern and reliable and could withstand the exuberant treatment meted out to them by a young man with pretensions of being a racing driver. I had no experience of the lighter touch needed for a car that was older than me and I also couldn't work out why a tank of fuel only seemed to last about 5 minutes in a car with only a 1300cc engine. Still, I drove that car as if it were a Porsche: wringing every last ounce of power out of it; racing along in the fast lane at 80 miles per hour and discovering the delights of power-sliding on gravel.

Soon enough though, things started to go wrong on me. First of all, the gearbox collapsed in on itself, no doubt as a result of the racing gear changes I had used in drag races at traffic lights. Then the carburettor needed to be replaced as my high-revving driving had dragged all sorts of impurities through the system and clogged it up beyond repair. So it went on: the 18 months that we were together were punctuated by frequent and expensive trips to the filling station and the workshop. My poor, aged car just couldn't keep up with being driven in the red.

Soon enough, the time came for me to trade the Beetle in for something with a bit more oomph: a GTI. I trundled my little VW along to a specialist in Norfolk in the hope that he would give me close to what I had paid for the car. He started examining it. 'Does the car shudder when you pull away?' 'Yes' I replied. 'That's because the clutch is knackered.' 'Oh' I said, my pride starting to bruise. 'Is there play in the steering when you drive along?' 'Yes' I said. 'That's because the steering box is knackered.' 'Oh' I said, a feeling of complete mechanical inadequacy beginning to creep in. 'Plus, the chassis is about to give up and, er, there's no oil in it. I'll give you £200 for scrap and parts.' 'Oh' I said, crestfallen, tail between my legs and thoroughly embarrassed.

The first and fundamental principle of well-being is that we must care for the organism that transports us around from place to place: the extraordinary human body. If we do not live according to the demands and limitations of the body we inhabit, we can expect things to start going wrong, just as my poor little VW began the slow and miserable descent towards the breaker's yard through being driven beyond its capabilities. The human body is organic and it is governed by laws of nature: to act in harmony with those laws of nature will increase our chances of being healthy and to act out of concert with those laws will dramatically increase our chances of developing ill-health.

Just as you would service a car, there are activities which we can choose to do which will enhance our body's chances of working properly. We will look at some of those in a moment. Just as you shouldn't constantly drive a car in the red, or, indeed, try to fuel it with pesticide, there are activities we ought to avoid to ensure that the body is working well; for example, excessive stress, consuming toxins (alcohol, tobacco smoke, etc.) and poor diet. Just as there are warning lights and mechanical indicators that something is wrong with a car, the body has an elaborate alarm system (called the somatosensory system) that tells us loud and clear when there is something wrong: in fact, for many of us, the only time that we *really* notice our body is when something is wrong with it.

The human body, if we reduce it down, is a biological machine the express evolutionary purpose of which is to replicate its own DNA through reproduction. Even if this aim is not achieved or not chosen, the survival instinct exists to make this happen. Staying alive requires our body to perform certain functions. The significant features are as follows:

- The taking in of energy and nutrients in the right quantity to enable movement, growth and regeneration of cells and move those nutrients to appropriate organs.
- The maintenance of the body's water content (about 72 per cent in men and 68 per cent in women).
- The taking in of oxygen for dispersal throughout the body's organs.
- The processing and expulsion of waste.
- The maintenance of the body's temperature: 37°C.
- Movement and exercise.
- The sensing and processing of information about the outside world (including alert to risk through the sympathetic nervous system and alert to benefit through the parasympathetic nervous system).

Machines need to be cared for to keep them working and the human machine at its most basic level simply needs fuel, exercise, shelter and rest and the ability to carry out associated processes, such as releasing waste and passing on its own DNA. So long as we act harmoniously with our body's express aims, our chances of living healthily are increased. Anything that gets in the way of meeting these basic needs is likely, in the long term, to lead to health problems. Before we look at what we can consciously do to ensure we remain healthy, it is worth briefly thinking about how the body does a pretty extraordinary job of this already.

The elephant beneath us: the subconscious mind

Just as with a car, there is a huge amount of activity in the human body that we don't know about and over which we exert little or no conscious control. In any given second, our brain processes a mass of information and executes scores of decisions and starts off myriad courses of action. So why don't we notice much of this happening? It is partly due to the brain's structure. Humans have what Paul MacLean has called a triune brain:[19] a brain which is in three parts but is one overall. At the core, is the reptilian brain, which controls basic life functions. Around this, sits the limbic system, which has a role in emotions and memory amongst other things. These two areas at the heart of the brain are responsible for doing many of the jobs that keep us alive, such as regulating organ function and getting us out of harm's way.

Many of the things that happen in our bodies and, indeed, many of the things that we do, happen subconsciously, especially in an emergency when the reptilian brain and limbic system take over completely. The emotions, for example, start off in the limbic system and in their early stages are beyond our control. I'm sure you've all see someone fly off the handle in a rage, or seen someone recoil with fear. These initial reactions are *autonomic*; in other words, the brain has systems which kick into action before we've even had time to think about it. This of course makes sense evolutionarily: the early humans who asked themselves, 'Oooh, is that a lesser or greater crested sabre-toothed tiger?' tended to survive less well than those whose bodies took over, flooded their muscles with adrenalin and got them running before they had time to think.

Provided we care for our brains by living healthily and provided that the brain hasn't suffered any disease or trauma, many of the processes that we take for granted will happen successfully without our noticing.

Putting it into practice: body awareness

- **Body-map**: get the students to team up in groups to produce a life-sized diagram of the body on large sheets of paper. They should represent what different areas do, suggest what we need to do to care for the various parts and also look at how different parts of the body affect each other. This can be an ongoing work of art that takes several lessons to complete as they compile evidence.

- **Under the radar**: ask students to briefly think about and list the processes that are happening in their body, which they do not usually think about.

- **Specifics**: ask the students to notice the functions of a particular part of their body over the course of a week. What does it do? What improves/reduces the quality of its function? Ask them to look out for particular phenomena, such as heart rate or perspiration and notice what affects it.

- **Audit**: pick an aspect of healthy living – diet, exercise, sleep, recreation and so on – and get students to compare what they are doing with what they should be doing. Are they getting enough sleep? Are they exercising enough? You will need to exercise caution here and be alert to the risk of body image problems. There may be students in your classes who already exert a high degree of control over diet and exercise and it is important to draw a distinction between what is healthy and what is about control and appearance. Get parents involved: let them know that you are doing this, assure them that there is no element of blame or confrontation, just awareness and ask them to help their children to audit themselves.

- **Toxins**: ask students to think about the different substances and activities that are toxic to flourishing. Get them to explain in detail what the effects of these toxins are. Students should then think about the cure for these toxins. How can they get them out of their lifestyle? Where will they need to go to get help and advice?

- **Films**: *Supersize Me* is a documentary about a man who tries to live on McDonalds' food for one month, to test their claim that it can form the basis of a nutritious diet. It is a very helpful way of exploring the importance of good diet and putting the right fuel into the body. *Thank You For Smoking* explores the cynical tactics used by the tobacco industry both to keep people in the dark about the adverse effects of smoking and to prevent themselves from being sued for failing to protect people from the ill-effects of tobacco smoke. It is helpful for looking at the toxic effect that cigarette smoke has.

Keeping the body healthy: exercise and sleep

There are some very basic, very simple things that we can *choose* to do that will greatly increase our chances of developing a harmony not only within ourselves, but with the outside world too. They are:

1. meditation
2. regular exercise
3. getting enough sleep
4. good diet
5. the avoidance of toxins (e.g. excessive amounts of either alcohol or stress)
6. harmony with the outside world.

Evidence to back this list up comes from a study published in *The Lancet Oncology* in 2008. This study suggested that a diet rich in fruit, vegetables, whole grains, legumes and soy products,[20] coupled with a regime of regular exercise and meditation contributed to lowering the risk of cancer by producing an enzyme called telomerase, which controls longevity and some immune cells.[21] Good diet, exercise, sleep and stress relief seem to be the key ingredients to enabling the body to function optimally and even though they are just the basic building blocks of a healthy life-style, getting them right has far-reaching consequences. For example, a study carried out by Bernard Gesch with young offenders showed that multivitamin and fatty acid supplements contributed to a reduction in offending of between 25 per cent and 37 per cent, whereas the control group demonstrated no such reduction.[22] Diet also affects learning, memory, coordination, the ability to be active and behaviour.

Young people can quite often find it difficult to get these basics right, as they manage the competing demands from school, family, the need for stimulation and excitement, restrictions on play and what their body wants, which changes from moment to moment during puberty. Healthy, harmonious living will not be an overnight process, because we have to temper young people's desire for experimentation and love of big flavour food with their long-term aim of not dying young. And the long-term aim will probably not seem as important as the short-term one. Let's face it, young people often like to experiment with things that aren't very healthy for them and no amount of telling them to eat five portions of fresh fruit and vegetables a day will stop them preferring pizza. I prefer pizza, but I also don't like acne or being overweight, so I don't eat it very often.

However, young people must be encouraged and helped to get enough sleep, eat properly, get enough exercise and take time out through recreation, play and relaxation: a number of the problems they face can be at the very least ameliorated by servicing the body's needs first. Through repeated experimentation, evaluation and reflection, hopefully young people will come to realize the benefits of a healthy lifestyle.

Exercise

Unfortunately, modern life in the Western world is not always conducive to keeping our bodies in the best shape. Most of our evolution finished tens of thousands of years ago when the human diet was meagre but varied and when exercise was a fact of life, not a leisure pursuit. It was easier to be healthy (in one respect at least) in the year 8000 BC. It was only the extremely rich who were able to indulge themselves to unhealthy levels. The 2008 film *Wall-E* explores the consequences of the modern Western lifestyle with characteristic Pixar brilliance. In the future, humans have filled the planet up with rubbish and so have built a vast space station to escape to. People travel around the space station on small hovering sofas and have little robots to provide for their every need. They are permanently entertained by a video projection just before their eyes with speakers just behind their ears. The result? Blob-like, amorphous, obese humans who have smaller ears, smaller fingers and who are barely able to stand upright. The lack of challenge and adversity also seems to have led to a dullness of intellect. Whilst this is a parody, there is quite a bit of truth in it. In the West, we enjoy surplus food and we don't have to cover vast distances on foot any more. Drugs can be taken to mask us from reality or we can bathe ourselves in the soothing cathode glow of the television. Being healthy is a lifestyle choice, not a natural consequence of living in accordance with our body's demands. Sure, in the ancient world, people were plagued by pestilence, famine and a lack of civilization, but, by and large, they lived according to their body's needs.

Research shows the importance of exercise to mental health and longevity. In a now famous and oft-cited study carried out in 2000 by Michael Babyak and others, 156 patients with major depressive disorders were split into three groups of 52. One group was prescribed medication (SSRIs) for their illness; another group was prescribed 30 minutes of exercise three times a week and medication; and the third group was prescribed just exercise (three times, 30 minutes weekly). After four months, all three groups' depressive symptoms had eased by 60 per cent. After ten months, however, out of the medication only group, 38 per cent had relapsed into depression, out of the medication and exercise group, 31 per cent had relapsed into depression and out of the exercise only group just 9 per cent of the 52 patients had relapsed into depression. The human body has evolved to move and be exercised, so not exercising the human body can have the same effect as taking a depressant. Physical exercise releases our body's reward chemicals (dopamine and serotonin), so by not exercising we are depriving ourselves of the body's system for creating pleasure. Exercise also prolongs life: insufficient exercise increases your chance of premature death by up to 50 per cent. It also turns out the younger you start, the greater the benefits against problems such as osteoporosis later in life as the musculo-skeletal system is strengthened through exercise.

What is not so widely known is the importance of exercise for improving brain function. When we exercise, the chemicals needed for creating and strengthening the connections between neurons in the brain are released, and when new connections are made in the brain, we learn. A number of schools in the US have introduced daily exercise programs for all students and the results have been dramatic: Titusville school went from being below the state average on standardized tests to being 17 per cent above it in reading and 18 per cent above in maths. Another school in Kentucky reduced its behavioural problems by 67 per cent. Exercise also increases the rate at which we can learn: German researchers found that people learn vocabulary words 20 per cent faster after exercise than they did before it.[23] However, as John Ratey argues in *A User's Guide to the Brain*, it is not enough to just go for a walk; we should engage in exercise which involves us developing a skill as well, as this stimulates the development of new neural connections. Activities such as climbing, dance and martial arts are excellent for this because of the complex and fine motor work required.

There is another important aspect to exercise and this is the role it plays in switching off our minds, or at least turning the volume down. It is not possible to have higher brain function whilst exercising vigorously, because blood is shifted away from the neo-cortex, making rumination and worry an impossibility. This insight is present in Eastern religions. Meditation plays a vital part in the Hindu and Buddhist traditions' vision of a fulfilled life, but it is always accompanied by physical move-ment. The physical movements in yoga were developed in the Hindu tradition and we have various martial arts such as Kung-Fu and Karate in the Buddhist tradition. These physical movements are basically stretching exercises designed to unite body and mind as it was realized that meditation is too cerebral: too much in the mind. Indian head massage plays a similar role. In households across India, the day begins with massage of various pressure points on the head and torso. Not only is this a gift of love, reminiscent of the grooming rituals we see in the animal kingdom, but also it helps to join body and mind at the start of the day. This takes place not just in the Eastern traditions. In the West, it has been noticed that some depression stems from patients being too 'cortical': spending too much time up in their own heads with their anxieties and touch therapies have been developed to try to overcome this tendency.

So, regular exercise (and the British government's current recommendation is 30 minutes vigorous exercise five times a week) can heal and prevent stress, anxiety and depression, it also makes us learn better and live longer.

Putting it into practice: exercise

- **Just do it**: there is only one way to appreciate the benefits of exercise and that is to feel them by doing it. Many students will already lead active lives, but some will be sedentary and can only get out of that if they taste the benefits of exercise.
- **Comparison**: students should be encouraged to exercise regularly and compare the effects with sedentary activities such as playing computer games and watching television.
- **Journal**: they should keep a journal of comparisons. They should also record changes in physiology and the effects on their emotions and academic progress.
- **Variety**: make it fun and vary the types of exercise.
- **Eliminate the competition**: encourage the kids to compete with themselves only. Many students hate exercise because they associate it with ridicule and failure: those who are good at sport sometimes do a good job of making the less sporting feel deeply uncomfortable.
- **Collaborate**: team up with your PE department to offer early bird or twilight exercise clubs. Target particular kids and get their parents on board.

Sleep

Another important contributor to health is sleep, and especially for teenagers coping with huge physical and psychological change. When I was younger, I was spectacularly good at sleep. My room mate at university was staggered by how much time I spent in the land of nod and he often said that if sleeping were an Olympic sport, I should represent Team GB. I would regularly sleep for more than 12 hours and sometimes, I'd even notch up an 18-hour snoozing bender. It got to the stage where I went to see my GP about it. Needless to say, he rolled his eyes and told me to discipline myself, although I was pleased to hear that the condition had a name: hypersomnia.

Sleep is vital, as it is our body's chance to rest from physical exertions. The mind also makes use of it to process the myriad experiences of the day, which it does through dreaming. If we deprive ourselves of sleep, it makes us uncoordinated and as unable to function as if we consume alcohol or narcotics, and in extreme cases will lead to mental illness. It is no accident that sleep deprivation has been used as a means of torture. The human body needs 8 hours sleep per day, although this need does decline as we get older. Children and adolescents require more sleep than adults as their bodies are in the process of so much change: a 5 year old needs 11 hours of sleep in a night and this need gradually declines to 8.5 hours needed at the age of 16; 13 year olds are still likely to need up to 9.5 hours of sleep per night.[24] Excessive sleeping (as I well know) can cause problems too: it has side-effects such as lethargy and headaches and it can lead to depression if the body's natural rhythms fall out of sequence with the natural rhythms of light and dark (see below); it can also be lonely sleeping in until 6 p.m. and writing essays through the night.

Sleep is also vitally important to learning. The results of a study published in May 2007 and carried out by researchers from Harvard and McGill universities show that a period of deep sleep is important for pattern recognition and it is suggested that Stage 2 sleep, which comes between rapid eye movement (REM) sleep and light sleep, can also help with learning motor tasks, such as playing a musical instrument or a particular move in sport. Healthy sleepers usually fall into deep sleep after about 20 minutes, so even a nap can help with our ability to make connections between ideas and learn things.[25] Avi Karni and Dov Sagi at the Weizmann Institute in Israel found that when they interrupted REM sleep 60 times in one night, the learning process was completely blocked, but that interrupting non-REM sleep just as often did not have the same effect.[26] Other research conducted by Allan Hobson shows that during sleep, memories are rehearsed by the brain, helping to strengthen connections made during the day. This is often why, upon waking, we are surprised by how much we have learned the previous day.[27]

Even though the body needs sleep, it can sometimes be impossible to drop off. There are a few things that can be done to enable sleep:

- Try not to consume stimulants of any kind in the hours before bedtime: caffeine should be avoided and it is surprising how many drinks and medicines contain it.
- Avoid using bright screens (laptops, television and mobile phones for example) just before bed: the light sends a signal to the brain that it is time to be awake.
- Get plenty of exercise during the day.
- Avoid situations that will irritate, arouse or wind you up before bedtime: being in a state of emotional alert makes it difficult for you to relax and sleep.
- Practise breathing and relaxation techniques once in bed: there are some excellent guided relaxation techniques available.

Putting it into practice: teaching about sleep

For obvious reasons, much of the learning about sleep will have to happen outside the classroom. Here are a couple of activities that students could be encouraged to do in their own time:

- **Sleep journal**: keep a diary of sleep patterns over one week. Make a note of the things that happen in the lead up to sleep and then make notes on times and duration of sleep. When do they go to sleep, when do they wake up? Do they snooze at particular times? What seems to get in the way of a good night's sleep? How does a bad night's sleep affect them the next day?
- **Sleep and learning**: experiment with attempting to learn something the evening before sleep and then see how well it has been remembered the next day to test the hypothesis that sleep aids learning and memory. Try learning a variety of things such as lists of vocabulary or a new piece of music.

Harmony with the outside world: the human body and the environment

The human organism is intimately connected to the environment and the world around us, both natural and man-made, and a healthy life is one which, as far as possible, tries to live in harmony with the natural world.

A little while ago, one of our cats caught a bat and brought it into the house. It was about 10 p.m. and our living room lights were on. Because bats are nocturnal, the light made it sleepy. As soon as we got it outside in the dark, it perked up and flew away. Humans react similarly. Deep in the brain, in the hypothalamus, is an organ called the pineal gland. Descartes believed the pineal gland to connect the body and the soul. He was wrong. The pineal gland is responsible for setting our body clock and it acts in response to levels of light and dark outside. The human body has certain rhythms (called circadian rhythms) which happen alongside the natural rhythms of day and night (called diurnal rhythms). When it gets dark, the pineal gland releases a chemical called melatonin, which induces sleep. This is why sleep patterns are disrupted by being around too much light at bedtime (for example, by watching television or checking emails and text messages). In fact, in one study, checking text messages or emails before bed was likened to drinking a double espresso: the bright light from a computer or phone screen has an extraordinary effect.[28]

It's not just sleep patterns that are altered by chemical releases in the body. At dawn, the body releases cortisol to increase blood pressure and blood sugar to wake us up. At around noon, our intellectual ability is at its peak and in the afternoon, our body temperature is at its highest. All of these changes are brought about by our relationship to the environment. Mood is also evenly distributed throughout the day in cycles in order to conserve energy (being really cheerful uses up energy) and some people find that in the winter, when the days are shorter, that their prevailing mood is less positive than in the summer.

Alongside changes in light and natural rhythms, there is the simple fact that just being in or even near the natural world is good for us. There are interesting studies into how simply having a view of the outside world can improve our health. In 1984, Roger Ulrich published the results of research that he carried out on patients recovering from gall bladder surgery at a Pennsylvania hospital between 1972 and 1981. Of the 46 patients he followed, he found that the 23 whose hospital window overlooked nature took less time to recover from the surgery than the 23 patients whose window looked out onto a brick wall. They also asked for fewer painkillers and had fewer symptoms of headaches and nausea.[29] It's not just the inanimate natural world either. Great Ormond Street Hospital in London uses pet therapy to help children to reduce stress and recover from illness and a study conducted in Israel has suggested that caring for an animal can help to alleviate some of the symptoms of schizophrenia.[30]

Another benefit brought to us by the outside world is that of perspective. This idea is neatly summed up here by the philosopher Iris Murdoch:

> I am looking out of my window in an anxious and resentful state of mind, oblivious of my surroundings, brooding perhaps on some damage done to my prestige. Then I suddenly observe a hovering kestrel. In a moment everything is altered. The brooding self with its hurt vanity has disappeared. There is nothing now but kestrel. And when I return to thinking of the other matter it seems less important. And of course this is something we may do deliberately: give attention to nature in order to clear our minds of selfish care.[31]

Nature provides us with a very simple way of overcoming stress and obtaining perspective on many of the petty concerns that can come to dominate our lives. For nearly everyone, within minutes it is possible to be in a place that seems untouched by human hands; once there, the intractable problems of the week suddenly became smaller problems with a straightforward solution. When we are outside we should take time to notice things: to look up at the sky, to pay attention to the activities of wildlife – all of these things help us to gain perspective on our problems and enable us to calm down sufficiently to find ways to overcome them.

Putting it into practice: the outside world

- **Get out there**: as with exercise, the only way to fully appreciate the benefits of being outside is to experience being outside and reflect on it. Take your class outside for a walk; ask them to (alone and in silence) notice birdsong or the gentle, rhythmic song of the pneumatic drill. Take them back inside and ask them to compare how they felt before with how they felt afterwards. Ask them to notice specific things such as heart rate, mood or feelings about other people.

Choosing harmony: decision making and executive function

So as long as we are fed, watered and sheltered and get enough rest, we'll be OK. Not that tricky really. So why do so many of us abuse our bodies? The problem is that we are not machines. If it were simply a case of pre-programming robots to feed themselves, we'd be fine. And even though we have been pre-programmed to an extent, some people still manage to crack the code and override the programming. Unlike my cats. My cats operate according to instinct and whatever the present moment throws at them. There is a reason that my cats don't smoke cigarettes: my cats don't smoke because they don't have an imagination to make them think it would be a good idea. They don't take crack cocaine because they don't have a neo-cortex to produce the idea that a drug can numb the pain of their existence. They also don't have opposable thumbs to hold the little pipe. Our evolution out of ape-hood has come at a price: the imagination to find things that will poison our bodies under the illusion of pleasure and the free will to choose to ignore our body's pleas for the right fuel, for enough exercise and for rest.

I won't waste your time by telling you that we should teach young people not to smoke, not to take non-prescribed, illegal drugs and not to have unsafe sex. For starters, I don't think that telling someone not to do something will stop them from doing it (just as right now, my telling you *not* to think of a shimmering white polar bear hasn't worked). People avoid harmful behaviour for two reasons: 1) they have learned not to from experience (which may be borne out of experimentation) and 2) they have a strong enough set of values to make them choose not to. Or it will be a mixture of the two. I am not going to dwell on the topic of toxins: too much time is spent in schools looking at drugs and promiscuity at the expense of understanding the underlying physiological and psychological causes for these behaviours. Later on in this chapter, when we look harmony between the mind and body, we will explore why it is that some people feel the need to press the self-destruct button. For now, suffice it to say we shouldn't poison our bodies and young people should be given markers about the trap-doors which lead us into consumption of destructive substances.

Icebergs and elephants

In order to understand why we do not always choose what is good for us, we need to look at how the brain is structured and how it helps us to choose through what is called 'executive function'. On the top of the brain sits the neo-cortex, which is largely responsible for all the jobs that make up the conscious, thinking self, such as choice, reasoning, imagination and language. This is the part of the brain that we notice the most because it is the part that supports our conscious selves: the bit that makes us who we are, that creates and sustains our personality. The personality does not just reside in one part of the brain: like most brain functions, it is spread over a vast network of neural connections and it is this constant and unique pattern of firing neurons that makes us who we are.

The part of us that *thinks* doesn't always do what the part of us that *does* wants it to. The relationship between the thinking part of the brain (the neo-cortex) and the parts which take care of everything else is often characterized as an iceberg, with the conscious mind being the little bit poking out of the water and the unconscious part being the Titanic-sinking mass hidden away below the surface. As we saw in Chapter 1, Jonathan Haidt characterizes the relationship as that between an elephant and its rider: the little rider on top represents the conscious self (sometimes called the ego) who believes he is in control of the lumbering pachyderm beneath him. But in fact the elephant generally does what it wants, following pre-ordained pathways and serving its own biological needs, chief among which is survival.

Jonathan Swift allegorized this relationship in *Gulliver's Travels* when he wrote about the population of the floating island of Laputa. The island of Laputa hovers above the land of Balnibarbi. The majority of the male inhabitants of Laputa live purely intellectual lives and in fact they are so stuck in their own thoughts that they need a person called a *flapper* to follow them around and tap them whenever their immersion in thought poses problems for them:

> This *Flapper* is likewise employed diligently to attend his master in his walks, and upon occasion to give him a soft flap upon his eyes; because he is so wrapped up in cogitation, that he is in manifest danger of falling down every precipice, and bouncing his head against every post; and in the streets of jostling others, or being jostled himself into the kennel.[32]

The Laputians are solely concerned with music and mathematics and have no interest in anything non-intellectual and, as a consequence, their lives are disharmonious:

. . . although they are dextrous enough upon a piece of paper in the management of the rule, the pencil and the divider, yet in the common actions and behaviour of life, I have not seen a more clumsy, awkward, and unhandy people.[33]

Swift's point is clear: to be too intellectual means to lead an incomplete life. To fail to attend to the body as well as the mind is a mistake; interestingly, the wives of many of these Laputians are so dissatisfied with their intellectual husbands that they descend to the world below to take lovers, to which, of course, the husbands remain oblivious.

Executive function

Executive function (EF) is our ability to regulate our behaviour, emotions, thoughts, feelings and desires in any given situation and by doing this, it helps us to keep our short- and long-term goals in mind and overcome internal conflicts. For example, if I am at a dinner party but the next day I am running in a half marathon, it is my EF that will help me decide to not get drunk and not eat too much. It is a cognitive or thinking skill which, obviously, is vital for our well-being. EF is thought to have its seat in the frontal lobe[34] and indeed, patients with frontal lobe damage do sometimes have difficulty regulating their behaviour. EF skills are really important for a variety of things:

> Good EF skills are important for personal development, wellbeing and achievement in the workplace, as well as for academic success. Fostering EF skills in early childhood will create learners with better coping and resilience skills . . . stronger EF skills should also promote a flexible approach to learning.[35]

EF is also something that we learn through our experiences and the foundations are laid in early childhood. According to the 'Foresight Report into Mental Capital and Well-being', EF skills are based upon a positive self-concept (i.e. an image of the self which is positive), good self-esteem and good social and emotional skills. Children cannot acquire these skills by direct teaching, they have to be coached in them; in other words, as real-life situations arise, children are guided in how to deal with them. It is essential that a child's interaction with their care-giver or teacher is warm and responsive and 'negativity, sarcasm and verbal punitiveness' are avoided, as are restrictedness ('stop doing that') and directiveness, where the child's focus is directed towards what the care-giver thinks is more suitable.

Interestingly, the Foresight Report argues that the art classroom may provide the model environment for developing EF skills:

Art teachers work from the interest of the pupil, fulfilling the key aim for fostering wellbeing of individual engagement in a task considered fulfilling and worthwhile. The interactions around the learning are therefore responsive, involving listening to the ideas and opinions of the child. Art teachers appreciate that pupils want to create something of aesthetic significance, they encourage them to take risks, and they help them to learn from their failures. They teach pupils how to persist and how to work through frustration.'[36]

Putting it into practice: decision making and executive function

- **Anatomy of a decision**: give students a decision that they have to make (e.g. to get pizza or not/to do homework or not/to do something nice for your Mum or not, etc.) and then get them to break it down into its constituent parts. Ask them to speculate how much goes into each decision they make. Ask them to differentiate between the involvement of elephant and rider. Get the students into groups and ask each member of the group to play a role in the decision (e.g. 'I am Jack's values, I help him to decide what is right and wrong. In this situation . . .').

- **The elephant in the room**: explain Jonathan Haidt's elephant and rider analogy. Ask students to think of a time when something happened to them, where it was a case of the elephant taking over. Get students to act the scenario out in groups and ask the audience to speculate whether it was elephant or rider responsible for what happened to their classmate.

- **Deliberate or accidental?** Explain that a deliberate life is one where a person takes control of what happens to them, whereas an accidental life is one where the person does not control their decisions and has poor EF. Ask the students to characterize a person who lives deliberately/ accidentally. How do they walk/talk/interact with people? What kinds of thing happen in their lives? Use forum theatre to create a scenario where the audience help a character with poor EF skills to work through a difficult scenario.

- **Biography**: ask students to find out and write about a person who has good EF skills. What is their life like?

Film resource

- *Charlie and the Chocolate Factory*: the ghastly characters who share Charlie's visit to Willy Wonka's factory all show very poor EF skills because they are spoilt. They are a lovely way to exemplify decision making and EF.

Decision making and risk

One of the main reasons many people find themselves in trouble with their health is that they have the ability to think and the ability to override their body's basic needs. When I was 17, I started to smoke cigarettes. Just three years earlier, my dad had nearly died from heart disease exacerbated by smoking and notwithstanding the emotional trauma that should have galvanized me against smoking for all eternity, I tried it. I hated the taste of it the first time. In fact, I hated the taste for the first hundred times I smoked cigarettes, but my desire to appear cool in front of my friends helped to switch off my body screaming at me to never do this crazy thing ever again. It took me 14 years and the love of a good woman to stop.

In the next chapter on philosophy, I will write much more about how the mind doesn't always help us to see things as they really are (which is one of the goals of philosophy). But at this stage, whilst we are looking at health, I just want to mention a couple of things about how the mind can get in the way of making the right decisions.

The three key ideas that might help to illustrate how the mind doesn't always help us when it comes to harmful behaviour are these:

1. we prefer pleasure to pain
2. we aren't very good at predicting the future
3. we like to feel in control.

Humans are in many ways hedonistic creatures: pleasure seekers. When I started smoking, it was because I craved the pleasure of improved acceptance by my peers. Once I had become addicted, it was because I craved the pleasure of nicotine replacement. The trick in avoiding harmful behaviour is to replace harmful pleasures with less harmful ones. Instead of smoking a cigarette for pleasure, I now go for a run. This is easier said than done because of the next reason.

We are not very good at predicting the future. Humans suffer from something called presentism: we look at the future and the past through the lens of the present. I used to find that my resolve to give up smoking was usually much stronger after I had just finished a cigarette, when of course my desire for nicotine was sated. Our perception is also slightly skewed if we stand to lose something. If I ask you to give up your addiction to chocolate and take up my addiction to running, your mind will focus on what it stands to lose, not what I think you will stand to gain. The only thing that will stop someone from engaging in behaviour that is harmful is if you get them to re-frame the amount of risk they are willing to take in order to experience pleasure. The best way to do this is to provide a person with an incentive to stop taking the risk. My incentives to stop smoking were stopping my wife from being upset with me and becoming a father (and not wanting to be a wheezy old git who couldn't climb trees with his kids). The future without smoking suddenly seemed brighter than a future with it, although thinking I would never smoke again was terrifying in the first few days of giving up.

There is one small caveat here. Research suggests that during adolescence, people find the concept of long-term negative consequences harder to deal with and are more concerned with short-term rewards, and in the main, short-term rewards provided by their peer group. In other words, teenagers are more likely to choose something which produces pleasure now or soon, or approval or disapproval from their friends, than the prospect of cancer aged 60 when deciding about that cigarette. The crowd you fall in with really is important to decision making and risk assessment.[37]

The third spanner in the works is the need to feel as if we exercise control over our lives. I resented giving up cigarettes, because smoking was something I thought I could choose to do and giving up felt like giving up that choice. Feeling as if we have control impacts upon our health. In a study of elderly residents in a nursing home, the patients who were given control over the feeding and nurturing of the house plants lived longer than the patients who were given no control over the care and feeding of houseplants.[38] A sense of control is vital to our well-being and it is often this desire for control that leads people into harmful and destructive behaviour like smoking, eating disorders and self-harming. It is probably no accident that I started smoking at around the time I was under the most pressure from an external source: the commencement of my A levels.

The beauty of the whole system is that the human brain is plastic and can be changed. With work, it is possible to re-wire many of the connections in the brain and undo some of the bad experiences we have that can act as barriers to learning.

Putting it into practice: the mind

- **The fun police**: ask students in groups to imagine that they are to establish a police force whose job it is to arrest and punish people who take risks that seem like fun at the time, but which result in bad health and cost the NHS (and therefore the taxpayer) money. What actions would they prosecute? Why would they prosecute those actions? What punishments would they put in place? What mitigating circumstances or exceptions would they allow into the system?

More than a machine: learning, love and attachment theory

So far, we have explored the basic maintenance we need to perform on the body to keep it healthy and we have looked at the process of choice, decision making and executive function. It is at this point that we need to turn our attention from maintenance to thriving. The human organism is capable of achieving extraordinary things and the rest of the book will concentrate on what we have to do to enable ourselves to flourish. We'll start with two ingredients: learning and love.

Learning

Learning about our environment and creating new ways to master it is one of the things that makes humans unique. Those of us that teach are in the business of getting people to learn, but often we don't know exactly how that happens.

Learning takes place when nerve cells wire together in the brain and form synapses (connections between nerve cells). When we learn something new, a network of nerve cells join together and this creates a template in our mind. The more we do something and the more we use those networks of nerve cells, the stronger the networks become. Have you ever felt that magical moment as the penny drops and the light switches on as you learn something new? In order to remember something, a connection must be made between the cortex and either the corpus striatum for unconscious memories or the hippocampus for conscious memory: the things we can call to mind quickly, such as the capital of France.

The synaptic links are formed when two chemicals are released: glutamate and dopamine. Glutamate starts off the learning process and dopamine helps it to continue. If there is too much glutamate, the cells required for learning will die. If there is glutamate and dopamine present, you will learn whatever you are paying attention to at the time, whether you like it or not.

There are a few important ingredients to successful learning.[39] Alongside basic physical health resulting from getting enough sleep and eating the right things, there are three in particular:

- movement
- positive emotional states and avoiding excess stress
- repetition and practice.

Movement and learning

Movement plays a large part in learning. As we saw earlier, exercise ↳ chemicals in the brain which help to stimulate learning. There is also evidence ↳ learning a musical instrument creates more connections in the brain which in turn assists our ability to handle the cognitive aspects of learning required for academic work. Aside from complex sequences of movement, simply walking whilst thinking, humming, mouthing words or gesturing with the hands can assist in learning and the development of memory:

> The famous example of this is Albert Einstein, who played the violin regularly. At times he would suddenly stop playing, jump up from his chair and scribble down an idea or part of an equation. People who hum or whistle a tune while they are contemplating something – or walk the Stairmaster exercise machine as I do – are using motor programs in the brain to help them wander along in search of neuronal connections.[40]

Learning, positive emotions and avoiding stress

The enemy of this whole process is stress. Stress prevents learning from happening effectively by either driving memories into the corpus striatum and making them subconscious (and therefore difficult to access) or by causing the production of steroids which kill off cells in the hippocampus and damage our conscious memories.

The right conditions for learning are being in a safe and secure environment where we feel secure and where we trust the person from whom we are learning enough to start to explore. Creativity happens when we are in a good emotional surrounding. The most important skill to have in order to learn is the ability to manage our stress levels and this is a skill that we acquire from our primary care giver in the first few years of life. In her brilliant book *Why Love Matters*, Sue Gerhardt presents compelling evidence that children who do not have secure relationships in the early years of childhood find it difficult to regulate their cortisol levels. High cortisol levels are a significant barrier to learning.

Repetition and practice

Another barrier to learning is not practising or rehearsing new knowledge or skills. Every new experience we have causes the firing across some synapses to strengthen and others to weaken. The more a certain activity is repeated, such as holding down a C chord on a guitar, the more that neural pathway becomes strengthened and the more that skill becomes 'hard-wired' into the brain.[41] In his book *Outliers* Malcolm

Gladwell writes about an interesting study that was carried out in schools in America. A researcher tracked progress in reading over a single academic year to see the effect that schooling was having versus parental input with a view to testing the hypothesis that state-funded schools were failing children from deprived backgrounds. The results were staggering. Children from more deprived backgrounds made as much, if not more progress than children from less deprived backgrounds during term time. The problems arose in the long school holidays, where children from deprived backgrounds, whose parents generally did not encourage reading or other academically challenging activities at home, lost all the progress made in school during term. The children whose parents encouraged reading and other academic activities in the holidays kept progressing out of term and got further and further ahead. Practice makes, if not perfect, certainly more proficient.[42]

Putting it into practice: learning

- **Experiment**: suggest that students try some of the different strategies mentioned above in areas where they find learning difficult. Get them to keep track of their progress at weekly intervals and keep a record in their journals of any differences in their feelings about learning in those areas.

Love and attachment theory

Love is a pretty unwieldy word that means many things to many people. At the core though, we all understand love to mean being securely attached to another human being or group of human beings through family, friendship or romantic partnership. It is these bonds which may hold the key to securing everything else mentioned in this chapter: which may motivate us to live healthier lives, which may prevent us from lapsing into destructive behaviour and addiction.

In the late 1950s, a researcher called Harry Harlow was studying the behaviour of the Rhesus Macaque monkeys that he had bred in captivity. In order to prevent infection, Harlow and his team had separated the infant monkeys from their mothers, but they discovered that these separated infants had developed very poor social skills.

Acting on a hunch, the team believed that the infants lacked something to hug and hold close (an important feature of the early stages of development in most mammals) and they devised a clever experiment to test this. They created two 'mothers' for the infants: one made from wire that wasn't very nice, but which provided milk and another one covered in towelling which produced no milk. The result was that the infants went to the uninviting mother just for food and clung to the soft mother for the rest of the time. In a now famous photograph, you can see a baby Rhesus Macaque clinging to the towelling mother whilst feeding from the wire one.

Two other researchers heard about Harlow's findings and used them to develop what has come to be called 'Attachment Theory'. John Bowlby and Mary Ainsworth were interested in how children form bonds with their primary care-giver and wanted to test the hypothesis that children will only play and explore when they have developed a secure attachment to whoever that person may be.

Ainsworth conducted an experiment which she called the 'Strange Situation'. A mother would be invited into a room full of toys to play with her toddler. After a while, a stranger would enter the room and talk with the mother for a while, then join the child in play. Then the mother would leave her child alone with the stranger for a few minutes before returning. The stranger would then leave. After a while, the mother would get up and leave the child alone and the stranger would return before finally the mother returns for good.

As a result of this experiment, Ainsworth devised three categories of attachment between care-giver and child:

1. secure attachment
2. avoidant attachment
3. resistant attachment.

Secure attachment is the ideal. The toddler showed some distress at being left, but as soon as the mother returned, the child showed delight and returned to play. Avoidant children seem to show little interest when their care-giver leaves, although they are stressed, and resistant children get extremely agitated when separated. What's more, research seems to indicate that these attachment styles follow us into adulthood: the attachments we learn from our care-givers as infants help to define how we form all subsequent relationships.[43]

What is the upshot of all this? In order to flourish and thrive as an organism, we need to be shown love and we need to show love to others. By love I do not mean fanciful or whimsical love or infatuation or obsession. Felicia Huppert of the Cambridge Institute for Well-Being uses the term 'authorattentive', which means an attitude that is authoritative and disciplined but which is attentive to the needs of the human you are in relation to. She here uses it in the context of a parenting relationship:

> These are parents who are child centred – they really care about their child, they are warm parents, but they are very clear about values, and very clear about

boundaries. I think we need to make sure more parents are aware of the value of authorattentive parenting.[44]

More will be said about this in Chapter 8, which covers relationships, but the key point is that in order to really make the machine operate to its full potential, it needs to be shown love.

So we have come full circle.

Our bodies are set up for us to survive and lead healthy lives. We have an amazing organism at our disposal which takes care of the basic processes and provided we do a few simple things, leaves us free to learn about the world and enjoy beauty. The only slight problem is that every now and again, we try to live out of synchronization with our body's rhythms: it is this asynchrony and the occasional unforeseen circumstance that can lead to a lack of well-being. However, if we listen to and meet our body's demands we put the basic building blocks in place to enable ourselves to flourish.

4   Philosophy and well-being

Chapter preview

- Case study: David Shayler
- The benefits of teaching philosophy
- The elephant in the room: the hurdles to thinking philosophically
- Getting started with teaching philosophy
- The philosopher's toolkit: strategies needed for clear thinking
- Moral philosophy

Case study: David Shayler

In 1997 a former MI5 agent named David Shayler achieved media notoriety when he passed classified documents to the British national press suggesting that the government had been complicit in an assassination attempt on Lybia's Colonel Gaddafi in 1996. Shayler achieved the reputation of being a whistle-blower and fled the UK to live in exile in France. In 2000 he returned to the UK and was promptly charged with breaking the Official Secrets Act. Shayler's image was of a man of principle who was willing to make huge sacrifices to stand up for truth and justice.

In 2007, the story took a turn for the bizarre: David Shayler announced in a letter to *The Times* newspaper that he was the Messiah – the spirit of God incarnate on earth. In 2008, Jon Ronson interviewed Shayler about his being the Messiah for his BBC Radio 4 programme 'Jon Ronson on . . . States of Mind'. He had this to say:

> I know that people will find this absolutely extraordinary because I was an atheist three years ago and I would find it extraordinary if someone suddenly said 'I am the Messiah' . . . there are ancient documents showing that phonetically, someone called David Shayler or Shyler is the Messiah. Now when you put that in conjunction with the work I have done over the last ten years standing up for truth and justice and I'm called David Shayler, you don't have to be a brilliant journalist or intelligence officer to put two and two together to make 4 . . . After I'd been to the crop circle and accepted in my heart that I was the Messiah, I felt a sense of peace that I had never felt in my life before.[45]

Whilst Shayler was speaking, Belinda, his former landlady, challenged his assertion that he was the Messiah. She said that he had made three mistakes based on the precedent set down by other so-called messiahs and prophets: 1) he was not taking time out to meditate and work out his mission; 2) he didn't have a following of disciples; and 3) he had announced his own messiahship. Shayler responded by arguing the following:

> I know I'm the Messiah. It's up to you to look into your own heart and find out why you can't accept that; why you feel the need to come to the Messiah and tell him he's not the Messiah; why you feel the need to judge the Messiah . . . There is no precedent for the Messiah because I am the only Messiah.[46]

Our instincts tell us that David Shayler is probably deluded. Given that he has also claimed to be the reincarnation of Leonardo da Vinci, Che Guevara (whose death he was born before), Plato and Tutankhamen,[47] the evidence would suggest that Shayler's grip on reality might not be what it once was.

The benefits of teaching philosophy

This chapter is about teaching philosophy to young people as a part of a well-being programme. Philosophy might not be an obvious candidate for inclusion on a well-being course, perhaps because many of us associate it with impenetrable prose written by people who seem hell bent on confusing us. This is not what I mean by philosophy. I began this chapter with the David Shayler story to show what it is like when someone loses their grip on reality, when they stop perceiving things accurately, and whilst his is an extreme case, I would argue that many of the problems we encounter in life arise when we don't see things clearly. Take the last argument that you had with someone: I'll bet that the argument happened because you both thought you were right. Right? Chances are, both of you were partly right and partly (or mostly) wrong and it wasn't until you got a clear and accurate view of what had happened that you could patch things up (if indeed you have yet). It is philosophy, or critical thinking that can help to train the mind to see things more or less as they really are.

Philosophy starts when we ask 'why?' Anyone who is curious about why certain things happen is a natural philosopher and many of you will realize that this includes most children because they spend much of their time asking why certain things are the way they are. A lot of children become afraid of asking that question, simply because an infuriated adult closes it down for them through their own feelings of insecurity or incompetence in discovering why the world is how it is. One alarming study cited by Guy Claxton found that in the space of a lesson, children asked two questions compared to the teacher's 84.[48] As soon as children stop asking questions, or feel uncomfortable doing so, they are closing down avenues of curiosity and connection with the world outside them, they are also beginning to rely on their own opinions and received wisdom instead of trying to get to the truth.

Sound arguments and meaning

Once the question 'why?' has been asked, the next move is to construct an argument and this is the second job of the philosopher: the construction of sound arguments. If you listen closely to people, or if you take a more forensic look at what many people write on blogs, much of what is said or written is what is called assertion: a bald statement masquerading as fact. Although it is a masochistic pleasure, I particularly enjoy listening to people who hold bigoted beliefs for this very reason: they simply do not realize that their arguments are made up of assertions which bear very little similarity to what happens in the real world. Once equipped with philosophical tools, you have the ability to tackle the bigoted, the prejudiced and the opinionated.

There are other benefits of learning philosophy. Principal among them is that by training ourselves to ask why and create coherent arguments in response, we are engaged in an activity which has *meaning*. It is no accident that all of the great philosophers wrote about happiness, as most philosophical roads lead us to the question of what the fulfilled life is. If you develop the habit of asking 'I wonder why that is?', it forces you to be engaged with what it means to be human and what it is to exist in the world. It stands to reason that a person who is actively *and positively* engaged with their own purpose in life and with their place in the universe will live a happier life. This is borne out not only by arguments in Aristotle's *Nicomachean Ethics*[49] and Bertrand Russell's *The Conquest Of Happiness*,[50] but also by research carried out to verify these arguments, some of which is attested to by Martin Seligman in *Authentic Happiness*.[51]

Values and evidence

This moves us on to the second benefit of philosophy: citizenship. Unfortunately this has become something of a dirty word in British education, as it is the name of a course that has been introduced into schools by the government in an attempt to increase the positive involvement of young people in society. Some teachers find their hackles rise when they hear the word, as some of the materials are quite dull: learning about the constitution, whilst important, may require a Herculean effort to bring it to life. I was not taught 'Citizenship' at school and I do not really know how the British constitution works, certainly not in enough detail to tell you the difference between a white paper and a green paper. I don't think that this makes me a bad citizen. A good citizen is someone who is willing to stand up for certain principles that can be rationally shown to be good, such as truth, justice and prevention of harm to the innocent. In the film *V for Vendetta*, we meet a man who has been horrendously wronged by a tyrannical government that has come to power in Britain. He becomes a modern-day Guy Fawkes: a man motivated wholly by justice and the desire to remove a corrupt administration. His devotion to justice is visceral. It is part of his character. We can arrive at the principles and values that should govern the life of a good citizen through philosophy, either by dint of reasoning, or through experience: good citizenship is a natural consequence of successful philosophical enquiry.

The third benefit of philosophy is that it requires us to weigh up the evidence for our beliefs. This afternoon, I took a group of students out of school to help to keep a National Trust site tidy. On the way back, one of the students was telling me about her fear both of heights and of spiders and her refusal to participate in a high ropes course on a recent activity weekend. She believes that all spiders pose a direct threat to her existence and that all heights, despite ropes and harnesses, are inherently risky and are to be avoided. No amount of 'but the British house spider is harmless' or 'the rope is strong enough to hold a double-decker bus' would dissuade her of her belief that all spiders have to be killed and harnesses and ropes aren't enough protection because 'you just never know'. It must be difficult to be imprisoned by beliefs like this and this is the beauty of philosophy: by requiring that we substantiate the claims we make with evidence, it can often help to release us from the prison of unhelpful beliefs. This is very important for teaching children resilience and optimism.

The elephant in the room: the hurdles to thinking philosophically

Before we take a closer look at exactly how to teach philosophy, I would like to take a little time to point out how our minds are not always set up to help us to be philosophical. Because our mind is, amongst other things, trying to ensure that we are protected from any threats in the outside world, it has various inherent biases built into its perception of the world to enable us to feel happy enough to engage in life. Daniel Gilbert refers to this as the 'psychological immune system'.

> Rather than thinking of people as hopelessly Panglossian, then, we might think of them as having a *psychological immune system* that defends the mind against unhappiness in much the same way that the physical immune system defends the body against illness . . . We need to be defended – not defenceless or defensive – and thus our minds naturally look for the best view of things while simultaneously insisting that those views stick reasonably closely to the facts.[52]

You might be thinking to yourself that an entirely accurate perception of the world and of events is the most desirable situation to be in, but you'd be slightly wrong: the people with the most accurate perception of events and of their role in them are the clinically depressed. It turns out that people who do not suffer from depression have a slightly optimistic and, dare I say it, inaccurate perception of their own abilities. It is this bias, it seems, which helps us to view the world as an inherently friendly place over which we can exert some control.

It is for this reason that this section is called 'The Elephant in the Room'. If we return to Jonathan Haidt's analogy of the elephant and its rider, it seems that the mind, over which many of us will believe we exert complete control also has, if you'll pardon the pun, a mind of its own.

There are numerous examples of the hurdles that our mind can place in the way of seeing the world accurately and I will cite just a few here.[53]

Wishful thinking

Derren Brown is a British performance artist specializing in psychological conjuring tricks. In 2004 he travelled to the US to see if he could convince representatives from religious and new age movements that he had special powers, when in fact he was a fraud using techniques learned from psychology. He visited some psychics in Nevada and managed to persuade them that he could read minds; he visited evangelical Christians in New York and showed that he could 'convert' atheists and agnostics with the simple touch of a hand; he met with UFO spotters and told them he had special insight into people's medical conditions without referring to notes or conducting physical examinations and he made a medium believe (along with members of the audience) that he could contact the spirits of dead relatives.[54] The upshot of all this? People believe what they want to believe. Even though the representatives of these movements made a show of being sceptical, they were extremely easily persuaded that Derren Brown was the real deal because deep down they wanted to believe that God can convert people quickly and that the dead can contact the living and this British man provided just the evidence they wanted.

Wishful thinking is something that we all do: we find facts and people to fit in with our way of seeing the world. Imagine for example that you have just taken an IQ test and you have scored badly on it. Afterward, you are taken to a room and on the coffee table lie various articles about IQ testing, some favourable, some not. The chances are you will spend more time looking at the articles which are critical of IQ testing than those that endorse it. In fact, this very test was carried out in 1986 by D. Frey and D. Stahlberg with just those results.[55] The quest for justification does not end at magazine articles: many of the people whom we gather around us in our lives are people who agree with our worldview. My wife and I share broadly similar political, educational, religious and other perspectives and one of the reasons we fell in love was that in the other we met someone who confirmed everything that we had thought to be true.

Mind the gap

The memory is a funny old thing. We rely on it probably more than we realize for providing us with information about past events, but it can be surprisingly unreliable and have a tendency to let us down and not remember things quite as they were.

In the 1970s there were a large number of cases of people 'remembering' being abused as children as a result of therapy. Psychologist Elizabeth Loftus smelled a rat and constructed an experiment to show that the human memory is not all it's cracked up to be. She showed volunteers a series of slides of a red car heading to a give-way sign, turning right and then knocking over a pedestrian. One group of volunteers was asked if another car had passed the red car as it approached the *stop sign*. The other group was asked nothing. Both groups were then shown a picture of the red car at a stop sign and a red car at a give-way sign and were then asked which picture they had seen. Eighty per cent of the volunteers in the group asked about the *stop sign* responded that they had seen a slide of a red car at a stop sign, which of course, they hadn't. Interestingly, 90 per cent of the group not questioned pointed to the correct slide: the one with the give-way sign.

This study shows that, with a bit of priming, the memory will re-shape events to fit what it believes to be true, it fills in the gaps and will often completely fabricate situations. This is called confabulation. My students and I often debate the ethics of the killing of Jean-Charles de Menezes – the Brazilian man shot dead by Metropolitan police officers at Stockwell tube station in 2005. My students were convinced that de Menezes, whom they believed to be wearing a puffa-jacket, ran through the tube station carrying a rucksack and jumped the ticket barriers with armed police in close pursuit warning him to stop or he would be shot. They even believed that they had seen CCTV footage of de Menezes jumping the barriers. Of course, none of this was true. De Menezes had no idea that the police were pursuing him and he was calmly going about his business as usual. Yet my students, primed by stories in the press in the days after the events, felt able to justify the actions of the officers who shot him based on the evidence they believed they had seen.

Because memory is so important in recalling the facts that we use to construct our arguments, we need to be alert to the fact that it does, every now and again, fill in the gaps for us.

In my day . . .

Humans are deeply subjective: the world is not just the way it is, it is the way it is according to us. How often have you heard someone regale you with tales of the halcyon era when school children were immaculately behaved and respected their elders, when you could leave your back door unlocked and not worry, when children could play in the fields without fear of paedophiles, when you could do all of your shopping for thr'pence ha'penny and still have change to buy a house in the country? The thinking mistake being made here is quite a common one and it gives us an insight into why opinionated grandparents shouldn't be school governors and also why if you're on a budget, you shouldn't go shopping when you're hungry: it's something called 'presentism'.

Our view of the present is the perspective through which we see everything. My beliefs about taking risks now are very different to my beliefs about taking risks when I was 17, which is why I don't smoke or go hedge-hopping anymore. Our beliefs and attitudes change, but because they do so imperceptibly over time, we don't really notice and make the classic mistake of thinking that we have always believed the same things. Why do middle-aged people often disapprove of what youngsters are doing, despite the fact that they probably did it themselves? Because they are viewing their own past through the lens of their current beliefs about how teenagers should behave and conveniently forgetting their ancient history.

Not only does our view of the present affect our recall of the past, but it skews our view of the future. Especially when I go to the Mango Tree. The Mango Tree is the favourite restaurant of my wife and I and they serve great Indian food. When we go, I am usually ravenous and everything on the menu looks delicious. I always forget that the restaurant serves enough food in a single portion to fell a camel and blithely order prawn dishes, chicken dishes, lentils, rice, naan bread and anything else on offer. And who is it that can hardly walk at the end of the meal? I overstuff myself, because my empty, growling stomach makes my mind a little bit more optimistic about how much food it can fit in. I have predicted the future based upon the present.

Now that we have looked at some of the little hurdles to philosophical thinking that we ought to be aware of, we can look more closely at how to teach it.

Getting started with teaching philosophy

Starting children off on philosophy is easy. A philosopher does not have to have read every last sentence written by Plato or understand every nuance of Kant, they simply have to start asking questions. The process is so easy that even a 5 year old can do it, and indeed, there is a lot of successful teaching of philosophy happening in UK primary schools, where children learn to debate and help each other to form good arguments.[56]

The first step is to stimulate questioning with the students and to do that you just need to give them something interesting to look at or to do. You would be surprised at how simple the stimulus can be: a pine cone, a box, a photo of a boxing match, a watch – anything.

The next step is to ask the students to come up with questions based upon the stimulus. They do need to come up with the right kind of questions though: the more open-ended the better. If you put a clown's shoe on the table and a student asks the question 'How do you spell shoe?', any discussion will be short. But if they ask 'Do clowns feel pain?', you may have a more open-ended debate.

Once the question is asked, the debate can begin and this is where the philosophy can happen, because the students will begin to construct arguments. As soon as we have arguments on the table, we can start the process of refining arguments and making them more and more successful.

The philosopher's toolkit: strategies needed for clear thinking

This section looks at ten of the things that trainee philosophers either need to do, or to watch out for when they are putting their arguments together. A good argument is one where the premises support the conclusion and it is surprising how often we put a bad argument together, based on many of the errors listed below. A good argument has premises which lead to a conclusion and all of the premises should be open to scrutiny and supported by evidence. This is not an exhaustive list and there is a lot of excellent material available to assist in the teaching of this.[57]

The Devil's Advocate

In the Roman Catholic Church, the Devil's Advocate is the person charged with collecting evidence against the canonization of a candidate for sainthood just to double check that those being made saints have led a truly holy life. They turn over every stone they can to make certain that there are no skeletons hiding in the closet. In philosophy, devil's advocacy is an important job, as the person who takes on the role helps to iron out shaky thinking and point out mistakes in arguments. Any philosophy class needs either one person, or preferably the whole group, to adopt the role of devil's advocate when another person is putting forward an argument. The job should be carried out in a respectful way, not a sneering one, and it must still be done even if the advocate agrees with what is being said.

Assumptions

This is where you take something to be true or false without looking at the evidence. There is an old saying: 'never assume, it makes an ass out of you and me'. This is partly wrong: some assumptions are good, such as the assumption that the sky won't cave in on us in the next 30 seconds, and we make assumptions all the time based on our past experiences. There is nothing inherently wrong with assumptions. However, some assumptions are bad; for example, the assumption that all poor people are stupid or lazy. This assumption does not have evidence to support it: a person making this assumption is guiltier of stupidity and laziness in their argument.[58]

Authority

This is believing something to be true or false because someone with 'authority' told you. For example, trusting everything that teachers say without question might get you into trouble if one day you have an evil teacher. Some people believe things on TV or in the newspapers because, well, they wouldn't lie would they? This problem is particularly significant in dictatorships or where genocides are committed. Questioning, or standing up to authority figures who ask us to do bad things is a vital skill to learn.

Bad company fallacy

This is where you say something like 'you can't agree with euthanasia; Hitler used euthanasia. Arguing in favour of euthanasia is being as bad as Hitler'. You are arguing that something is bad because bad people have done it. The problem with this is that bad people sometimes do good things too: Hitler dramatically reduced unemployment and poverty in Germany. Just because a bad person has done something it does not necessarily mean that it is a bad thing to do.

Black and white

Believing that there are only two options in a situation: it's either this or that. George W. Bush once famously said 'You're either with us, or with the terrorists'. What if you're neither with the Americans nor the terrorists? This mistake in thinking is linked to making a false dichotomy, where you suggest to someone that there are only two options available to them; for example, 'you can either be gay, or be a Christian'. It could be argued that this is a false dichotomy, because there are individuals who are both gay and practising Christians.

Circular arguments

This is an argument which doesn't take us anywhere. For example, someone might argue that there is a God because the Bible tells us so. You might then ask why we should trust the Bible, to which they might respond 'the Bible is the word of God and has to be true'. The argument has taken us nowhere as we are no closer to knowing whether or not God exists.

Rash generalization

Where you argue that something is true for everyone or in every situation. For example, it would be a rash generalization to argue that all state-school pupils are badly behaved and all public-school pupils are perfectly behaved (or vice versa). Rash generalization is a rhetorical technique, often used by teenagers to try to get something they know they aren't really supposed to get: '*all* my friends are allowed to play Playstation for as long as they like' or 'you *never* listen to what I want', etc. etc. *ad nauseam*.

Fencing off

This is an old favourite of religion. Fencing off is where you make a subject out of bounds, often on the grounds of holiness or sanctity: the old blasphemy laws in Britain did this and the Monty Python film *The Life of Brian* was banned as a result for supposedly ridiculing the life of Jesus. Some people might argue that you cannot question the truth of a holy book because it is the word of God. This is a philosophical mistake because it assumes that some pieces of knowledge are inherently more valuable than others, which is not the case without sound argument. Whenever we are told 'you can't say that' or 'you can't think that' we should be very suspicious. It's usually an indication that the information they are trying to protect lies on fairly shaky philosophical foundations.

Getting personal

This is where you reject someone's argument because of a piece of personal information. This is a common and slightly underhand technique in arguing. For example, I might argue to you that smoking is bad. If you know that I used to smoke, you could say 'you can't argue that, because you used to smoke'. It would be a mistake to use that argument because the anti-smoking argument might be a good one regardless of whether or not I used to smoke. It also diverts attention away from the issue at hand.

The straw man

This is where you set up a caricature of your opponent's argument to show that their position is ridiculous. For example, Richard Dawkins, the famous atheist, made a documentary once in which he tried to argue that religion is the root of all evil. In the first episode, he interviewed two fundamentalists with extreme religious views – one from Christianity and one from Islam – to try to show that all religious people hold extreme views. He made the straw man mistake because he didn't destroy the credibility of religious belief, he only destroyed a 'straw man' version of religious belief.

Once you have started questioning, argument and debate in your classroom, the process of developing philosophical muscles is underway. Begin with quite open-ended topics, just to give your students the chance to practise arguing. Once you are happy that they are confident, you can move on to more sophisticated problems, such as time travel, whether or not robots can think or the Sorites Paradox.[59]

Moral philosophy

Case study: Stanley Milgram's 'Obedience' study

In 1961, a young professor of psychology at Yale University in the US placed an advert in the local newspaper asking for participants in an experiment on learning. When the all-male respondents arrived, they were introduced to another man whom they believed to be another volunteer but who was in fact a confederate of the organizers of the experiment. They were told that they were going to be experimenting in the learning of word pairs and that the learning would be reinforced by the administering of electric shocks rising in increments from 15 to 450 volts. One man would be the learner and the other the teacher and the situation was rigged so that the genuine volunteer was always the teacher. Taken into adjacent rooms separated by a thin wall, the teacher would read out a list of words and the learner would have to read out the words that corresponded to them: 'LAKE, LUCK, HAY, SUN. *Tree, loon, laughter, child.*'[60] If the learner made a mistake, the teacher would administer an electric shock that climbed in increments with every wrong answer, up to a total of 450 volts. The UK mains supply is 240 volts.

In each experiment, the learner wasn't very good and made mistakes. As the voltage increased, pre-recorded screams and eventually silence was to be heard on the other side of the wall by the teacher. A man in a white coat sat next to the teacher and encouraged him to carry on. Some of the teachers protested, but they were told that the experiment had to continue, that no serious harm was coming to the learner and that the organizers of the experiment would take the responsibility if there was. How many men continued to 450 volts? An alarming 65 per cent.

Eventually, the 'teachers' were shown that the experiment was a sham and that the electrodes weren't connected up. Immediately, the real aim of the experiment dawned on the volunteers: it was a test of how easily a rational adult human can succumb to an immoral authority. For many of the volunteers, this caused a profound sense of awakening to an unpleasant truth:

> The experiments caused me to reevaluate my life. They caused me to confront my own compliance and really struggle with it . . . I saw how

essential it was to develop a strong moral center (sic). I felt my own moral weakness and I was appalled, so I went to the ethical gym, if you see what I mean.[61]

Stanley Milgram's 'Obedience' experiment gained notoriety quickly and there was an explosion of similar experiments in the post-war years as, in the aftermath of the holocaust, academics tried to understand how ordinary human beings could be tricked into doing bad things. What is startling is that even though there is a huge body of literature on how easily we can be tricked into doing evil (Philip Zimbardo's *The Lucifer Effect* is among the best) it still happens. Take the Jonestown massacre, the genocide in Rwanda, the massacres in the former Yugoslavia at Srebrenica, the torture carried out by US soldiers in Abu Ghraib prison in Iraq and the genocide in Darfur to name but a few.

The above quotation from the participant shows the importance of philosophy. The experience of being tricked into doing evil catapulted this man into trying to regain his moral centre and it is philosophy that enables us to do this by equipping us with the following tools:

1. The ability to ask questions of authority and received wisdom.
2. The ability to develop values that can be tested.
3. The ability to spot fallacious arguments and form sound ones.
4. The ability to argue our way out of difficult situations.
5. A logically coherent view of life.

Relativism

There can be little doubt that young people must be given opportunities to develop an understanding of right and wrong: it would seem ridiculous to argue otherwise as a society cannot function if its members do not have a clear understanding of morality. The greatest problem that our young people face with morality, though, is who to trust. Modern society broadcasts conflicting messages about morality and it must be excruciating for the young to try to navigate their way through what appear to be conflicting messages. So what are we to do?

I think that the approach to be avoided is one that has relativism at its fulcrum. The relativist argues that there is no one single truth and that all opinions are equally as valid. I often come across this style of argument when marking the work of 15–16 year olds: because they do not want to have their own views criticized, they extend the excessively liberal right to hold any opinion to everyone else. This approach to morality is mistaken as it prevents us from condemning things that are quite obviously wrong, such as the torture of innocent children for pleasure. It is good to allow people to practise moral autonomy and arrive at decisions of moral rightness and wrongness for themselves, but as a society we do need to reserve the right to praise and condemn certain actions and indeed to tell people that they are wrong.

Whatever works best

The philosopher Peter Vardy has also cautioned against a kind of 'whatever is useful' morality or utilitarianism. In the television series *24* Kiefer Sutherland plays a counter-terrorism agent called Jack Bauer who always seems to find himself in extremely awkward moral situations that have life or death consequences. In the first series, the first time that torture was used to extract evidence from a suspect, there was a sense that this was a momentous and highly unusual event. However, once the floodgates had been opened to torture in series one, by series four torture was being used quite regularly to gather 'intelligence'. It is important for young people to question this. After the atomic bomb was dropped in World War II, it has become easier to use the old adage 'you can't make an omelette without breaking eggs'. Young people find it difficult to take a stand on principle as our culture lends itself to the belief that if the consequences are slightly better than the action, then the action is permissible. This is not the only way in moral philosophy and we should encourage investigation of the possibility that there are some actions that are inherently wrong.

But perhaps this is where the problem lies. Our vision of moral philosophy is sometimes all about actions: which footballer has put rohypnol in whose drink, which politician has embezzled public money, the rightness or otherwise of abortion, is it right to attack burglars in our own homes as self-defence and so on. We have to face up to the fact that some of these moral dilemmas will never be resolved. The abortion debate will continue to rage as it rests upon two very important features of human life: whether or not it is right to kill and whether or not humans (in this case women) have complete freedom of action over their bodies – people will always fall on one side of the fence or the other.

Character building

If we focus on actions all the time in moral decision making, we can also end up with a very narrow, short-term view of life which lurches from one moral dilemma to the next and life is just not like this. Life is a narrative that is continuous and is underpinned by our character. Every decision we make is informed by a thousand other decisions and a thousand other memories, all of which have been slowly subsumed into our character through the course of our experiences.

This leads us to a third way between a society which allows everyone to think what they like and morality that is obsessed with right and wrong actions and this is an ethics which focuses on what kind of person we should try to become. This approach to ethics is commonly referred to as virtue ethics or aretaic ethics, because it focuses upon the development of virtues (good habits of character) or excellence (arête) and is most associated with Aristotle and Alistair MacIntyre. Virtue ethics forces us to take a long-term view of our actions and consider what kind of character we are developing. Virtue ethics also has the capacity to move us away from a focus upon immediate pleasures on to an understanding of what a good life might involve and how we might flourish and excel over time by cultivating certain habits.

It is taking this long-term view that is really so essential to living a good life. Once we ask ourselves the question 'what sort of person do I want to be?' our answers provide us with the values and principles that guide us through life and which we can start to act in accordance with. We often see people who appear to be buffeted about by strong winds without anything to hold them in place, rudderless and lurching from one bad decision to the next because there is no depth of character to make them resilient to the lure of transient pleasures. Sure, the process of developing character takes time and experience, but it has to start and it should start as early as possible.

Moral philosophy and character building should not be about handing over a vast code of outlawed actions, nor should it be about simply avoiding the least bad action or doing what brings about the best consequences. Schools should get students to think about *their* character and about how this is formed over a long time by habits and they should move away from the red herring of moral dilemmas such as 'unprotected sex or not?' or 'cannabis or not?' These moral dilemmas shorten and stymie our ethical muscles by taking our attention away from what *really* matters: the question of what sort of person I want to be. Students should also be required to *be* ethical: to do things that will help them to form character and to reflect upon and learn from the successes they have and the mistakes that they make, because despite what the puritans say, we all make mistakes and they are one of the best ways to learn.

I would also challenge the argument that as teachers we must remain impartial on moral issues. To feign impartiality is to model moral apathy to our students and I believe this to be a mistake. Of course, we must not be bigoted, but provided our argument is based upon sound reasoning, we should show our students that part of the life of a responsible adult is to hold reasoned opinions about issues of moral weight. In Quaker schools, children are encouraged by their teachers not only to hold moral opinions, but to participate in campaigns and protests to defend their points of view, particularly on peace-related matters.

Before we move on to look at some of the ways that philosophy can be taught to young people, I'd just like to include a quote from A.C. Grayling's book *The Choice of Hercules.* The book gets its title from the Greek myth of Hercules, who was supposedly given the choice between a life of duty and a life of pleasure. Grayling argues that this is a false dichotomy and finishes his book with these words:

> The point of making good societies and good communities is to make conditions right for there to be good individual lives . . . the focus remains with real people, individuals in relationships with each other, all seeking and meriting a chance to realise the good . . . And since that is so, it is worth repeating – again and again – the point that the life best worth living is the informed life, the considered life, the responsible life, the chosen life, in which sound the notes that together, in harmony, make for fulfilment in the active sense of well-being and well-doing that Aristotle nominated as the mark of moral success. It might be a Herculean labour at times to achieve this success; but the choice any would-be Hercules of the good life should make, is at least to try: for it is the endeavour itself which is the greatest part of the good.[62]

Putting it into practice: teaching philosophy

This really isn't as daunting as you think and it certainly doesn't require you to read the complete works of Plato or Bertrand Russell. The only qualifications needed for this are, first, to have an open and enquiring mind and, second, to be willing to let your students experiment with ideas and make mistakes.

Starting out

Philosophy starts with the ability to ask questions and to be aware of our own understanding of knowledge. Here are some ideas for starting this process off.

- **The right type of question**: philosophy starts with questions that will spark debate (e.g. are school uniforms necessary?). Closed questions (e.g. what colour is my blazer?) while important (as they set the limits of what we can know) don't lead to that much discussion, which is what we are trying to engender. Ask students to come up with a list of philosophical questions they would like to have answered.

- **Philosophy is everywhere**: give your students an array of mundane objects and see what kinds of questions they come up with. Hopefully they will see that you don't need a beard, some sandals and a toga to start the philosophical process.

- **Spot the difference**: set out three objects with absolutely nothing in common. Ask the students to spot the difference/odd one out. Just because they don't know that there isn't an odd one out doesn't stop them thinking. They come up with amazing answers and it's a great warm-up exercise.

- **Knowledge**: give students a series of statements which mix up knowledge, beliefs and opinions such as 'water boils at 100°C', 'there is life after death', and 'Liverpool are the greatest football team', and ask them to separate them into knowledge, belief and opinion and then ask them where we get these items of knowledge/belief/opinion from.

Observation

- **Philosophy diary**: ask your students to keep a diary for a week (or more) of philosophical questions and what prompts them. For example, they might be watching an episode of *The Simpsons* and wonder about something, or they might be climbing a tree and suddenly have an idea. In the following lesson, ask the students to volunteer philosophical observations that they have made.
- **The philosophy of others**: once you have taught some of the problems of arguing philosophically, ask the students to observe the arguing style of others: family, friends, philosophers, politicians, football coaches, and get them to keep a diary of the philosophical mistakes that other people make.

Arguments

- **Spurious arguments**: type 'the case for banning bread' into an internet search engine – hopefully your search will yield a set of spurious arguments for banning bread. See what your students make of it. See if they can spot why these arguments are fallacious using their philosopher's toolkit. Alternatively, type 'dear Dr Laura' into a search engine. This will bring up a great example of how you can challenge received wisdom.

Discussion

- **The discussion lesson**: give an entire lesson over to discussion. Start with some stimulus and ask the students to come up with a series of questions based upon it. Sit in a circle and slowly work your way through the questions in order of class preference (perhaps having voted on it beforehand). Take a backseat role as teacher and let the group lead the discussion: just intervene when more than one person is speaking at once. The content of the discussion is secondary to the quality of the discussion: encourage the group to construct good arguments, avoiding the mistakes we have seen above. Give them crib sheets if needs be to remind them of arguments that don't work.
- **Texts and imagination**: provide students with extracts from books or newspaper articles that are provocative or that raise questions – this could be anything from Harry Potter to an editorial in *The Times*. Ask one half of the group to speculate on the implications for us if the author is right and the other half to speculate if the author is wrong. Science fiction and fantasy might be particularly good for this exercise.
- **Imaginary dialogue**: ask students to adopt a character and argue as they would. The character

could be a historical figure, a current figure, a stereotype or someone imaginary. They should then set up a dialogue with someone else, also in character, and see how long they can maintain authentic argument.

Moral philosophy

- **Who's right, who's wrong?** Provide students with a controversial story from the news, one which really divides opinion. Before discussing, ask the group to divide themselves up into those who hold one opinion, those who hold the opposite opinion and those who are neutral. They should stand/sit in different parts of the classroom. Open up the debate by asking particular students why they are standing in a particular place. Allow students to move if they change their opinion.

- **Campaign**: ask students to organize an imaginary campaign on a moral issue. What would they do? What are they allowed to do by law? What would be the most effective way of gathering support? How can their campaign retain moral integrity (i.e. is it right to have a violent demonstration against war?)?

Evaluation

- **Reflect**: ask students to reflect on how finding out about philosophical thought has affected them. How has it helped them in other subjects? How has it helped them in their personal lives; for example, in negotiating in disagreements?

5   Emotions

Chapter preview

- Case study: Tom
- Emotional awareness: knowing what emotions are and how they work
- Emotional management
- An emotional management case study: Phineas Gage
- Emotions and other people
- Back to Tom

Case study: Tom

Tom sat at the table in room 17 of Marlton Community College. It was about 8.45 a.m. in the morning and registration would happen at 9 a.m. He usually sat at the same table, on the left-hand side of the room, just out of the morning sunlight which streamed in through the windows in the back. The school buildings were poorly designed and built in the 1960s and the furniture was utilitarian and battered. The tables had brown formica surfaces with graffiti etched into them by the tips of pairs of compasses, most of it initials only, but some of it was profane and several of the tables had lost one or two of the plastic feet which sat in the ends of the legs, making them wobble. Every day folded up pieces of file paper were placed between leg tip and floor, abating frustration, until the frustrated cleaners removed them when the school was in twilight and silent. The room was a double, divided by a concertina-like screen in the middle, and at lunchtime the screen was withdrawn and rooms 17 and 18 became the school dining room. As a result, when the time came for afternoon registration, the room smelt of chips and vinegar and there were sometimes brown, acrid puddles of Sarson's to be avoided.

There were already a few people in. Lindsay, Jo and Mel sat together at the back and talked. Tom couldn't hear what they were talking about, they were usually quite quiet. He was also slightly wary of them: he had said something insulting to Lindsay earlier in the year and the three of them had shunned him and said unpleasant things to others in the tutor group about him. This had mostly blown over, but it was still quite a raw wound and some of the insults that the girls had dreamt up were occasionally shouted across the classroom.

Some of the early buses had already brought kids in from Caldwood, but the Barnleigh lot had yet to arrive. Paul, who was from another tutor group, sat holding hands with his girlfriend Emma and a couple of others sat with them, including James, the social star of the group. Tom felt awkward in their company as he didn't know them well and found that they were not interested in the things he was interested in. Also, they were considered cool and popular and while Tom wasn't socially inept, he certainly wasn't cool.

Soon enough, Toby and Euan, Tom's best friends in the tutor group, appeared in the doorway and quickly they were sat together around the table. All three had seen the same comedy programme the night before and were busy repeating funny lines and correcting each other when they got them wrong. This ritual, accompanied by sharing new and exciting bits of information about cars and each other's exploits went way back to primary school, it was the favourite part of the day for all three and was repeated at break and lunchtime and on the way home at the end of the day. After a couple of minutes, James came over to join them and immediately showed not only that he had remembered the best lines from the programme, but could do the voices too. This impressed all three.

A loud cacophony in the corridor outside the room heralded the arrival of the kids from Barnleigh. They had gone to different primary schools to Tom, Toby and Euan and much of the nine months they had spent at the school so far involved getting to know these strangers. The Barnleigh kids felt a bit rougher and a bit more know-ledgeable about dangerous things than the Marlton kids. Already, a few of them smoked and Tom knew that a couple of them had broken into boarded up derelict houses and also went shoplifting. It seemed to Tom that when there was someone who hadn't done their homework, it was a Barnleigh kid. If someone got sent out of class, it was a Barnleigh kid. He always felt slightly on edge around these newcomers to the town and he knew that Euan felt the same way, although Toby always seemed much more interested in getting involved when there was mischief afoot.

Finn and Danny came to join them. Finn sat down. He stank of cigarette smoke, not just from his parents, but from the cigarette he'd had on the walk up to school from the bus stop with Danny. Finn was small for his age and where Tom was awkward in some social situations, Finn appeared confident, but tended to make people around him uncomfortable. He was keen to impress others with stories of his accomplishments, but many of them were obviously untrue and in any case the events he related usually revolved around rule-breaking, cheating or lying or showing that he could challenge authority where others wouldn't. This didn't impress those who were genuinely bold enough to do the things Finn thought cool and worthy of approval, and alienated those who complied with authority. Danny, who was from the year above and who liked to think he impressed kids in the year below with his street wisdom, stood behind Finn with a grin on his face. 'Go on Finn; show them what's in your bag.' Finn obliged and opened up his school bag. On top of the broken pencils and tatty exercise books sat two full shop-sized boxes of chewing gum and ten packets of 20 cigarettes. 'Nicked them from my Nan's shop. I'm going to sell them.' Tom immediately bristled with fear. Not only was he not allowed to chew gum by his parents, not only did smoking strike him as the most rebellious thing a young person could do, but Tom was also absolutely petrified of getting into trouble and being associated with wrongdoing. The thought of being caught, by their tutor, with an open bag full of illicit items *in school* filled him with dread. He also knew that he didn't want the lives that Finn and Danny had. Tom thought about moving to another table to protect himself, but was also worried about losing face in front of his friends. Toby and James were already showing a deep interest in what Finn had in his bag, while Tom and Euan shared concerned glances and tried to conceal their feelings.

'Robson's coming!'

At the warning of the form tutor's approach, the bag was zipped shut. Tom could feel his heart thud in his chest and the blood drained from his face in anticipation of being caught in the act by their form tutor. Danny left the room confidently saying 'Morning Sir' as he went through the door. Robson strolled in, register in hand, smug and spoiling for a sarcastic outburst as usual. They all knew he didn't like them: they were insignificant and uninteresting and until they could dissect literature at A level, weren't worth talking to in any meaningful way. As his register opened, they all felt the school day beginning.

'Finn.'

The tutor group all looked at Robson who was holding a piece of red paper above his head. All apart from Finn who was trying to engage Toby, Euan and Tom in conversation about his new money-spinning venture, and who hadn't picked up on their facial cues that his attention was wanted elsewhere.

'Listen to me when I'm talking to you Finn. There's a note here from Mr Parmenter telling you to go to his room now to hand in those homeworks that are late.'

Finn's face fell. It was obvious that he hadn't done the work. He didn't move.

'Well off you go then!' Robson shouted. Tom, Toby and Euan edged away from Finn in their seats. Tom's stomach turned somersaults. Even by association with a troublemaker he felt uncomfortable.

'I'm not going sir.'

'What?! I suppose what you mean is, "I haven't done the work sir."' Robson mimicked a snivelling tone at this point. 'I've told you once to go and I don't want to have to keep telling you like you're some kind of moron!'

Robson's tone had escalated in volume and force to anger by the end of the sentence. The rest of the tutor group all knew what was about to happen: this had become quite a regular occurrence.

'I'm not going! Alright!' Finn slammed his fists on the table, and then sat back in his chair, arms folded across his chest, eyes wide open, face red and breathing heavily. He muttered an expletive under his breath.

'What did you say?! Get out! Get out of my classroom!'

Finn stood bolt upright knocking his chair over in the process and stormed out, slamming the door behind him.

Robson took the register swiftly and in a state of obvious agitation. He then strode out of the classroom and the tutor group turned to each other with muffled, cautious giggles as a heated exchange between the two of them took place in the corridor. Finn came back into the classroom, shoulders sloped down, avoiding eye contact with the others. Tom handed him his bag as he came over to collect it. Finn muttered a barely audible 'thanks' as he choked back some tears. Robson stood at the door, looking imperious and authoritative as he ushered the boy he had reduced to tears out and off to the head of year's office.

Emotional awareness: knowing what emotions are and how they work

At the root of the teaching of emotional intelligence to young people lies the need to enable them to avoid getting caught up in situations like this and to equip them with the skills *and* the opportunity to practise them, which will help them to avoid making mistakes with their emotions. This chapter will explore what the emotions are, how they work and what children can do to heighten their emotional awareness and skill.

What is an emotion?

In terms of the repertoire of emotions, it has been suggested that there are roughly eight main emotions, each having a family of shaded varieties. These eight emotions are:

- anger
- fear
- sadness
- enjoyment
- love
- disgust
- shame
- surprise.

As with any system of classification, there is disagreement about the exact number of emotions, with some arguing that there should be more and others less. What is known, however, is that these emotions are for the most part universal across cultures; if someone is surprised in Papua New Guinea, their eyebrows raise in the same way as someone's eyebrows in Frankfurt.[63] Throughout the chapter I will refer to positive and negative emotions; by this I mean emotions which either help us or hinder us. For example, disgust is to be viewed positively if it helps you to avoid eating something that will do you harm and enjoyment is to be viewed negatively if it results in harming another person. Matthieu Ricard puts it like this:

> If an emotion strengthens our inner peace and seeks the good of others, it is *positive*, or constructive; if it shatters our serenity, deeply disturbs our mind, and is intended to harm others, it is *negative* or afflictive.[64]

Evolutionary theory and evidence is not conclusive about exactly when the brain structure of *homo sapiens sapiens* was moulded into the shape that we now have, but it is at the very least tens of thousands of years old. Emotions evolved to perform two basic functions: they draw us towards objects, people and events that ensure our survival and drive us away from objects, people and events that threaten our survival. The emotions act as an alert system, much of which operates at the subconscious level, to keep us on the right course for a flourishing existence. Of course, any alert system that is not properly maintained will either not work, will not work at the right time or will be overactive. Tom's alert system was primed for any threat to the way he was perceived by others. He had been brought up to be moral and desperately avoided situations that threatened this – probably due to emphatic reinforcement from his parents. As well as alerting through the sympathetic (fight, flight or freeze) system, the body soothes itself through the parasympathetic system, which regulates heart beat and breathing once the perceived threat has gone. Our responses to both of these systems can be augmented through practice.[65]

By early adolescence, children should be in a position to recognize emotional states. They should be able to accurately interpret the myriad signals that we give off to others through facial expression, body language and tone of voice enabling them to detect and respond accurately to others in social situations. Some, however, have had more practice at this than others. Finn is a character whom we all recognize as someone who is so desperate to ingratiate himself into a group that he neglects to read how others are feeling (Tom and Euan's nervousness for example). James on the other hand is clearly well-versed in moving effortlessly between different social situations and reading the cues given off by others, enabling him to successfully blend into new surroundings without making others feel uncomfortable. One might also suggest that the form tutor behaved in an emotionally unintelligent way and that the stand-off that we witnessed was caused by his failure to deal with a clearly volatile child in an appropriate way.

How do emotions work?[66] Primary emotions

By the time children reach early adolescence, a lot of their emotional development has already taken place, and in fact many of our pre-dispositions to emotional behaviour are set at birth via our genetics and in the infant years by our primary care-givers and the way that they interact with us. With emotions, Haidt's analogy of the elephant and rider is particularly apposite as while we may believe we are in complete control of our emotions, the reality does not quite correspond with this.

Antonio Damasio, a distinguished neuroscientist has argued that there are two types of emotions: primary and secondary. The primary emotions are likely to have been present in our most distant primate ancestors and find their root in the limbic system of the brain. The limbic system has been characterized as a bagel with a bite taken out of it, and it sits on top of the brain stem, which leads down to the spinal column and is the first and last vestige of the life signals: physical death is determined by brain-stem activity. The limbic system controls all the basic functions that keep us alive and that we never think about until they come under threat. The key part of the brain relevant to an understanding of primary emotion is the amygdala, two of which sit on top of the limbic system: one on the left, one on the right. The amygdala, vital to an understanding of how emotions work, has been described by Daniel Goleman as the 'neural tripwire',[67] because it is responsible for marshalling the body's initial response to external stimuli. When the body perceives an object, person or event that is either beneficial or detrimental to survival, the percept is received by the brain from the sensory apparatus in the thalamus. The thalamus directs this percept to two areas: the amygdala and the neo-cortex.

When Tom saw the bag open in front of him, his amygdala would have marshalled the fear response (or a close relative such as apprehension or foreboding). It would have caused certain physical reactions to take place before he became aware of it: a surge of catecholamines (chemicals such as adrenaline, epinephrine and nor-epinephrine) would have flowed through his bloodstream enabling a quick physical response. His eyes would have opened wide and his eyebrows would have risen to take a wider view of the threat. Blood would have flowed to his large skeletal muscles to enable flight – this would have accounted for his face blanching as the blood flowed to where it was most needed. In Finn, when he was challenged by Mr Robson, his amygdala would have begun the anger response. Similar chemicals would have been released, but this time with the intention of fighting. Blood would have flowed to his hands to enable him to grab an object to fight with, hence his slamming the desk.

This situation is what Damasio calls a primary emotion. It is the emotional system that saves our lives for us when we step out in front of a bus and find ourselves on the pavement seconds later, mysteriously un-squished with not much idea how we did it.

It is also the system that may cause us to jump into a river to save the life of a drowning child without thinking about it. This primary system is in part formed by genetic instructions which determine brain structure, size and function and in part by our learning experiences, which start from the earliest moments of childhood.

Learning emotion

In the first few years of life, infants pick up on cues for emotional management from their parents and primary care-givers. The affective styles[68] of child and parent will influence the way that they interact with each other and it is through the thousands of little exchanges that later emotional proclivities are shaped.[69] When a baby gazes attentively at its mother and father, part of what the baby is doing is learning how its parents act emotionally. The child who is brought up in a safe, secure, calm and loving environment will, according to some psychologists and psychotherapists, begin to adopt these emotional patterns in their own lives.[70]

Also 'attachment theory', developed by John Bowlby and Mary Ainsworth (and explained in more detail in Chapter 3), suggests that a child who is securely attached to his or her primary care-giver will develop emotional competency later in life.[71] Secure attachment is shown in children who feel happy to explore and experiment in the presence of (in Ainsworth's experiments) their mother, who are able to adjust and cope when left by their mother and replaced by a stranger and who return to exploring and experimenting when their mother returns. Statistics relating to American children suggest that approximately 66 per cent of children develop secure attachment styles. Bowlby and Ainsworth's research has been augmented by Cindy Hazan and Phil Shaver who have suggested that children who are securely attached as infants replicate these secure patterns of attachment in their adult relationships.[72]

We do not stop learning and modifying our emotional behaviours. Because of this, it is vital that children of adolescent age not only have the opportunity to learn about their own emotional systems, but that they also have opportunities to practise different emotional management techniques and crucially for us as adult role models, that they have the opportunity to see how adults regulate and manage their emotions so that they themselves can learn appropriate emotional responses to situations. In this sense Mr Robson was not a good emotional role model.

Secondary emotions

Given that emotions are generated by the same system in all of us and that emotions are largely universally experienced and expressed, it should be no surprise that children of adolescent age can, in general, recognize emotional states effectively.[73] It is with what Damasio terms 'secondary emotions' that the real issues lie for the majority of children of adolescent age. As well as sending a signal to the amygdala for a quick, often subconscious response, the thalamus also sends a signal to the pre-frontal cortex in the pre-frontal lobe area of the brain. As our ancestors evolved from apes to humans, something triggered the brain to develop an area that became capable of language and reasoning. This is the rippled 'grey matter' that sits on top of a brain – it is the bit that we can see. Evidence shows that the pre-frontal cortex, in the thinking part of the brain, has a responsibility for dealing *intelligently* with emotional responses and turns brute emotion into feeling and moods that can be manipulated.

Why is this such an issue for adolescents? While the sensory and limbic systems are generally developed by puberty, the pre-frontal cortices which provide the more nuanced emotional levels continue to mature into the mid-to-late teens (16–18). To be sure, the human brain has qualities of plasticity and continues to be altered by experiences throughout its lifetime, but to nothing like the same extent as during childhood and adolescence. Adolescence is the perfect time for children to be exposed to experiences that help them develop and reflect upon their emotional skills, and helping the pre-frontal cortices to develop properly allows a degree of control and feeling of emotional states which is socially invaluable.

> In short, feeling your emotional states, which is to say being conscious of emotions, offers you *flexibility of response based on the particular history of your interactions with the environment*. Although you need innate devices to start the ball of knowledge rolling, feelings offer you something extra.[74]

This 'something extra' for adolescents is the opportunity to not let their lives be dominated by unpredictable mood swings, which they arguably would be if we only had a primary emotional system. It is the opportunity to, with practice, choose the mood that they are in. It is the opportunity to choose which emotions are appropriate in particular situations, thus enabling us to create and maintain positive relationships. It is the opportunity to train ourselves out of potentially crippling emotional reactions from the primary system (excessive anxiety for example) by using the secondary system to immediately ask the questions 'why do I feel like this?' and 'why did I react like that?'

Emotional memory

Another interesting function of the pre-frontal cortex which has been suggested by Antonio Damasio comes via his theory of the *somatic marker*. Damasio's research has shown that the emotions play a crucial role in our ability to make decisions, so much so that it appears that the philosopher Immanuel Kant's assertion that emotion should not be involved in moral decision making may have been misguided. There is emotional memory in the limbic system: the amygdala, in collaboration with the hippocampus, stores information about past events which have generated large emotional responses, so that when similar events occur we are made cognisant of the past and know to be drawn to or avoid that experience. However, Damasio argues that the pre-frontal cortex lays down what he calls *somatic markers* which, based upon past experiences, direct us away from courses of action that prove disastrous and reduce our options in decision making. Some people may refer to this as gut instinct. Damasio has put a very convincing argument forward that, without the secondary emotional system in the pre-frontal cortex, our ability to make decisions that serve us well is dramatically reduced. Opportunities to fine tune our pre-frontal cortex are of the utmost importance.

So, what does all this mean for adolescents? During the secondary-school years children will become aware of complex emotional cycles, where one emotional state proceeds from another (for example, feeling guilty about feeling angry). Adolescents will learn to regulate their own emotions and this will be informed by their emotional memories right from early childhood, their moral beliefs and by their concerns about the way that they appear to others. They may also distinguish between different groups when doing this; for example, Tom became fearful because his moral beliefs about theft and smoking prompted this reaction. Had Finn been challenged or mocked by a peer in the same way that his tutor challenged him, he would almost certainly have reacted violently. Adolescents get better and better at 'packaging themselves' emotionally to gain approval from peers and adults; they also become better at talking about feelings with each other to create and strengthen relationships.[75]

Putting it into practice: teaching emotional awareness

- **Self-awareness**: get students to complete an emotional inventory to develop an awareness of their emotions. These are available online for free at www.authentichappiness.org: the PANAS scale is a useful tool.
- **Identity parade**: using images from an internet search, a film clip or an extract from a book, ask students to 'diagnose' emotional states in the characters and justify why they believe it to be a certain emotion. Ask students to look for a range of evidence from tone of voice to facial expression and body language. (Pixar films usually have good and easily identifiable emotional outbursts in them, e.g. Donkey in *Shrek*.)

- **Under pressure**: ask students to perform a challenging task against the clock (such as building a house of cards) and ask them to name the emotions that arise during the task and notice how their emotions change while completing it.

- **Sculpture**: using a pair of volunteers, ask one student to 'sculpt' the other student into an emotion, paying particular attention to facial expression and body language. Ask the class to diagnose the emotion and explain the symptoms.

- **Sculpture 2**: give students a piece of paper divided into six sections. Using modelling clay of different colours, ask them to sculpt six different emotions one by one, three 'positive' and three 'negative'. It might help to use guided imagination for this to help them imagine the emotion.[76]

- **Emotions and morals**: in the time between lessons, ask students to notice how their body employs emotions when they are faced with moral decisions. Does the emotion of disgust appear when they are offered something they know they shouldn't take? Can they find any somatic markers of their own?

- **Journal**: between lessons, get students to observe emotions 'in the wild' and make observations on what they see in both themselves and others. They should record what the emotion was, the activity that caused it, the beliefs that caused it (e.g. school bags full of stolen cigarettes get people into trouble), what the physiological symptoms were, how long the emotion lasted and what, if anything, caused it to come to an end. Feedback in the following lesson.

Emotional management

> With the help of experience, we can deal with negative emotions *before* they surface. We can 'see them coming' and learn to distinguish those that bring suffering from those that contribute to happiness . . . In order to prevent forest fires in times of drought, the forester cuts firebreaks, lays up stores of water, and remains alert. He knows very well that it is easier to extinguish a spark than an inferno. (Matthieu Ricard)[77]

Noticing what is going on for us emotionally is a very important skill to develop and as Matthieu Ricard suggests, the important skills are those of noticing and managing emotions as or even before they arise. Young people should be able to name emotions as they arise and they should also be able to associate physical and mental symptoms with particular feelings and moods, both in themselves and in others. These are the basic and fundamental building blocks of forming successful relationships: if we know our own emotional state and can read the emotional states of the people around us, we can behave appropriately and enable meaningful interaction. The overall aim of emotional management is to enable us to bring about the right kind of emotional state to enable us to perform optimally in any given situation. It has been suggested that there are four emotional zones, which are set out as follows:[78]

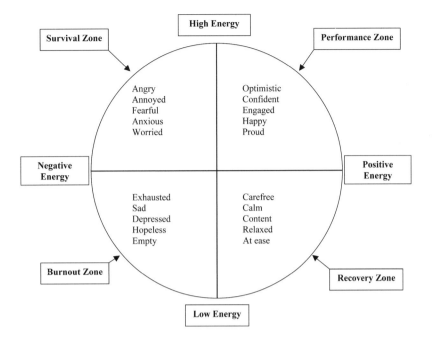

We will spend a mixture of time in each zone in our lives, but what is important is the ability to recognize which zone we are in and act either to remain in it, or take steps to get out of a zone that is undesirable. It is not appropriate to remain exclusively in one zone: accomplishment in life relies upon us being able to move between zones to achieve different things. Obviously, it will be appropriate to spend some time in either the burnout zone or the survival zone, if someone has just died or we are about to be run over by a bus for example. The trick is to restrict the time we spend in the negative energy zones to necessity and aim to get ourselves in the positive energy zones as much as possible. The skills we need to do this are encompassed in emotional awareness, which has just been described, and emotional management, which is described next.

Emotional management builds upon emotional awareness by enabling us to take charge of our emotional states. Very often we see people who are at the mercy of their emotions and seem to exhibit no control over them at all, or we see people who control their emotions so much that they appear to be emotionless. An example illustrating this is that of Zinedine Zidane, the French footballer. Zidane is arguably the greatest footballer to have played the game and to watch him in full flow is to watch a man in complete control of his emotions. A film was once made which followed Zidane for an entire 90 minutes of a football match: the camera tracks him alone. While he plays, Zidane is in an almost trance-like state of concentration: he is utterly focused; all unnecessary emotions and feelings are subdued in order for him to maintain complete absorption in his play. Famously, Zidane's concentration was broken in the 2006 World Cup final by the Italian player Marco Materazzi, who cast a slur against Zidane's sister causing him to lose his temper. Zidane head-butted Materazzi in the chest and he was sent off for the foul. France lost the game. In the split second where Zidane reacted, he lost control of his emotions.

How often do we see this happen in schools? How often do we see children let their emotions get the better of them, causing barriers to their learning, either by getting them excluded from a lesson, or by being so intense during a lesson that they cannot concentrate on the academic work in front of them? Lack of emotional skill disenfranchises children. While Finn may have known he is prone to angry outbursts, it is clear that he was not able to manage those outbursts as they arose. There are a few simple tactics that children can learn that will help them to manage their emotions and spend the right amounts of time in the positive and negative energy zones:

- positive actions
- broaden and build
- self-soothing.

Positive actions

This technique for managing negative emotions involves being aware of a negative emotional state and choosing to do something positive, which stops the negative state being prolonged. There are several approaches to it that children ought to experiment with:

- **Pleasures**: engage in an activity that brings pleasure, such as reading, watching comedy, listening to or playing music. Bear the distinction between pleasures and gratifications in mind and remember that we adapt to pleasurable activities eventually. Also distinguish between constructive and destructive pleasures.
- **Exercise**: exercise releases chemicals in the body that increase positive feeling and mood.
- **Accomplish**: complete a task, do something *simple* you've been meaning to do for ages, e.g. tidy up. The feeling of success at having completed something raises positive affect.
- **Flow**: do something that you become completely absorbed in.
- **Stillness**: practise meditation. Bear in mind that this intervention works better for breaking the cycle of high-arousal emotions such as anger or fear. For emotions linked with sadness and depression, while meditation can be enormously effective, it may not help to *break the cycle* in the same way as exercise, a high-arousal activity, can.
- **Altruism**: do something to help someone else. Frequent experiments have shown long-lasting positive affect results from being altruistic.

Broaden and build

Barbara Fredrickson argues that experience of positive emotions helps to broaden our horizons and build our social, physical and intellectual skills; in other words, the more that a person experiences positive emotions, the more creative and the more able they become. This is illustrated in a simple experiment where subjects were split into two groups. Each group was given a candle, matches and a box of tacks and were asked to attach the candle to the wall in such a way that the candle didn't drip wax onto the floor. One group was shown a funny video beforehand, the other group was not. The group that benefited from the positive emotional state before attempting the challenge was invariably the group that succeeded at the challenge because the laughter and release of associated chemicals in the brain allowed them to be more creative and avoid 'functional fixedness' where they use the objects conventionally. The solution is to empty the tacks from the box, tack it to the wall and use it as a candleholder.[79]

Martin Seligman refers to similar research showing that doctors were better able to diagnose liver problems when they had been primed to feel positive beforehand: their peripheral awareness was heightened and they were more creative. Seligman argues that when we are positive, we tend to see more of what is right around us and we are more competent at synthesizing information and seeing links between ideas; when negative, our ability to be creative is closed down. Positive emotions, when experienced, create virtuous cycles as Sonja Lyubomirsky explains:

> positive emotions beget upward spirals – for example, you feel invigorated after aerobic exercise, which boosts your creativity, which gives you a new idea about how to enchant your partner, which strengthens your marriage, which shores up your satisfaction and commitment, which leads you to be more grateful and forgiving, which fuels optimism, which creates a self-fulfilling prophecy, which buffers the sting of a setback at work and so on.[80]

Self-soothing

Self-soothing is the skill of lessening the effect of negative moods or reducing the impact of negative emotions. The aim is to engage the parasympathetic nervous system, which calms us down and through the vagus nerve slows down heart rate and breathing. Self-soothing is a skill that we begin to learn in early childhood by observing how our parents or care-givers respond to our basic needs and, in mimicking this, we in turn learn how to manage our own moods. While we may not have complete control over when a particular emotion seizes us, we certainly have control over how long that emotion or mood lasts. Self-soothing depends upon being emotionally self-aware and also being willing to try the emotional management techniques mentioned above.

Here are some of the self-soothing methods to help us cope with unhelpful emotional states:[81]

- **Distraction**: emotions exist, for the most part, in the mind – they are cognitive. In order to overcome undesired emotions, we must either think about something else, or do something else to distract us from it. Suggest to students that if an undesirable emotion arises, they ought to do something else: go for a walk or a run, play a game with friends, watch a (funny) film, read a book, meditate – engage in activities that take their mind off the emotion they don't want to experience. Emotions build themselves up the longer we experience them: it is up to us to dissipate them. It is also worth remembering that it is not possible to experience a positive and negative emotion at the same time: the one will replace the other.

- **Touch**: there is some evidence that the vagus nerve might be activated by feelings of love.[82] We can all remember times when being held by someone we love or trust has calmed us down or slowed down the process of a fight, flight or freeze emotion. Being held by a family member, a friend or someone trusted might therefore help to soothe heightened negative emotional states.

- **Catch and write**: as you notice unpleasant thoughts arising, write them down. Once you can see them in front of you, they can be challenged or re-appraised.

- **Angel's advocate**: as unpleasant emotions surface, stop and ask yourself why you are having this feeling and challenge it. What has caused it? Are the causes legitimate? Nine times out of ten, the negative feeling can be easily challenged. This works best in the early stages of the emotion arising and so depends upon practice in emotional self-diagnosis.

- **Re-frame**: at the end of one of P.G. Wodehouse's Jeeves and Wooster stories, Bertie Wooster is bemoaning the end of his engagement to Honoria Glossop, when all of a sudden, with the help of his trusty servant Jeeves, he realizes that he didn't want to be engaged to her in the first place. This is a form of re-framing, which simply means altering our focus from the negative aspects of an event, onto the positive, and thereby gaining a new perspective.

- **Channel**: emotions, as we know, are signals to act. A good way of dissipating unwanted emotions is to use the impetus given to us by the emotion to act to change some part of our environment: to channel the emotion into action. *Touching the Void* is a film about a mountaineer stranded on a mountain with a badly broken leg. There is a superb sequence which illustrates the skill of channelling. Joe Simpson, after falling into a crevasse having had his rope cut by his climbing partner, channels extreme levels of fear and anger into summoning the energy to crawl back to base camp. This channelling of negative emotion into positive ones saved his life.

It is important to point out that managing emotions is not the same as masking or suppressing them. Emotions are essential markers for us, indicating whether we are safe or in some kind of danger: we ignore emotions at our peril. However, it is possible to be over-indulgent with emotions and allow them to continue beyond their use-by date. Learning how to manage our emotions and use them efficiently is an important skill to develop.

An emotional management case study: Phineas Gage

Emotional management is a skill that has to be learned through practice and it appears that the skills reside in a specific part of the brain, as demonstrated by the celebrated story of a nineteenth-century rail worker.

Phineas Gage was 25 years old in 1848 and the Rutland and Burlington Railroad Company who employed him as a construction foreman said that he was the most efficient and capable man in their employ. The Rutland and Burlington were expanding their railroad network across Vermont and the gang that Gage was in charge of were blasting a path for the tracks through rock using explosive charges. The process of blasting was simple, but it had to be carried out in stages with precise accuracy and high levels of concentration. First, a hole was drilled in the rock. Second, explosive powder was poured into the hole so that it was half full. Third, a fuse was inserted. Fourth, sand was poured into the hole and tamped down with an iron rod, to ensure that the blast went into the rock, and not straight back out of the hole. Finally, the fuse was lit and the rock blasted to desired effect. Gage was described as being a virtuoso at laying explosive charges. On 13 September, Gage was busily laying charges. In the middle of one charge, someone distracted his attention. He turned back to the job and began tamping before the sand had been poured in. As the iron tamping rod, hand-made to Gage's personal specification, struck into the hole, it caused a spark to ignite the powder and the metre long, 3.5cm diameter iron rod was blasted out of the hole, through Gage's left cheek, traversing the front of his brain and exiting the top of his head at high speed, landing some 30 metres away. Miraculously, Gage survived.

Here is how Dr Edward Williams, who treated Gage initially, described what he found an hour after the accident:

> I first noticed the wound upon the head before I alighted from my carriage, the pulsations of the brain being very distinct . . . the opening through the skull and integuments was not far from one and a half inch in diameter; the edges of this opening were everted, and the whole wound appeared as if some wedge shaped body had passed from below upward . . . Mr Gage then related to me some of the circumstances, as he has since done; and I can safely say that neither at that time nor on any subsequent occasion, save once, did I consider him to be other than perfectly rational.

The story of Phineas Gage not only shows the remarkable ability of the human brain to survive seemingly fatal injuries, but it also demonstrates the role of the pre-frontal cortex, the part of Gage's brain that was taken with the rod as it exited his head. Before the accident happened, Gage was a reliable, hard-working and morally upstanding man. Even though he survived the accident and did so seemingly with his ability to reason and his memory intact, there was something different about him. 'Gage was no longer Gage.' He became foul-mouthed, aggressive and generally unpleasant to be around, so much so that women were advised not to stay long in his company.

After the accident, the change in Gage's personality meant that his former employer would not take him back. He worked on farms and ranches with horses, but couldn't hold a job down for long because he fell out with his colleagues or his employers. For a while he became a circus attraction, but this didn't last and after a spell in South America, he returned to the US, and moved around different labouring jobs before dying, aged 38 in 1861.

Research into the life of Gage, and into patients exhibiting similar changes in behaviour caused by either brain damage or unwanted growths such as tumours, show that the pre-frontal cortex[83] plays a very important role in regulating and managing emotions, making decisions relating to our futures, assessing risk and in ensuring that we act in accordance with the moral norms of our culture, particularly those associated with sexuality and appropriate sexual conduct.

Putting it into practice: teaching emotional management

- **Mimic**: split the class in half. Ask one half to take a pen and clasp it horizontally between their teeth, mimicking a smile and ask the other half to grip the pen horizontally between their puckered-up lips, mimicking a frown. Then, give them some funny cartoons to watch and see the effect. The children with the pen between their teeth should find the cartoons funnier because the smile and the emotion have already been prompted.[84]

- **Mimic 2**: find the 'laughing quadruplets' video on the internet. This, just by itself, shows how emotions are infectious and should influence most of your students.

- **Just do it**: try out some of the 'positive actions' mentioned above with a class. Ask them to practise them in their own time and reflect on their effectiveness in their journals.

- **Random act of kindness**: ask the students, between lessons, to practise a random act of kindness for someone they don't know and compare the intensity and duration of the feeling that results with a pleasure such as eating a bar of chocolate. Take feedback.

- **Problem solving**: run the experiment with the candle holder quoted above (or something similar) in class. Ask students to reflect upon the impact of the funny stimulus (or its absence) on their ability to complete the task.

- **Zone change**: ask the students to picture themselves in one of the emotional zones. Ask them to think about what might have put them there, how long they ought to stay in that zone and what they might need to do to move to one of the other zones.

- **Journal; broaden and build**: the most powerful way to explore this is to ask students to be on the look-out for positive and negative emotional spirals between lessons. Ask them to observe and record times when, for example, their mum said/did something nice for them when they got home from school, this helped them complete homework/music practice really well, which led to a really absorbing and positive conversation with a sibling/friend, etc. Ask the children to pay particular attention *to the way the positive emotion impacted upon the subsequent task/interaction*. Obviously, the same process may occur with negative spirals of affect, and some children may report this, but encourage them to balance their report with a positive experience. Use the anonymous feedback method (see Chapter 1) and read out some examples in class the following lesson.

- **Journal; self-soothing**: ask students to try some of the self-soothing strategies suggested above and evaluate their effectiveness for preventing the experience of negative emotions being prolonged.

Emotions and other people

The topic of relationships has an entire chapter devoted to it later on in the book, but emotional intelligence is arguably *the* essential skill in forming meaningful relationships with other people and young people who are able to create a number of good relationships are generally characterized as being popular. A popular child will usually be described as being helpful, friendly, considerate, warm, humorous, sensitive to social cues and capable of following the agreed rules in games and play. They will also be good at joining in games or group activities: instead of barging in or silently spectating, they will take time to work out how the game is being played and pick the right time to become involved. This is contrasted with unpopular children, who are generally divided into two groups: the aggressive child and the victim, both of which are unable to tune in to social cues, but one decides to disrupt and fracture relationships, whereas the other will be withdrawn and avoidant.[85]

But it is not just about being popular with other kids. A growing body of research shows that the qualification most valued in the workplace is not academic, it is interpersonal as Daniel Goleman explains:

The new rules predict who is most likely to become a star performer and who is most prone to derailing . . . These rules have little to do with what we were told was important in school; academic abilities are largely irrelevant to this standard. The new measure takes for granted having enough intellectual ability and technical know-how to do our jobs; it focuses instead on personal qualities, such as initiative and empathy, adaptability and persuasiveness.[86]

Mimicry

Emotions and moods are contagious. We can all think of people that we love spending time with because they are infectiously and unflappably positive: we enjoy being with them because their moods invariably rub off on us. The human body is alert to the emotions of others from birth. As we watch other people, the emotions they express flash across our own faces as we mimic them subconsciously.[87] If two people sit down together, they will quite naturally attempt to tune themselves in to the emotions of the other, with the person who is more forceful holding sway over the more passive.

> Just seeing someone express an emotion can evoke that mood, whether you realise you mimic the facial expression or not. This happens to us all the time – there's a dance, a synchrony, a transmission of emotions.[88]

Simply being around others who display positive moods can help lift someone out of a bad mood, provided they are prepared to mimic and attune to them. Of course, the opposite is also true and we must be aware of that.

Putting it into practice: teaching about emotions and relationships

- **Listening and empathy**: in pairs, students read fictional stories in the first person containing emotional aspects (e.g. the break up of a relationship, an argument) to each other. The other student in the pair listens and 'mirrors' (notices and describes) the emotional states back to their partner once the story has finished (e.g. 'you felt sadness when your girlfriend said she didn't want to be with you any more, you felt this because . . .'). The listener then allows the speaker to correct any points where they have misinterpreted and the listener then corrects him/herself.

This activity encourages students to listen to the details of each other's stories first, and then pick up their emotional states and feelings. After emotional awareness, this is the next step to positive relationships as it shows another person that you know how they feel. A good way to bring this to life even more is to use clips from television series such as *Fawlty Towers* or *The Office* or films like *As Good as it Gets*. One of the main themes in these programmes is the complete emotional incompetence of characters like Basil Fawlty, David Brent and Melvin Udall: we cringe because they get it so badly wrong.

- **Cues**: when interacting with other people they give us cues as to how they are feeling through facial expressions, body language and tone of voice. Get students into groups. Ask them to consider what cues a group might give to an individual in the following scenarios:

  1. the group is enjoying your company

  2. you have annoyed someone or more than one person in the group

  3. you have disclosed something too personal to the group too early

  4. the group respect you

  5. the group trust you

  6. you are ill, unhappy or in distress.

  Ask them to pay particular attention to body language, and perhaps distinguish between 'open' and 'closed' body language with them.[89] Ask the groups to then devise a 30-second scene where this situation is acted out. Play these scenes out and offer advice and commentary from the audience.

  After observing the scenes, ask the groups to decide how an individual should react upon noticing these cues. Act this out.

  As a journal activity, ask students to pay attention to cues in their own social interactions; observe what the cues are, whether peers and adults gave different cues and describe how they then responded to them. Use anonymous feedback in the following lesson.

- **Three into two**: get students into groups of three. Ask one of them to leave the room, or stand in a corner (creating a new group). Ask the pairs to choose and start talking about one of the following topics listed on the board (their favourite holiday, their best Christmas present ever, their favourite film, what I did last weekend, if I had a million pounds). Leave them talking for 3 or 4 minutes, enough so that a rapport is built up. Then ask the third student to come in and try to find a way into the conversation successfully.

  Ask the students to reflect on how successful the newcomer was by thinking about the following questions:

  1. Did they wait, observe and try to mimic the emotions in the situation they were joining?

  2. Did they pay attention to non-verbal cues?

  3. Did they join in, try to take over or contribute nothing?

  4. Did the other two try to involve the third person?

  5. Could it have gone better or worse? If so, how? If not, why was it successful?

- **Emotional packaging**: by this stage, students should be aware of their own emotional tendencies. An exercise to consolidate this is for students to design their own emotional packaging which displays how they package themselves emotionally to the outside world. The form of packaging itself is really up to them: it could be clothing, a placard, or it could be things that they do and the emotional signals they send out.

As an ice-breaker try to find a picture of someone who is heavily pierced or tattooed, or who is clearly into death metal and ask the students to describe their emotional impressions of that person.

The key point is how our actions inform others about our emotional state. Perhaps a homework exercise for the journal could be to get your students to dress up differently and observe the different reactions elicited.

- **Journal**: ask students to do two things and observe them. First ask them to observe how they approach joining in a conversation with a group of friends: how do their friends accommodate them? How do they involve themselves? Then ask them to strike up a conversation with a group of people they don't normally talk to. How do they go about it? How does the group react? How well does the conversation go? In their journals, students should compare the two situations. What cues were given? How were the cues different? How did they follow cues? How long did it take to feel accepted in each situation? Use anonymous feedback in the next lesson.

Back to Tom

It was two days after the last GCSE paper. Tom, Gavin, Toby and James had agreed to go off camping together one night in one of the fields on the outskirts of town. At about 6 p.m., after some supper at home, Tom slung a tent, a sleeping bag and a small rucksack over his shoulder, patted his pocket to check for some money and his door key, said 'thanks for tea' and 'see ya later' to his parents and set off to call at Toby's house.

By the time they all met James at the foot of Herd Lane, the sunlight had softened and become golden. They strolled up the track together, kicking stones and leaving columns of dust hanging in the air which shimmered in the early summer evening light. They talked about exams, girls, the school band breaking up as the end of an era (artistic differences over a Bryan Adams cover version apparently). The track passed above the humming electricity substation and Tom wondered what it would be like to throw an old bike into it. He pictured the sparks flying everywhere and lights going out one by one in town, disappointed faces in front of darkened TV screens. He smiled and of course dismissed the idea as idle fantasy.

The track narrowed and passed some allotments on the right hand side. Tom remembered one Saturday afternoon, aged 8, playing there with some previous friends, two brothers, whilst their father tended his plot. It had been in the autumn, but he remembered feeling warm and safe and excited about what discarded things they might find hidden in the tree-covered valley behind the allotments.

Toby pulled the lever from the catch to open the five-bar wooden gate, which creaked on its spring as they went through and negotiated the rusty, bent bars of the cattle grid. They had done this countless times over the years, but it never ceased feeling like a challenge to avoid the gaps that were supposed to foil bovine escape plans. 'Last one through shut the gate.'

The plans for the evening were simple. Put the tents up, get hold of some beer and food, go into town and see who was about, perhaps take the opportunity to flirt with some of the Caldwood girls whom they knew were coming over that evening to sleep over with friends and generally spend some time together. The first stop was the off-licence, but instead of the usual girl who didn't know their age, believed their fake IDs and served them, a sixth former called Chris whom they knew was standing behind the counter. The four of them turned to each other, openly disappointed with this turn of events. Various solutions were offered, including raiding parents' stock, but Toby remained unflappable; they would go into the off-licence as planned and use the 'five-finger discount' at which they all knew Toby had become practised. He would need Tom and James to distract Chris while he secreted beer, kept at the back of the shop, into his rucksack.

Tom immediately felt uncomfortable. A variety of images flashed through his mind, all of which, even though fleeting, were deeply disquieting. Although drinking beer was a long-standing part of the plan for the evening and he didn't want to put a dampener on this, Toby's (brave) solution and the undeniable excitement of theft, every fibre of his being was telling him to get away from this situation.

'Mate, I'm sorry, I can't do it. Let's just get some of Gavin's dad's beer.'

'Don't be a pussy,' said Toby. 'It won't take long and I've never been caught.'

There was a noticeable pause. Tom knew he didn't want to do this, but he felt pulled by his loyalty to his friends and their enjoyment of the evening, which judging by the looks on their faces, he knew he was about to ruin. He was also worried that his fear would cause him to make a mistake in the shop and give the game away while he was distracting Chris, getting them all in trouble. He looked at Gavin, who had moved slightly away from them and was looking in a shop window. Gavin was the cleverest of the four of them, but didn't particularly enjoy this messy kind of situation resolving. He knew his own mind and because he enjoyed risk-taking, Tom knew he would have wanted to carry out a successful theft. But Tom also knew that Gavin's imagination and opportunism would offer him other possibilities and when they caught each other's eyes, the one instantly knew what the other was thinking.

Toby on the other hand was becoming agitated. This wasn't just about getting the beer, it was a matter of pride for him. He had suggested the idea and he knew he could walk out of the shop without the staff ever knowing he had taken anything. Tom's nervousness around risk-taking had been a constant source of irritation to him throughout their friendship and while it had got better over the years, situations like this infuriated him. And Tom knew this. By this time, Toby was scowling and had turned away, his shoulders hunched, hands thrust into his pockets.

Tom decided to tackle it head on.

'I'm sorry mate; I know it pisses you off when I get like this. I'm just worried that if I go in there, all pasty-faced and sweating and looking around nervously, Chris will spot what's going on and we'll all be in trouble. Let's go in there, buy some fags and crisps, I've got the cash, then we go to Gavin's house and get some beers, we can get more there anyway and have two each instead of one and when it gets to midnight, let's go hedgehopping. I've got my balaclava.'

James, ever alert to someone who needed support, especially when it chimed with his own desires, pitched in with 'sounds like a plan mate'.

Toby's shoulders had relaxed and his mouth had broadened into a smile. He

> punched Tom hard on his left arm, then put an arm around his shoulders and gave him a shake.
>
> 'Well, we don't want to spend the night we celebrate finishing our GCSEs banged up do we?'

How has Tom developed emotionally in the five years since the first story? Instead of just being aware of his fear response to external stimuli and riding it out as he did aged 12, he is able to notice its arrival, and even predict that it will arise based on an assessment of the way events are shaping up. He knows to use his fear response as an indication that something is perceived to be wrong and he takes steps to either manage his emotion or manage the situation. He is able to read the emotions of others accurately and respond to the needs that those states generate, no doubt bolstered by emotional memories warding him off saying or doing things to upset them. He also recognizes the importance of being honest in a situation like that: he has learned that it is difficult to conceal emotions and that to do so will only cause more problems in the long run. However, he is controlled: the knowledge that he can do something about the situation soothes his fear and he doesn't go about disclosing his feelings in the pathetic or exaggerated way that would cause instant alienation and the usual 'here we go again' expressions of the friends – tolerant but deeply irritated by unaddressed weakness.

After a few years of trial and error and the safety net of secure friendship, Tom has been able to practise his strategies. In this situation, Tom tried to defuse Toby's anger by admitting to his own 'shortcomings' and by offering a solution to the problem that his fear response had generated: in short, he negotiated. He was only able to do this because of the secure foundation of self-awareness and awareness of the strength of bond with his friends: he knew he couldn't go through with the shoplifting for moral and emotional reasons, he knew that the only way to soothe his fear was to remove himself from that situation as theft was always going to arouse fear for him; he also knew that the friendships he had around him were strong and elastic enough to allow him to bargain the situation.

And it is in the crucible of those friendships that the situation was formed. Gavin was intelligent enough to recognize his own feelings of dislike about negotiation and arbitration and he withdrew, knowing that the others would sort it out. Toby was conciliatory with Tom and was willing to let go of his own pride to preserve the friendship and James saw the importance of defending someone vulnerable whom he cared about. This kind of result can only come after the thousands of little interactions with other people that allow us to become emotionally skilful.

6

Resilience

Who is your enemy? Mind is your enemy.
Who is your friend? Mind is your friend.
Learn the ways of the mind. Tend the mind with care.

The Buddha

Chapter preview

- Resilience defined
- The work of Martin Seligman
- Explanatory style
- Thinking traps
- Self-soothing and coping strategies
- Self-efficacy: be the change you want to see in the world
- Post-traumatic growth
- Implications for teachers

Resilience defined

Optimism, pessimism and resilience

My younger brother is one of life's optimists. He believes that the world is not a place populated with insurmountable obstacles, but challenges to be overcome. I'll illustrate what I mean with a couple of examples. When we were young, my brother, sister and I all had to attend church on a Sunday with our parents. My brother used to go to the Methodist church with my mum, whilst my sister and I went to the Catholic church with dad. My brother did not like church and he certainly didn't like Sunday school. He soon realized that simply complaining about it wasn't getting him anywhere, so, aged 13 he came up with an ingenious solution. My brother had discovered that the local rugby club trained its youth squad on Sunday mornings and knowing that mum and dad were rugby fans, chanced his arm. My brother discovered a love of rugby and is now a very good player. He hasn't attended church since.

This optimistic streak has served him particularly well recently. My brother has long harboured an ambition to work in the yachting industry. To do any meaningful work, you need what is known as a 'Yacht Master' qualification, which consists of three months of intensive training and costs about £10,000. My brother has been saving up for this for a long time and had also taken out a bank loan to help to pay for it. He had researched the courses on offer and had picked one that started on the Isle of Wight and finished up sailing a yacht down the Australian coast to Sydney Harbour. We were all very excited about it. There was just one minor hurdle: my brother is colour-blind. We were hoping that this would not be a problem, as it had been with his previous desire to join the Merchant Navy and there was a test for him to sit to find out. When the results came back that he would not be able to take part in the course, he was predictably very upset. However, I spoke to him two days later on the phone and he was back to his chipper self. Far from letting an immovable obstacle get him down, he had just shifted his focus. He knew he wanted to work in the outdoor leisure industry and had always fancied scuba diving, so he is now getting set to train as a scuba diving instructor, which he will do in some fabulous locations around the world.

This is what psychological resilience is all about: it is a cognitive skill which enables us to climb over life's obstacles, instead of being blocked by them. Physical resilience is covered in Chapter 3 on harmony. People who display resilience or optimism believe that the world is a changeable place over which they can exert their influence. The opposite of this is pessimism, where people believe that the world consists of immovable obstacles which they can do nothing about and it seems that whether you are an optimist or a pessimist is one of the best predictors of conditions such as depression and heart disease. A number of studies have been conducted on people undergoing significant and potentially traumatic medical treatment such as open heart surgery, IVF and abortion. What has been found is that those who show the signs of optimism before the medical treatment are much less likely to develop depression before, during and after the treatment than those who display the signs of pessimism.[90] Furthermore, optimistic people live, on average, eight and a half to nine and a half years longer than pessimists, which is the equivalent (statistically) to smoking three packets of cigarettes a day.[91]

Why is this? It appears that people who are optimistic tend to see life's problems as hurdles to be overcome and challenges to be resolved, whereas pessimists tend to avoid the problem or try to deny its existence. The distinction is explained here by Charles Carver and Michael Scheier:

> people who are confident about the future exert continuing effort, even when dealing with serious adversity. People who are doubtful are more likely to try to push the adversity away as though they can somehow escape it by wishful thinking; they are more likely to do things that provide temporary distractions but do not help solve the problem; and they sometimes even stop trying . . . While optimists reported a tendency to accept the reality of stressful events, they also reported trying to see the best in bad situations and to learn something from them. In contrast, pessimists reported tendencies toward overt denial and substance abuse, strategies that lessen their awareness of the problem.[92]

It is this basic optimistic mindset, that the future can be changed for the better, that can transform the world from being a hostile place, to a place of opportunity.

It is important to point out that generally speaking, people adopt a mixture of optimistic and pessimistic attitudes in their lives and this will generally correlate with how much mastery one feels one has in particular theatres of life. For example, a person may be pessimistic about academic study, but they may be extremely optimistic about skateboarding simply because they feel that they have more control over their successes and failures riding a board.

It should be clear that optimism and resilience are two of the most important skills that we can teach to young people. Adopting, learning and practising an optimistic worldview can help to fend off depression, substance misuse, risky or harmful sexual behaviour and criminality and can foster deep, meaningful and lasting positive relationships and a sense of meaning and purpose in life.

The work of Martin Seligman

The name most associated with the teaching of resilience is Martin Seligman. In the 1960s, Professor Seligman was involved in research into a phenomenon known as 'learned helplessness'. What psychologists had discovered through experiments with dogs was that there comes a point where dogs and people give up on a task and stop learning. Dogs were placed in cages with electrified floors and were given random electric shocks over which they had no control. Twenty-four hours later, the dog was returned to the cage and given a lever to stop the shock. The result was as follows:

When shock is inescapable, the dog learns that it is unable to exert control over the shock by means of any of its voluntary behaviors [sic]. It expects this to be the case in the future, and this expectation of uncontrollability causes it to fail to learn in the future . . . When the animal learns that it has no control and expects this to be true in the future, it undergoes motivational and cognitive changes that are responsible for its failure to learn escape.[93]

In other words, when a dog learns that it has no control in a given situation, it expects to fail and gives up; resigned to its fate. This was in complete contrast to dogs in the control group who were given the same lever from the start, which they learned to use to stop the electric shocks, and did not give up. What Seligman realized was the need to equip people with the psychological defences to withstand the feelings of helplessness that can lead to depression. The brilliance of his work was to realize that you can teach people to be optimists and help them to develop resilience to feeling a lack of control and develop mastery of the circumstances of their lives.

Seligman's work into 'learned optimism' or 'resilience' has been most associated with combating depression in young people and his Penn Resiliency Program has had remarkable results in helping children to avoid depression. In 17 studies of the PRP involving over 2,000 students it was found that two years after learning the PRP skills, students had half the rates of moderate to severe symptoms of depression as the control group.[94] Also, after 30 months, students of the PRP were half as likely to show behavioural problems as those who had not taken part in the programme.[95]

Seligman's approach is cognitive (to do with thinking and beliefs) and, to be sure, not all forms of depression are caused by cognitive factors – by our way of seeing and perceiving the world. Some forms of depression are best tackled by addressing underlying chemical imbalances in the brain,[96] or indeed by looking at diet, sleep, exercise and other aspects of one's lifestyle. However, much depression arises from a feeling that, ultimately, the world is a place which is set up to make us fail. The teaching of resilience attempts to overcome this feeling of learned helplessness by equipping young people with a new way of thinking about the world. It is not only depression that can be addressed by the teaching of resilience. Academic progress is often hampered by the holding of pessimistic beliefs. If those beliefs can be challenged and shown to be either false, or at least inaccurate, this might help to increase a student's ability to learn.

Seligman's PRP encourages participants to examine their explanatory style: the way that they explain the causes of events in their lives and the beliefs that they hold about the world. Through a series of cognitive practices, the PRP attempts to get children to re-shape unhelpful, negative or pessimistic styles of thought.

Explanatory style

You have probably met the child that I am about to describe to you; you have probably spent time either worrying about them, or tearing your hair out in frustration having spent hours trying to help them. The child I am about to describe to you is the classic pessimist. We'll call her Lorna Doom. Lorna sees the world as an essentially hostile place: every situation presents an opportunity for her to fail publicly. When something goes wrong, it is not just irksome, it is a disaster. When Lorna gets a bad set of grades, it is because she is rubbish at school, her teachers hate her: she'll never succeed at anything. When Lorna gets work back, she immediately looks for the criticism to reinforce her view of herself that she is a failure. Success is ignored and takes second place to criticism. It is also often seen as happening by chance, whereas failure is deserved. Lorna might be excessively angry or aggressive or she might be passive and gloomy. She finds it difficult to trust people and it always requires effort to get Lorna to overcome any problems that she might have.

Why is Lorna like this? In Chapter 1, we saw that our temperament is in part set at birth by our genes so it may well be that she has inherited a depressive temperament. However, we also saw that a significant proportion of our personality is determined by our voluntary contributions: by the things that we choose to think and do. Much like the poor dogs who found their paws getting electrocuted, Lorna has *learned* the responses to the 'adverse' situations that she finds herself in. We have to ask ourselves, why do some children take a hurdle, such as failing an exam, as an opportunity to learn and why do others see it as the end of the world? The answer, quite simply, is because they have learned different responses to adversity from their parents, peers, teachers, or from their experiences.

Our explanatory style derives from what happens to us in our interactions with people and things. Take for example a student that I teach who tends to focus on the negative. She recently got her termly report and the majority of the grades were good and a couple were excellent. However, her attention went straight to the bad grades and she started to cry. Time was spent with her to focus first on the positive comments and she was asked why she looked straight at the subjects she was doing less well in: 'that's where my parents will look first' was her response. She had learned that criticism was more important than praise. The more often something happens to us and the more often we think in a particular way, the more it becomes a part of our worldview.

Our response to adversity is known as our *attributional* or *explanatory style*; in short it is how we explain adversity and where we apportion blame (if any). Explanatory style divides into two types: pessimistic and optimistic.

A pessimistic explanatory style has three aspects to it and Seligman uses three 'P's to show this: *permanence*, *pervasiveness*, and *personalization*.[97] The permanent explanation sees bad events as always happening. The pervasive explanation sees this as a problem that affects everything and the personal explanation places the blame fully on the explainer's own shoulders. Let's use an example to illustrate this. Lorna agrees to meet Sarah in town at 2.30 p.m. It's 2.40 and the friend is not answering her phone. Lorna, as a pessimist will react like this:

Permanent: 'This *always* happens to me.'

Pervasive: 'I haven't got *any* friends.'

Personal: 'It's all *my* fault that she's stood me up/Sarah's a bitch.'

Because Lorna chooses to explain the situation in this way, she exacerbates her feeling of helplessness and that, essentially, the world is a hostile place where things are out of her control. No matter what she does, bad things will always happen to her. Holding this view of events dramatically increases a person's chances of experiencing depression. It is vital that Lorna learns optimism.

The optimist has a different explanatory style when they encounter adversity. The optimist sees adversity as something that is unusual or temporary as opposed to something that *always* happens or is long-lasting. They believe that adversity is due to specific causes rather than universal ones and they believe that adversity results from a combination of factors: it is not just down to one person.

Were Lorna to view this situation in an optimistic way, she would probably react as follows:

Temporary: 'It's unusual for Sarah to be late.'

Specific: 'Still, my other friends are always on time.'

Impersonal: 'She might be having a problem. I'll wait a bit longer and try phoning again.'

The main difference between the optimistic and the pessimistic approach is that the former sees adversity as something that is temporary and which can be resolved, while the latter sees adversity as an immovable object. Optimism is nicely summed up in this quote from the Dalai Lama: 'If the problem can be remedied, then there is no need to worry about it. And if there is no solution, then there is no point in being worried, because nothing can be done about it anyway.'[98]

Optimism and pessimism work with the good events in our lives too. Pessimists will tend to view positive events as being the result of fluke and that they didn't really deserve them: in that sense, they are simply trying to confirm their own belief that their life isn't very good, or that they are not worthy. An optimist on the other hand sees good events as being deserved and is ready to show appreciation to themselves or to others when they happen. Above all, the optimist *examines the evidence* and is able to see events and their causes and the beliefs and judgements which result from them clearly.

Thinking traps

Explanatory style is to do with *beliefs* and *perceptions*. When Lorna's friend was late, all of her reactions such as 'I haven't got any friends' or 'Sarah is a bitch' are beliefs and perceptions: they are not *facts*. Upon stepping back and examining our world-view, we discover that much of what we think is true is in fact belief or perception and is entirely subjective: it is a construct that we have been busily creating based on our judgements of the events that happen around us. A lot of our beliefs are helpful, healthy and normal such as 'If I go for a walk in the woods at night without a torch, I may fall down a deep hole and hurt myself. Perhaps I will take a torch.' Other beliefs that we have may not be so helpful such as 'Sarah is a bitch, I'll never speak to her again.' Many of the problems that we encounter in life are down to unhelpful beliefs that go unchallenged and many of these beliefs follow a particular style. See if you recognize any of these thinking traps:

- **Jumping to conclusions**: 'If she ignores me that means that she hates me.'
- **Tunnel vision**: 'I don't care what anyone else thinks, I have to get this finished.'
- **Over-generalization**: 'If I don't get into the seconds team this week, I am rubbish at sport.'
- **Magnification**: 'This is the worst thing that has ever happened to me.'
- **Minimization**: 'Plenty of other people fail their exams.'
- **Personalizing**: 'It's all my fault.'
- **Externalizing**: 'It was nothing to do with me; it was the teacher's fault.'
- **Mind reading**: 'I bet he's thinking I'm a complete idiot.'
- **Perfectionism**: 'If I get one bit of this wrong, the whole thing is rubbish.'
- **Me! Me! Me!**: 'I am right. If only everyone else could see things my way, the world would be so much better.'
- **Comparing**: 'Everyone else is better than me. Why can't I be as good as them?'
- **Arrogance**: 'I am better than everyone else.'
- **Ruminating**: 'My life is awful. Woe is me. Will this misery never end?'

These thinking traps are just *judgements* and they can be problematic, particularly if they cause us to become stressed, anxious, angry or afraid. When the student above looked at the negative comments and ignored the positive ones on her reports, she was operating under the belief that criticism is more important than praise. This belief led to her feeling anxious and sad about her progress, which in turn led to her believing that she was failing and that she didn't belong in the school. By falling into a thinking trap she had created an inaccurate perception of reality which was then hindering her progress: she was distracted and depressed in lessons because she had told herself that she was a failure.

Because the brain is plastic and our thought patterns can be undone and re-wired, with practice it is possible to notice when we are about to fall in to a thinking trap and start to look for evidence to either challenge or support our beliefs: old thinking patterns, even though they die hard, will die eventually. The skill is to tune in to the judgements as they arise and dismiss those that are inaccurate by finding evidence to counteract them: it is just like tuning in to (and out of) a radio station that plays our internal monologue all day. Remember though, that our beliefs might be accurate: it might be that a particular person who has just flatly ignored you in the street, does in fact dislike you: this presents an opportunity to question why and question whether or not their friendship really matters, but not until you have examined all the evidence for alternative explanations first. Perhaps they really didn't hear you. Awareness of our own thinking traps can also lead us to be compassionate towards others with a tendency to fall in to them: suddenly we become more aware of the subjective realities people create for themselves and can start to make allowances for them.

Self-soothing and coping strategies

Sometimes things don't go quite how we would like them to and one of life's most important skills is learning the ability to self-soothe: that is engage in thoughts or activities that lessen the pain or frustration we are experiencing. However, our choice of soothing technique is vital. Negative events and emotions can be difficult to deal with and, unless we learn the skills of understanding and managing these emotional states, we can be prone to the adoption of soothing techniques that are harmful. The most obvious of these are things such as drug addiction (including nicotine and alcohol), eating disorders (including over-eating), obsessive exercise, promiscuity or self-harm. Why do people turn to these behaviours? Very simply, because they lead to the body's production of the chemicals that make us feel happy such as dopamine and serotonin, or they introduce substances that do this artificially. They mask emotional pain in the short term and can help us to forget about it. The downsides are the desperate toll they take on the body and the fact that they don't do anything to deal with the underlying emotional distress, and in many cases will simply add to it.

It is not just masking that causes problems. People who suppress or ignore their emotional states are at greater risk of illness because suppressed emotions lead to physiological stress, which reduces the effectiveness of the immune system to fight off disease.

There are simple tricks, sometimes also called coping strategies, that we can employ to distract us from a negative mood. It is important that children learn *healthy* coping strategies that help them to engage with difficult events and overcome them, rather than masking or suppression strategies which simply store up further problems. These strategies fall into three categories:

- **Active**: these are strategies which may work as a temporary distraction, or which may produce the chemicals necessary in the brain to help us to resolve difficult situations. Exercise, play, humour, being out in nature and being in the company of others are all excellent strategies to use.

- **Calming**: these are strategies that help to overcome the body's fight, flight or freeze response and which can also quell anxiety or anger. Deep-breathing techniques, massage and meditation are all extremely effective, as can be the use of other treatments acting on the senses such as aromatherapy.

- **Thinking**: these are cognitive strategies used to help us re-think our approaches to certain situations by requiring us to re-evaluate our beliefs. Martin Seligman's ABC strategy (see opposite) has been shown to be very effective here as are strategies such as re-framing and writing about the event. One form of re-framing is called benefit-finding, where some time after a difficult event, a person is asked to think about what good has come out of it. Writing about difficult experiences has also been shown to have very positive results: '. . . people who write about their traumas show better immune system functioning, better health and fewer visits to the doctor compared with those who write about trivial topics'.[99]

In her book *Why Love Matters*, Sue Gerhardt argues that the skills of coping and self-soothing must be taught to children from as early an age as possible and this may require many parents having to think carefully about their own emotional skills. Children learn how to manage their emotions from their primary care-givers and if those care-givers model withdrawal, avoidance or suppression, this is what their children will learn. If, on the other hand, a child is taught to name emotions as they arise, to work out what has made them arise and think through what needs to be changed to make them go away, they will most likely avoid the need to either mask or suppress negative emotions.

Putting it into practice: teaching resilience and optimism

In order for students to develop the skills of resilience and optimism, the basic building blocks that they need are:

- to understand the difference between optimistic and pessimistic explanatory styles
- to notice thoughts as they arise
- to assess whether those thoughts are helpful or not
- to assess whether those thoughts are accurate or not by examining the available evidence
- to establish alternative thought patterns or courses of action that are preferable.

The trick to making this succeed is regular practice and approaching it from different angles. The more that students can learn that the beliefs that arise in their minds are open to being challenged if they are unhelpful, the better.[100] Absolutely key to the success of these sessions is the atmosphere within the classroom: it has to be supportive and encouraging so that students don't feel judged or vulnerable for volunteering personal material. Students will learn a great deal from each other as many of their classmates will already exhibit optimism to quite a high degree, having been taught to see the world that way by their parents, but they will only learn from each other if the atmosphere is one of support and encouragement rather than condemnation and ridicule. There are some suggestions for the different approaches you might take below:

- **Notice**: the first step is getting students to notice the thoughts that cross their minds while they do things – to tune into the internal radio station playing their beliefs and judgements. One technique that works well is to ask them to individually build a house of cards in silence and pay attention to the thoughts that cross their minds. Ask them to make a note of these afterwards and try to work out which thoughts are optimistic and which pessimistic.
- **ABC**: to develop resilience, Martin Seligman suggests the use of an ABC model, where 'A' stands for adversity, 'B' stands for beliefs and 'C' stands for consequences. On a sheet of paper, students should mark three columns headed A, B and C. In the 'A' column, students should think of a time recently when they encountered an adversity or challenging situation. In the 'B' column, they should record the beliefs that arose in response to the adversity and in the 'C' column, students should speculate about the consequences of holding on to those beliefs. For example, in 'A', a student might write 'got a bad mark on a piece of work'; in 'B' they might write 'I am bad in this subject'; and in 'C' they might write 'put in less effort, behave worse, drop subject ASAP'. You can then start to explore the positive consequences of holding optimistic beliefs and the negative consequences of holding pessimistic beliefs. This technique should be practised regularly for positive and adverse events so that students learn to observe and manage their beliefs.

- **Challenge**: provide students with a series of scenarios they might encounter which could result in adversity (e.g. being asked to go to the head's office, being ignored or stood up, getting a bad grade, trying out for a team, speaking to people you don't know) and ask them to make a list of optimistic and pessimistic beliefs that a person could have in those situations. Ask the students to try to challenge the pessimistic beliefs: what evidence might they need to counteract them (e.g. if a pessimistic belief arising from getting a bad grade is 'I'm rubbish at this subject', evidence to challenge might be looking for other grades that are good, or thinking carefully about the causes of bad grades, such as not doing any work or not asking for help when something is not understood). The emphasis should be on finding ways to challenge unhelpful or inaccurate beliefs.

- **ABC journal**: ask students to keep a journal of ABCs. They should pay particular attention to any patterns in beliefs they have and start to think about how they can summon helpful beliefs and challenge or overcome unhelpful beliefs.

- **Role play**: get students in small groups to invent two characters – one who reacts pessimistically and one who reacts optimistically in a particular situation. Ask students to have a narrator who plays the role of the internal radio station, the beliefs that cross each character's mind in the situation. The optimist and the pessimist should play out their reaction to the situation, including the consequences.

- **Forum**: role play as above, but ask the audience to get involved and instruct the characters how to respond to the situation. If they are experiencing negative or unhelpful beliefs, how does the audience advise that they can counteract or overcome them?

- **Self-talk space invaders**: when we take negative or excessively critical comments from others on board, they become part of our beliefs about ourselves. What we need to do is find a way of dealing with unhelpful comments, feelings, body language and so on. One way is to imagine yourself playing space invaders with them: if you can't remember the game, type 'space invaders' into an internet search engine. There are plenty of free versions you can play online. Get students to think up some phrases they can say to themselves which they can use to help counteract thoughtless comments from others and ask the students to imagine that their self-talk destroys those negative remarks, rather like the guns in space invaders destroy incoming alien fire.

- **Self-talk footage**: find some footage of athletes lining up before a race, of footballers before a game, of musicians tuning up before a performance or racing drivers before the green light and ask the students to speculate about the beliefs and judgements that are going through their heads as they prepare for competition or performance. What thoughts do the students think they ought to have to ensure a successful performance? What beliefs or judgements will hinder them? Can we work out their beliefs from their body language?

- **Sticks and stones**: ask for a volunteer from the class. Hand out some slips of paper to other members of the class – half with positive words such as 'confidence', 'happiness', 'satisfaction', 'respect' and the other half with words such as 'helplessness', 'despair', 'failure', 'wasted'. Be careful to avoid words that could be used directly as an insult. Ask the volunteer to adjust their posture as they hear first the negative words and then the positive words. Ask the audience to notice how the volunteer's posture changed: what does this suggest to us about positive versus negative comments? How should we go about speaking to people, particularly when we are trying to communicate difficult material (e.g. constructive criticism)?

- **Experiment**: ask the students to try out ACT (active/calming/thinking soothing techniques, see page 102) between lessons to overcome unhelpful beliefs. Which do they find the most successful?

- **Constructive and destructive**: ask students to differentiate between constructive approaches to self-soothing (e.g. ACT) and destructive approaches (e.g. drug abuse). How can destructive approaches be overcome?

- **Neutralize the trap**: ask students to think of as many different types of trap as they can (mouse trap/man-trap/hole in the ground, etc.); ask them to draw one trap and then draw a way of neutralizing it (e.g. plank of wood over a hole in the ground). Now ask them to think of an important event that is coming up and ask them to speculate about the thinking trap(s) that might open up in front of them. Ask the students to then think of ways that they might be able to neutralize the trap(s), using the visual analogy that they have just created (e.g. steady breathing before a music performance might be like putting a plank of wood over a hole).

Self-efficacy: be the change you want to see in the world

A self-efficacy case study: *Fantastic Mr Fox*

When I was five, my dad read *Fantastic Mr Fox* by Roald Dahl to me. It is the first book I can clearly remember, although I know there were others. I read it many times afterwards and the story had a profound effect upon me. If you don't know it, the story is about a family of foxes who live in a hollow under a tree. Mr Fox, ace poultry thief, was the nemesis of three farmers: Boggis, Bunce and Bean, all of whom were grotesque in a way that only Roald Dahl can portray grotesqueness. The three farmers eventually decided that they'd had enough of Mr Fox's antics and set about digging him and his family out of their home to be shot.

However, there was a flaw in the farmers' plan: the resilience and resourcefulness of Mr Fox. Instead of succumbing to a grisly fate at the hands of three brutal and sadistic farmers, Mr Fox saved his family by digging a deep tunnel. But not just any tunnel: a tunnel which ran directly under the store houses of the three farmers, which meant that the starving, besieged family could eat like kings right under the noses of those who wished them dead.

To use the language of psychology, Mr Fox was an optimist who had high levels of self-efficacy. Mr Fox believed that the farmers' cruel intentions did not amount to an inescapable fate and that with the application of brains and effort, not only could they escape doom, but they could also get one over on those who were trying to kill them.

Self-efficacy as a theory owes its existence to the work of Albert Bandura. 'Self-efficacy' refers to the set of beliefs that we have about our own ability to achieve goals that we set for ourselves. Bandura supposed that when it comes to actions, humans are motivated to act when they believe that they have a good chance of being successful and refrain from action when they believe that a particular goal is not achievable. Mr Fox believed that he could outwit and out-dig a trio of farmers with mechanical digging equipment, so he set about doing it rather than succumbing to a bloody demise. Self-efficacy beliefs determine how well we will perform at particular tasks and as Alan Carr points out, self-efficacy beliefs (which can be measured via questionnaire) offer a good indication of an individual's likely academic performance, control of habits and addictions such as eating and drug use and management of anxiety;[101] for example, how many smokers do you know who are now ex-smokers simply because they have *decided* that it is possible to succeed at quitting? Conversely, how many do you know who still smoke because they *believe* that giving up is impossible?

In the same way that optimism and pessimism vary across different areas of our lives, self-efficacy beliefs do too. I have high self-efficacy beliefs about learning to play 'Stairway to Heaven', but low ones about learning a ballroom dance for performance in front of a large audience. My self-efficacy beliefs are built up from a variety of sources. Bandura proposed four:

1. mastery experiences: actually succeeding at a given task
2. vicarious experiences: seeing someone else succeed at a task
3. social persuasion: being given encouragement to succeed by others
4. physical and emotional states: being healthy and happy enough to accomplish something.[102]

The implications for young people should be abundantly clear. We often meet students for whom the word 'can't' is an oft-repeated one. Our mothers were right when they said, 'there's no such word as can't', but it takes a little more to help young people see it. Firstly, they have to learn to adopt an optimistic outlook on life and challenge unhelpful beliefs and thinking traps as they arise. They must then be given opportunities to try, and to fail and to try again. Children should also learn new skills in the company of others so that they can see that whatever they are trying to learn *is* possible: they must also see that others make mistakes too and that this is OK. The third ingredient, persuasion, must be of the right character. Aggressive, judging and excessively critical coaching will bring about negative and defensive emotional states and *prevent* learning. Coaching must be clear, accurate and positive:

the learner must feel that they are safe and supported, but also that they will be corrected when they make a mistake and helped to refine their performance of the task. The last point about physical and emotional states returns us to the material on self-soothing above. A person cannot learn if they are exhausted, in pain or if they are experiencing a heightened withdrawal emotion such as fear or anger.

Self-efficacy beliefs need to be acquired over time. Some people have a head-start in life because they are born into families who help their children to develop these beliefs. Others don't and it will take time for those people to learn that Barack Obama's catch-phrase from the presidential campaign of 2008, 'Yes we can', is for the most part true. The rewards for the development of self-efficacy beliefs, as described here by Alan Carr, are great:

> Self-efficacy beliefs enhance the functioning of the immune system and lead to better physical health, greater resilience in the face of stress, and better psychological and social adjustment. Within specific domains such as work, sports, weight control, smoking cessation, alcohol use and mental health problems, the development of self-efficacy beliefs leads to positive outcomes.[103]

Putting it into practice: teaching self-efficacy

- **Plan for change**: ask students to identify an area of their life where they would like to be more successful. Ask them to make specific plans for how they are going to put Bandura's four ingredients for change in place (mastery, vicarious experience, persuasion and health). When are these things going to happen? What beliefs will they need to achieve their goal? What thinking traps do they need to overcome? Who will they need help from? How are they going to ask for it?

Post-traumatic growth

I recently watched a documentary in which two doctors travelled to countries such as Malaysia, Tibet and India and studied how people deal with pain without any anaesthetic. They watched Hindu devotees push large needles through their cheeks and watched a group of Indian rationalists attempt to show that there is no God, only mind over matter, by suspending themselves from butcher's hooks that had been pushed through the skin on their backs. The section that makes my students grimace and cringe the most is where a Tibetan doctor cauterizes a rotten tooth with a red hot poker without any anaesthetic at all. Of course, the patient experienced pain, but after the operation the pain subsided and the woman was smiling again within about 10 minutes, the rotten tooth having been completely fixed.

Western culture seems to take the view that pain and suffering are bad and that they should be concealed or eradicated at all costs. Pain relief is freely available and widely prescribed so that, if we choose, there is never any real need to feel any physical pain. The health and safety obsession tries to risk-assess away any prospect of danger, mistakes or failure. Many of our natural enemies such as disease and predators have been vanquished, so we need only look at them in a Petri dish or a cage.

However, there is compelling evidence that trauma helps us to grow and develop as human beings. This is not a new idea and many of the early explanations for suffering in the world involved the idea that God allows a degree of suffering in order to enable us to grow spiritually. Jonathan Haidt suggests that there are three main benefits to be had from trauma:

1. Adversity often reveals talents and strengths you didn't know you had. This can positively enhance your 'self-concept' or the picture of yourself you have in your mind. Many people report how fighting off a major illness like cancer gives them a surprising insight into their own reserves of strength.

2. Adversity strengthens relationships by acting as a filter. Suddenly all the petty and trivial concerns of everyday life become insignificant as Haidt puts it: 'Trauma seems to shut off the motivation to play Machiavellian tit for tat with its emphasis on self-promotion and competition.'[104]

3. Adversity re-aligns our priorities in life. Being faced with death or suffering often throws what is most important in life into sharp relief and this re-evaluation can often lead to people embarking on a new trajectory through life.

Of course, none of this is front-page news, but there is now a body of research and testimonies from thousands of people that show that it is true to say what doesn't kill you makes you stronger. However, Haidt makes a controversial suggestion. He argues that it is just possible that we *need* adversity to grow as humans; indeed, we need suffering to become fully what it is to be human. His thesis reminds me of a story that I was told once in assembly by my junior school headmaster, Clive Orchard. An old man tending to the plants in his greenhouse finds a chrysalis. Every day he spends time studying it closely, in the hope that he will see the beautiful butterfly emerge. One day, the chrysalis started to move. The movement got more and more intense and it struck the old man that perhaps the butterfly was unable to get out of the tough casing surrounding it, so he took his penknife and with the tip, made a small incision to help the butterfly out. Soon enough, the butterfly emerged, but something was wrong: it was unable to fly. The struggle to emerge is what causes a butterfly's wings to strengthen and work. Unwittingly, the old man had deprived the developing butterfly of an essential adversity.

For Haidt, adversity is the piece of grit in the oyster: although difficult, the psychological and physical benefits to be had from struggle can be hugely significant. Adversity can often provide the impetus needed to initiate long overdue changes in life and help us to discover meaning, purpose and value:

> Adversity may be necessary for growth, because it forces you to stop speeding along the road of life, allowing you to notice the paths that were branching off all along, and to think about where you really want to end up.[105]

Putting it into practice: teaching about post-traumatic growth

- **Experiment**: ask the students to do something they have been putting off for a while – one of those annoying jobs that has been hanging over them. Ask them to write about how it felt when it was complete and perhaps compare with a pleasure such as eating chocolate.

- **Research**: ask the students to find out about someone who has overcome an adversity and who believes that it made them stronger. This could be someone in their family or someone in the public eye. Ask students to write about what the person believes the benefits to be.

Implications for teachers

The implications for teachers as regards resilience are twofold: the first concerns their interactions with students and the second concerns their own personal well-being.

The pessimistic explanatory style holds that we should not have high hopes for the outcomes of future events. When this explanatory style finds itself being applied to students, the consequences can be devastating. The remarkable work of Carol Dweck into what she calls 'mindset' (explored in Chapter 7) cites an enormous wealth of evidence to suggest that if teachers take a pessimistic view of their students and believe that their intelligence and therefore their attainment has a ceiling, then it requires an almost Herculean effort on the part of the student to exceed the expectations that the teacher has of them. The opposite is also true. If we do not place a limit on a child's ability, if we recognize that intellectual ability is not fixed but is completely 'plastic' and if we praise students when they apply effort and perseverance rather than praising some notional inherent ability, students will surprise us with what they can achieve.

It is vital that teachers are optimistic about their students and that they encourage students to apply effort to effect changes to their achievement. As soon as teachers start to say things like 'well, you've got to consider the backgrounds these kids come from', or 'this is a very weak year group and we'll be lucky if we get good results with them', they put a ceiling and a label in place and are almost guilty of fixing the levels of attainment that the students can expect; we are left with the all too common self-fulfilling prophecy.

It is also important for teachers to adopt an optimistic attitude in order to safeguard their own well-being. I cannot repeat this point enough: a teacher who is not well is not an effective teacher and teachers *must* place their own well-being first and be supported by structures within the school to enable this to happen. Teaching has the potential to be a stressful profession: every day involves countless ceaselessly changing situations and interactions that cover the complete spectrum of emotions. We often find ourselves operating at full throttle for extended periods and sometimes whole working days can pass without a break. If teachers view their professional lives pessimistically, they will suffer. If they view their professional lives optimistically, they will thrive. It is as simple as that.

7　Strengths and flow

> ## Chapter preview
>
> - The importance of doing what you're good at
> - Dispelling myths about talent
> - Mindset: the work of Carol Dweck
> - Brain plasticity: old dogs and new tricks
> - Talent and children: openness and opportunities
> - Character strengths
> - Authenticity
> - Flow: the work of Mihaly Csikszentmihalyi
> - Motivation: intrinsic and extrinsic

The importance of doing what you're good at

For the beginning of this chapter, I'm going to take you back to the farm where Lawrence and I saw the fox on that frosty morning in February 2000. As I mentioned there, Lawrence and I spent three months working on that farm together to build a fence that was over 1 km long between the farmer's land and the mainline railway which runs between Bristol and London.

While we were working on that job, we met a young lad who was working as a labourer for the farmer. He was about 14 years old and he didn't go to school. I'll never forget the first time that I saw him. He was walking up the main track through the farm in camouflage army surplus clothes, wearing a black balaclava, carrying an air rifle with two Jack Russell terriers close at heel. He was off to catch rats he said. I met this young man in the 12 months between graduating and starting my teacher training. He taught me a very important lesson about the importance of school as it is in the UK.

I was good at school. My parents were teachers and taught me the skills I needed to get on well with those who taught me and to succeed at exams. I am naturally quite bookish and enjoy academic approaches to learning involving reading and writing. School, especially in the classroom, played to my strengths. Predictably though, the part of school that I found hard was the social side and my learning curve there was steeper and harder than it was for many of my peers. After school I went to a good university and found myself surrounded mostly by independent-school educated, middle-class, well-off young people who wanted to get an upper second and earn good money in London as soon as possible. I was living in the bubble of a largely cerebral world which was about the conventional view of success that schools very often inculcate in us.

And here I was, digging holes for fence posts, on a farm, talking to a boy in a balaclava who was skipping school to go and catch rats with his dogs. Something was amiss.

As I got to know this boy over the course of the job, I developed an enormous respect for him. He wanted to be an agricultural engineer and decided that he would learn more by doing the job he was already good at than sitting in a classroom learning things that he felt weren't helping him, from people he felt weren't sympathetic to his trajectory in life. I asked him the obvious question about needing GCSEs and other qualifications to get into college, to which he replied that he would attend night school should that be necessary. He wasn't academically unable; he had just decided to channel his efforts into learning on the job. What's more, he was happy, he was fulfilled and he was learning.

The memory of the boy that I met on that farm has stayed with me throughout my teaching career because he taught me an important lesson: humans are at their best when they are doing what they are good at, and that, sometimes, the education system either tries to funnel children into a narrow conception of what they *ought* to be good at, or it simply does not recognize what they are good at in the first place. I have no idea what that boy would have been like in a classroom. I doubt very much that he would have been disruptive. He probably would have been one of those very quiet students you never quite seem to reach, who hands in two out of three homeworks, done with a minimum of effort. And yet on that farm, he was engaged, creative and consumed by his work.

My intuition that this boy was making a wise decision, wise beyond his years, has been confirmed by a lot of the research that has been conducted into talents and character strengths. It seems that one of the secrets to well-being and happiness is to provide people with as many opportunities as possible for them to excel.

Dispelling myths about talent

Many people are of the belief that talent in a given area is genetic: that people are born with or without certain abilities and that if you don't have this birthright, you'll never have it. You may have heard it said that people with large or prominent ears have musical talent, as if there is some genetic connection between the way that people's ears grow and their ability to play an instrument. Similarly we often hear people say that such and such a person is a *'natural'*, again implying that they have some kind of pre-ordained destiny to be gifted in some way. We support this with the evidence that some people just seem to understand things or are able to pick up a skill more quickly than others. We even do it as teachers: we label certain children as being talented or otherwise in our subject. Much of the research shows that this attitude to talent is just wrong.

Nature versus nurture and the 10,000 hour rule

The BBC recently made a fascinating documentary series which looked at the role of nature and nurture when it comes to talent. They selected three people, each prominent in particular fields, and explored whether a particular aspect of their lives was due to nature or nurture. John Barrowman was picked for an exploration of homosexuality, Colin Jackson, the Olympic gold-medal winning hurdler, was picked for an exploration of sporting prowess and Vanessa Mae, the violinist, for musical ability. Aside from the documentary on John Barrowman, which concluded that his homosexuality was the result of factors largely beyond his control, the dominant theme was that while there may have been physical predispositions present due to genetic or other factors, the most significant contributor to excellence in any given field is *hard work*. Vanessa Mae and Colin Jackson are exceptional in their fields because, quite simply, they worked harder than anyone else to activate and perfect the abilities that they possess and it is reckoned that about 10,000 hours (about 10 years) of practice is what is needed to become really good at something.

This point is made by Malcolm Gladwell in his book *Outliers*, which looks at the few individuals who were so extraordinary that they helped to shape a generation. He cites the work of K. Anders Ericcson, who conducted a study at the Berlin Academy of Music. He found that what separated the elite violinists from the 'good' and the 'mediocre' was the amount of time that they had practised by the age of 20:

10,000 hours, 8,000 hours and 4,000 hours respectively. Gladwell does not deny that there may be some innate ability or propensity, but argues that it is effort which capitalizes upon this and that effort is driven by desire. He uses the example of the Beatles, and Bill Joy, founder of Sun Microsystems and one of the architects of the internet and the Mac operating system to make this point:

> A good part of that 'talent', however, was something other than an innate aptitude for Music or Maths. It was desire. The Beatles were willing to play for eight hours straight, seven days a week. Joy was willing to stay up all night programming. In either case, most of us would have gone home to bed. In other words, a key part of what it means to be talented is being able to practise for hours and hours – to the point where it is really hard to know where 'natural ability' stops and the simple willingness to work hard begins.[106]

If we return to Colin Jackson and Vanessa Mae, what was most interesting, particularly with Vanessa Mae, was that the revelation that effort is every bit as important as ability came as a bit of a blow. Throughout their lives, Mae and Jackson had been praised for their *gift* or for their *talent* and this singled them out and made them feel special, different, somehow other; as if they possessed something inaccessible to other mere mortals. Truth be told, we like it when someone praises a talent that we may have, don't we? It makes us feel somehow superior to others who do not have that talent to the same degree as us. However, as soon as our talent is put down to hard work, it becomes accessible to anyone who is willing to put in the time and we don't feel quite as special as we did before. The truth is 'what any person in the world can learn, *almost* all persons can learn, *if* provided with the appropriate prior and current conditions of learning'.[107]

Putting it into practice: teaching about talent

The only way that young people can learn that talent derives from practice is by doing it themselves and by studying talent in others. Here are some teaching ideas for exploring this.

- **The fertile plains of talent**: ask the students to think about what the best conditions for developing a talent are – both physical (care of the body, sleep, etc.) and psychological, beliefs and self-talk. Ask them to consider short-term and long-term goals: wanting to be able to juggle seven clubs, but having to start with two juggling balls to begin with. Look at resilience and self-efficacy skills for ideas here too.

- **Experiment**: ask the students to think of something that they would like to learn to do and challenge them to learn to do it. Ask them at regular intervals how they are progressing and ask them to measure their progress against the number of hours they have put into practice. Compare as a class: who has become most proficient and how many hours have they put in?

- **Case studies**: ask students to investigate people who have become really good at something. Did it come naturally, or did they have to put the hours in? It doesn't matter what the talent is either: it could be playing the piano or using a chainsaw. Look at famous examples too.

Mindset: the work of Carol Dweck

The problem with praising talent is that as soon as we do it, we are inadvertently causing problems for the person whose talent we praise. Fascinating research conducted by Carol Dweck into what she calls 'fixed mindsets' and 'growth mindsets' shows that as soon as we draw attention to ability rather than effort we cause that person to think that their success in a given area is due to factors beyond their control: that is, their innate predisposition to that field of expertise. For example, if a student does particularly well on a piece of work and their teacher praises their *talent* rather than their *effort* (by saying something like 'you're a natural mathematician'), the student is likely to feel certain things about themselves:

- I succeeded at that task because of an innate ability I have, about which I can do nothing.
- Others cannot be as successful as me because they don't possess the same degree of talent.
- I have to keep proving to others that I have this innate ability (even if it means deceiving them).
- The more effort I have to expend, the less able I am.
- If I can't do something, I give up to avoid embarrassment.
- If I fail, others are to blame because I am talented.
- I fear being shown up for not having this ability.
- If I fail, I am not worthy.

The more we praise talent, the more we encourage what Dweck calls a 'fixed mindset', which is the belief that success depends directly on *talent*. The healthier alternative to the fixed mindset is the 'growth mindset', which is the view that success depends upon *effort*. By praising the amount of effort a person puts into something and thereby encouraging the growth mindset, it prevents people from believing that certain fields of expertise are beyond their reach. Instead, it shows that success in a given area depends upon the effort you put in and the support and guidance you are given. Suddenly, areas of expertise that were closed off by the 'talent police' are opened up. The key difference is that people who show the growth mindset believe that hurdles can be overcome by the application of more effort; they believe that the world is a place containing challenges which are not insurmountable. People in the fixed mindset are more likely to believe that problems can only be overcome if you have the talent to do so: if you don't have the talent, the problem won't get solved and very often, those in the fixed mindset just give up. The world is a place full of opportunities for the untalented to fail.

Dweck has studied dozens of children and taught them the growth mindset. She has found again and again that this simple shift in beliefs about talent versus effort, for both students *and* teachers, stops children seeing the world as a place where certain things are closed off to them because 'well, God didn't bless you with that ability' and in turn raises their attainment in learning:

> One day we were introducing the growth mindset to a new group of students. All at once, Jimmy – the most hard-core turned-off low-effort kid in the group – looked up with tears in his eyes and said, 'You mean I don't have to be dumb?' From that day on, he worked. He started staying up late to do his homework, which he never used to bother with at all. He started handing in assignments early so that he could get feedback and revise them. He now believed that working hard was not something that made you vulnerable, but something that made you smarter.[108]

It's important to qualify all this. Dweck is not talking about simple 'boosterism' or the self-esteem movement, where one foolishly tries to convince people that they can achieve whatever they want to. I know that I am not going to win the Olympic 100 metres final, on land or in water, for men or women, ever. What's more, I can live with that because I know that no matter how much effort I apply to the challenge, I am about 20 years too late in starting and there are a few little physical factors like the fast-twitching muscle needed for top sprinters missing from my physique. However, I know that I could, with effort and training, complete the London Marathon. The growth mindset does depend upon accurate beliefs about the world and about oneself.

But what about the child who doesn't want to learn, or play sport, or pick up a musical instrument, or make friends with other kids, or speak up in class and so on? Dweck writes about 'low-effort syndrome', which is where children who believe in the fixed mindset, instead of applying their mental energy to growth and development, apply it to protecting their egos by avoiding any opportunity to be publicly shown to lack talent. But this is a paradox: human beings have evolved to learn. Remember the last time you learned something new? It felt good didn't it? Chris Peterson argues, citing the research of Robert White, that it is basically unnatural for humans to be disinterested because when we develop a competency in a given field, it feels good – especially if there is no external reward attached, because learning something new is an intrinsically rewarding process. Becoming competent in anything is an essential ingredient to the thriving life, but competencies need to be developed through supportive, yet challenging teaching which provides opportunities for learning new things (novelty) – tasks which are accomplishable but complex and which involve a degree of uncertainty. If the outcome is a foregone conclusion, we soon become bored or frustrated.[109]

> some teachers preached and practiced a growth mindset. They focused on the idea that all children could develop their skills, and in their classrooms a weird thing happened. It didn't matter whether students started the year in the high – or the low-ability group. Both groups ended the year way up high . . . The group differences had simply disappeared under the guidance of teachers who taught for improvement, for these teachers had found a way to reach their 'low-ability' students.[110]

Carol Dweck's research into mindset has enormous implications for teachers and students alike. Teachers who propagate the fixed mindset myths are hampering the achievement of their students and this has a direct negative impact on self-image and self-concept. Not only this, but they may be harming their own self-esteem by creating a deeply pessimistic view of education as being largely impotent and unable to effect individual change.

Putting it into practice: teaching about mindset

Because your mindset originates largely upon your perceptions and beliefs about yourself and the world, the skills required to develop a growth mindset are extraordinarily similar to those required for developing optimism. Many of the techniques for putting optimism into practice that were suggested in the last chapter will transfer across with very little alteration.

- **Speculation**: ask the students to speculate about what life might hold in store for a person with a growth mindset. Ask them to devise a timeline of their life and speculate about how they deal with adversities as they appear. Do the same for a person with a fixed mindset.
- **Inoculations**: ask the students to speculate about how having a growth mindset might help to inoculate them against destructive coping strategies such as drug and alcohol abuse or promiscuity, hopefully teasing out the idea that the growth mindset sees problems as resolvable, thus lessening the need to mask emotional difficulties with substances for example.

Brain plasticity: old dogs and new tricks

Of course, to be able to acquire new skills, such as marathon running, speaking Hebrew or throwing pots, we need to be able to create new pathways in the brain. It used to be thought that you couldn't teach an old dog new tricks: that the brain, after an initial period of growth and development in childhood basically became stable through adulthood. It is now clear that this is not the case and that the brain keeps on developing right into old age, as John Ratey explains:

> the adult brain is both plastic and resilient, and always eager to learn. Experiences, thoughts, actions and emotions actually change the structures of our brains. By viewing the brain as a muscle that can be weakened or strengthened, we can exercise our ability to determine who we become. Indeed, once we understand how the brain develops, we can train our brains for health, vibrancy and longevity. Barring a physical illness, there's no reason we can't stay actively engaged into our nineties.[111]

The current thinking in the world of neuroscience is that the brain is 'plastic': in other words, it can be changed. There are certain skills which, if not learned early enough, can never be fully learned – the learning of language, for example, is one of these skills – but apart from a few windows of opportunity that cannot be missed, humans are always open to learning. When we learn a new piece of information or acquire a new skill, new pathways are formed in the brain. The more we use the newly acquired piece of information or practise the newly acquired skill, the more reinforced those neural pathways become and the less likely we are to forget what we have learned: some skills become 'hard-wired' such as riding a bike and although the skills may get rusty, it doesn't take much to polish them up again.

Of course, the opposite is also true: lack of practice will mean that a skill can be lost altogether, especially if it has not become hard-wired. The brain is incredibly economical and it will adapt any of the 100 billion neurons to do other work if they fall idle. Homer Simpson was more or less right when he said that every time he learns new stuff, it pushes the old stuff out: so long as the old stuff hasn't been used for a while. This process has been called 'Neural Darwinism' and is an obvious quality needed of a brain with (albeit enormous) finite capacity and a need to constantly adapt to a changing environment.

It is vital for us to get away from the idea that abilities are fixed. The biological structures that underpin learning and skill acquisition are capable of being remodelled and while that remodelling might be tough to begin with, the perseverance does pay off.

Putting it into practice: teaching about neuro-plasticity

- **Reflect**: ask students to think about how they learn. Does the idea of brain plasticity ring true for them?
- **Application**: ask students how their finding out about neuro-plasticity affects their approaches, beliefs, judgements about their own learning. Using material from Chapter 3 on learning, how can they set up conditions in their own lives to make for optimal learning environments? Are there any ways of thinking or skills that they would like to acquire or get rid of?

Talent and children: openness and opportunities

'We need to be careful not to privilege some passions over others, even though many can be classed as low culture versus high culture.'[112]

Whenever I travel to London I arrive at Waterloo Station. If I have a spare few moments, I really enjoy walking along the South Bank by the Royal Festival Hall, getting a large cup of coffee and watching the skateboarders. If you don't know what I'm talking about, there is a place just by Waterloo Bridge which is given over exclusively to skateboarders and BMX riders; it's basically a concrete bowl with a few other obstacles and it's beautifully decorated with graffiti. The skateboarders who gather there vary in their skill levels, but one thing unites them: absorption – they are completely consumed by their love of skateboarding and of learning new tricks (and a little bit of playing to the crowd too).

When I was young, I was never allowed a skateboard. I think it's for the same reason that I wasn't allowed bubble gum: my Mum didn't want me to be the kind of child who rode a skateboard or chewed bubble gum. It was uncouth. But I do think she was missing the point a little bit. Surely, anything that offers someone the opportunity to develop a high level of skill and which positively contributes to developing character is a good thing? Good skateboarders have high levels of skill and are very graceful to watch. Learning a skill such as that also affords us the chance to try and to fail, a very important aspect of character development as it engenders the skill of resilience. Obviously, there are some things that enable us to develop high levels of skill that do not contribute positively to character development: injecting drugs intravenously, for example, requires skill, hacking into other people's computer systems requires skill, but neither *necessarily* positively contributes to character development.

The point is that we ought to be open to the types of talents that our young people possess or that they wish to develop. The benefits of becoming skilled at something are enormous and we should not close down some avenues of opportunity because the skills involved are not deemed worthy enough. To appreciate another's skill also transforms our relationships. You may have seen the film *Kes*, which is the story of Casper, a 13-year-old boy who captures and raises a young kestrel and is based upon the Barry Hines novel, *A Kestrel for a Knave*. Casper is a naughty boy who has a horrible home life, is disenchanted with school and regularly finds himself in trouble. However, none of the people who pester and harangue Casper know about the amazing aspect of his life where he has taught himself falconry and has hand-reared a bird of prey, apart from his English teacher who gets him to stand up in front of his class and talk to his peers about something that interests him. It is a magical moment of film where an otherwise disenfranchised boy is at last given the chance to show that he shines and the lesson is that, as teachers, it is imperative for us to find out what our students are good at inside and outside the classroom.

Strengthspotting

In his book *Average to A+*, Alex Linley makes some very important observations about the role of spotting and nurturing strengths amongst the young. According to Linley, only about 30 per cent of us have a meaningful understanding of what our strengths are and he suggests that we ought to give over much more time to what he calls 'strengthspotting'. The spotting of strengths should be a relatively straightforward exercise, although for some it might be such an unusual exercise that it takes a little longer:

> If you think about it carefully, you can probably spot the things that you really look forward to doing. The things in which you just lose yourself. The things that make you feel like 'the real you' – fully alive, fully engaged, fully immersed in the activity.[113]

He also describes the change that is noticeable in a person when they switch from discussing an area of weakness to an area of strength and, unsurprisingly, there is a marked increase in positive emotion and engagement. Of course, we know this, but in our culture of educational achievement measured by results, we can become a little fixated on discussion of areas for improvement while neglecting talk of the areas where we thrive, especially if the areas of thriving, like the boy we met at the start of the chapter, lie outside the classroom and the realm of five A*–C grades.

We do seem to be set up to find discussion of what we are good at difficult: in cognition, there exists a natural bias towards the less satisfactory side of life called the 'negativity bias'. The reasons for this are quite obvious: in order to succeed, we need to remove barriers and we can only spot barriers if we are tuned in to detecting them. It is easy to let the negativity bias get the better of us and for it to be on permanent high alert and if we do let it get the better of us, it can lead to a pessimistic outlook on life which eventually results in depression. 'Strengthspotting' is a great antidote to the negativity bias because it engenders a positive emotional state in us and in others. We enjoy discussing what we do well and, as teachers, we should encourage this activity as much as possible, not only with our students, but with each other too.

Linley explains very clearly what is needed to allow children to develop strengths. Initially, they should be given the room to explore and to make mistakes. We cannot discover what we are good at if we aren't allowed to find it in the first place. Some parents try to overcome this by providing a different activity for their children every hour of every day in order to engender talents and strengths. The only problem with this, as is explained below, is that the child derives its motivation to act from outside (the parents) and has not developed an *intrinsic* motivation to engage in this activity. Intrinsic motivation makes us much more likely to persevere with something when the going gets tough. The other extreme is the parent who doesn't care and takes no interest in their child's strengths, much like the parents in Roald Dahl's story *Matilda*. Linley writes about the importance of planting 'golden seeds', which simply means noticing, commenting on and commending strengths in others. This is especially important for children, as the encouragement they derive from having been praised for doing something well increases the likelihood of their persevering with that activity. The opposite of the 'golden seed' is the 'leaden seed', the unnecessarily negative and critical remarks which can stop exploration and creativity dead in their tracks and lead to us *believing* we cannot do something. As we saw in Chapter 6, false beliefs can be debilitating.

Developing strengths is a natural process driven by the human desire to be competent. Environments are either conducive or obstructive in helping us to find and develop strengths and it is important for schools to examine how well they enable their students and staff to employ their strengths every day. Not only this, but we must encourage students and staff alike to set rigorous challenges for themselves, as this quote from Mihaly Csikszentmihalyi argues:

> A community should be judged good not because it is technologically advanced, or swimming in material riches; it is good if it offers people a chance to enjoy as many aspects of their lives as possible, while allowing them to develop their potential in the pursuit of even greater challenges. Similarly the value of a school does not

depend on its prestige, or its ability to train students to face up to the necessities of life, but rather on the degree of lifelong learning it can transmit.[114]

The sense of satisfaction gained from achieving something we believed impossible is huge and contributes enormously to a personal sense of well-being and to the relationships we forge with people we may overcome these challenges with. The more that education is homogenous and focuses solely on fixed avenues of achievement, rather than providing diverse opportunities for exploration and expression, the more it reduces the ability of young people (and indeed of the adults who work with them) to find fulfilment through expression and development of what they are good at.

Putting it into practice: teaching about strengths

- **Play to your strengths**: ask students to write down the things that they are good at. Ask them to work out how much time they spend each week playing to their strengths and how they can use their experience of doing what they are good at to help them improve in other areas.

- **What are you good at?** Ask students in pairs to tell each other something that they do well that their partner might not know about. Ask them to tell each other about a time when they employed one of their strengths. Feed these stories back to the whole class. Create a map of the strengths in the room. Does it surprise the class? Can anyone do things they didn't think possible for people of their age?

- **Celebration**: ask the students to devise ways that the whole-school community can celebrate the diversity of strengths of the students and staff.

- **Strengths coach**: once students have found out about a talent that another student has, ask them to interview that student to find out how they acquired their strength and put together five pieces of advice for another person who wants to develop that strength.

- **Strengths and superheroes**: ask students to put together a case study of the strengths of a particular superhero. How do their strengths benefit society? Compare the superhero with their alter-ego (e.g. Superman and Clark Kent). What is it like for the superhero to have to refrain from playing to their strengths? Is there a link between alter-egos and people who are unable to show the world what they are good at? Why do superheroes have to hide their identities (and strengths); why can't they take credit for the good they do? The opening sequence of the Pixar film *The Incredibles*, looks at what life might be like for a frustrated superhero in a society which has banned superheroes and put them in witness protection.

Character strengths

The chapter so far has focused mainly on skills, talents and abilities. We have looked at Carol Dweck's work on mindset which is, to a greater or lesser extent, to do with strength of character and it is to character strengths that I would like to turn now.

At first glance, the topic of character strengths might seem a bit wishy-washy: the kind of thing that we all know about intuitively, but can't really quantify. However, work into categorizing strengths of character has been going on for centuries and arguably finds its greatest expression in Aristotle's *Nicomachean Ethics*, written in the fourth century BC, which takes as its focus human *excellence*. Character strengths are those personal qualities which allow us to achieve excellence: qualities such as perseverance, courage, belief in justice, loving and being loved, curiosity, humour, wisdom and so on. Interest in character strengths has resurfaced as part of Positive Psychology and a huge amount of research has been conducted into establishing a list of character strengths which holds across cultures. Chris Peterson is the person most associated with this work and, with others, has devised a list of 24 character strengths which fall into six categories:

1. wisdom and knowledge: e.g. open-mindedness, creativity
2. courage: e.g. authenticity, bravery
3. humanity: e.g. kindness
4. justice: e.g. teamwork, fairness
5. temperance: e.g. modesty, self-regulation
6. transcendence: e.g. appreciation of beauty.

The character strengths are in no way fixed: they can each be developed and we possess all of them to a degree, but as Aristotle argued we must practise them if we are to exhibit them. The repertoire of character strengths is a little bit like a toolkit that we dip into to get certain things achieved: I will employ different strengths when I am spending time with my wife to when I am putting up shelves. Schools must provide opportunities for staff and students to develop their character strengths: it stands to reason that if you allow people to discover their character strengths and find opportunities to employ them and stretch them, they will feel more engaged in life and are less likely to feel frustrated and disaffected.

It is a hugely positive experience to hold a conversation that focuses on strengths. My tutor group this year consists of 12 Year 9 girls and my favourite well-being lesson with them so far has been the strengths lesson. Beforehand, the students complete the VIA Strengths Test online[115] and they print off their strengths report, which tells them what their 'signature strengths' are – the five strengths that, according to their responses, they use most frequently. They arrived to the lesson (after lunch on a Friday) in a state of great excitement and were already talking about their own and each other's strengths. During the lesson, I ask the students to think of a time when they employed one or more of their strengths, to then tell that story to a partner and the partner tells the story to the group as a whole. We had some wonderful and highly amusing stories, but that wasn't the best part. The best part was the atmosphere of appreciation in the room: everybody had an aspect of their character publicly celebrated by someone else and that is a very affirming experience for anyone.

Authenticity

We know instantly when someone is being inauthentic and we usually experience extreme moral aversion to it, largely because being inauthentic is one of the best ways of stopping another person from trusting you. Authenticity is built upon knowing our own strengths and of living in harmony with them and it is also built upon appreciation of the strengths of others and having an appropriate reaction when they employ them. In her article on authenticity, Susan Harter lists the words that we tend to use for inauthenticity. It is a list of dark and delicious verbs, adjectives and nouns: fabricating, withholding, concealing, distorting, falsifying, posturing, charading, faking, elusive, evasive, wily, phoney, manipulative, calculating, pretentious, crafty, conniving, duplicitous, hypocrite, charlatan, chameleon, impostor.[116]

In Western culture, the two groups of people notoriously associated with inauthentic behaviour are politicians and second-hand car dealers. What unites them in their inauthenticity is the willingness to resort to Machiavellian strategies to achieve their goals: it often seems that they will do anything to influence an Act of Parliament or flog an aged Jag with a broken gearbox. Inauthentic behaviour is fixated upon achieving something else – it allows the ends to justify the means, as Harter points out:

> Various forms of 'facework' communicate to others that we are competent, likable, moral, or worthy of respect, motives designed not only to protect and promote the self but also to curry favour, obtain social currency or power, and preserve critical relationships.[117]

In the film *Thank You For Smoking* we see this 'facework' put to brilliant use by PR guru 'Nick Naylor' who is employed by the tobacco industry to lobby governments in order to allow the tobacco companies to continue making a profit at the expense of those addicted to nicotine. Duplicity and evasion are the main tactics used by Naylor and authenticity is the leitmotif of the film. We see the same process in *Jerry Maguire*, where Maguire, a sports agent played by Tom Cruise, realizes the chicanery that happens in the industry and puts together a manifesto for honesty. Both characters go through a denouement where they realize that they are being inauthentic: that they are living contrary to the beliefs and values that they hold and, indeed, contrary to their strengths.

Authenticity starts to become important to us in adolescence. Not only does society demand that we play different roles and therefore have different selves (how many teenagers are the same with their parents as they are with their friends?) but developments in the neo-cortex allow adolescents the cognitive resources to play different roles in different situations with different people.[118] Of course, this comes with the added pressure that others are going through the same process and are perhaps more attuned to inconsistency between selves. This is one of the causes of strife amongst teenagers: in the frantic grappling for a sense of self, there are sometimes casualties as they make mistakes and present themselves as one thing to one group and another thing to another group and get caught in the middle having been 'rumbled' by both groups.

Susan Harter has conducted research with adolescents where she interviews them on how they present themselves to different groups (e.g. parents, friends, teachers) and then invites them to see if they can see any conflict in how they present themselves (e.g. depressed to parents, cheerful to friends). She has found that the number of conflicts can range from 1 to 20 depending on the stage of development and gender of the adolescent; however, girls express more conflicts than boys do. Harter explains that it is not until later development, when we either learn to live with some of these apparent conflicts or resolve them that they become less painful.[119]

How can we help to foster authenticity? Harter writes about the creation of a life story and the importance of allowing children to create the narrative of this story for themselves by encouraging children to voice their opinion and by giving them the opportunity to be listened to non-judgementally. Where children are told how to interpret the events that happen to them and have their reactions named for them ('that was exciting', 'we don't like it when that happens do we?', 'you were disappointed by that'), they will feel the need to fit in with the narrative and the self that is being created for them.

> When asked directly why they engaged in false-self behaviour, many adolescents indicated that they did so because parents and peers did not like their true selves and therefore by suppressing their true selves, they might garner approval or support.[120]

If, on the other hand, young people are accepted and praised for the person that they are and for the strengths that they possess, as opposed to being approved of for playing roles (for example, the dutiful son, the studious scholar, the joker or the rebel) they are likely to be much more authentic because they will feel less of a need to act to gain approval.

Putting it into practice: character strengths and authenticity

- **Strengths lesson**: ask students to complete the VIA test online and bring their strengths reports to the lesson. In pairs, ask each student to think of a time when they employed their strengths and tell that story to their partner. Feedback some examples to the whole group.

- **Strengths in practice**: ask students to take their signature strengths and think of ways that they might use them in their everyday lives. Might they use them differently with different people? Are there particular situations where they can really make the most of them? How could they use their strengths to improve relationships? How can they use an awareness of other people's strengths to improve relationships with them?

- **Strengths talk**: ask students to role-play a conversation in which strengths are celebrated. Ask the students to reflect on how it feels to talk about another person's strengths. Does it feel natural? Does it feel weird? What needs to be in place in a relationship first before we can praise strengths (familiarity, trust, etc.)? Can we talk about the strengths of strangers? What kind of expressions and language can we use to praise another person?

- **Inoculation**: ask students to think about how their strengths can enable them to overcome adversity. Is there a particular problem at the moment that they might apply their strengths to? Ask them to think about how they might go about developing other strengths that they may need to face other challenges.

- **Role play**: ask the students to devise a short piece of role play containing both authenticity and inauthenticity. This could be real, celebrated (e.g. something from reality TV, often a good source of inauthenticity) or imagined.

- **Facework**: ask the students to think of the different faces they show to different people (and perhaps draw them as masks). Are they consistent, or do they change their behaviour slightly to suit what they believe different people to expect of them? Is there any danger of people seeing them as inauthentic?

- **Fame**: ask students to think of examples of people in the public eye who have to maintain one identity for the public and who might maintain another in private. Ask them to speculate about what that must be like. Celebrity magazines might be a useful source of visual stimulus.

So, the key messages so far are that:

- effort is what counts in the acquisition of new skills
- we must get away from the idea that humans have fixed talents
- the human brain is (given the right conditions) always ready to learn new things
- we should broaden our notions of what strengths and skills are worth acquiring
- anyone, given appropriate encouragement can acquire and develop new strengths
- a key ingredient of the happy life is the opportunity to play to our strengths
- children must be encouraged to develop authentic selves by praising them for their strengths.

Flow: the work of Mihaly Csikszentmihalyi

No matter how many times I write the name of the psychologist associated with 'flow', I always have to check the spelling. His surname is pronounced 'cheeks-sent-me-high' and he is the author of one of the most remarkable books on finding happiness in life.

All strengths work, essentially, is aimed at the production of states of 'flow'. I expect you will know very well the meaning of the expression 'time flies when you're having fun' and that you can call to mind any number of experiences where you have been so engrossed in what you were doing that time literally flew past. This is one of the characteristics of a 'flow' experience, which is where our ability and our concentration meet perfectly when doing something resulting in complete absorption in the task. Flow states are magical, even mystical and they are perhaps the peak form of experience that we enjoy as humans: they enable the boundaries between the self and the world to become dissolved as we reach the height of our abilities. Csikszentmihalyi cites this interview with a rock climber to illustrate what he means by flow:

> The mystique of rock climbing is climbing; you get to the top of a rock glad it's over but really wish it would go on forever. The justification of climbing is climbing, like the justification of poetry is writing; you don't conquer anything except things in yourself . . . The act of writing justifies poetry. Climbing is the same: recognising that you are a flow. The purpose of the flow is to keep on flowing, not looking for a peak or utopia but staying in the flow.[121]

There are enormous benefits to be had from experiencing flow and the remainder of this chapter looks at how we might go about enabling those experiences.

Csikszentmihalyi describes the eight foundations of generating a flow experience.

1. We must have a chance of completing the task.

2. We must be able to concentrate on what we are doing.

3. There are clear goals.

4. We get immediate feedback on success or failure.

5. The worries of everyday life are removed from awareness.

6. There is a sense of control over our actions.

7. Concern for self disappears, but the self emerges stronger afterwards.

8. Our sense of the passage of time is altered: hours pass by in minutes.

Once these features are in place, we can attain to the peak level of experience that Csikszentmihalyi calls 'flow'.[122] However, flow experiences are not just about pleasures. When our body's needs are met, the chemical dopamine is released and we experience a little reward for feeding, resting, exercising or attempting reproduction. Flow experiences go beyond the mere generation of pleasure and involve effort, dedication and repeated practice.

Csikszentmihalyi writes about the development of an *autotelic* personality: the *autotelic* person is able to generate and achieve their own goals; they live deliberately and do not have their goals dictated to them by nature, or by others.[123] This is very important. We often see people whose lives are almost accidental: they lurch from one disaster to another, sometimes fuelled by drugs or drink and it's as if they have no control over what happens to them; they have lost the ability to select the kinds of opportunity that will enable them to thrive. The *autotelic* person is not like this and Csikszentmihalyi argues that there are certain factors that can be provided in childhood and adolescence that can help to develop it:

- Clear goals and expectations set by parents or teachers: this prevents squabbling over rules, which is wasted energy.
- Interest shown in what the child is doing *now*, not what is hoped they will achieve in the future.
- A feeling of choice: that the child feels they can exercise control over what they choose to do.
- Trust: that the child does not have to feel self-conscious or excessively self-aware as they pursue activities which generate flow.
- Challenge: the provision of increasingly complex activities to stretch ability.[124]

Motivation: intrinsic and extrinsic

According to Csikszentmihalyi's research, children who grow up with these features present in their families find it much easier to be self-motivated. This argument is supported by the work of Ryan and Deci who argue that we become interested in new things or in mastering new skills 'when our needs for competence, relatedness and autonomy are satisfied'.[125] In other words, if we feel as if we have the right skills and knowledge (competence), what is new fits in with other things we do (relatedness) and we feel as if we have control over our choices (autonomy) and so we are more likely to be motivated to achieve something. What is also interesting is that rewards and punishments seem to *reduce* intrinsic motivation because they make us think that we performed well or badly *because* of the threat of punishment or the promise of reward, not because we wanted to succeed at a task because the task was inherently interesting.[126]

Ryan and Deci have shown very clearly that to be intrinsically motivated to perform a task significantly increases our chances of performing it well:

> Compared with people who are extrinsically motivated, those who are intrinsically motivated show more interest, excitement and confidence about the tasks they are intrinsically motivated to do. They also show enhanced performance, persistence and creativity concerning these tasks and more generally report higher self-esteem and subjective well-being.[127]

Csikszentmihalyi makes similar remarks about the occurrence of flow experiences: that they result from freely chosen activities, not ones forced upon us, that they often occur when engaged in inexpensive activities such as talking or gardening,[128] that they become increasingly challenging, that they require discipline and sometimes the rote learning of knowledge or skills,[129] and that the *autotelic* person can create an opportunity for a flow experience in even the most barren of places.[130] It is important to note that flow could be found just as easily while stealing cars (which is nicely explored in the film *Gone in Sixty Seconds*) as it could while performing surgery on the brain, so the choice of activities likely to produce flow must be governed by a strong set of values that are rationally arrived at and regularly scrutinized (see Chapter 8). Also, the finding of what can cause flow may be difficult and this is where I would return our attention to the idea of openness mentioned above. It may take the young people some time to find what really excites them in life, especially if the conditions for being intrinsically motivated have not been provided for them and knowing what we do about brain plasticity, it is never too late to learn something new. Furthermore, we cannot really predict what will cause people to experience flow and we certainly cannot impose it upon them. We ought to move away from the idea that there is a 'canon' of desirable pursuits in a society and anything falling outside that canon is unacceptable or boorish.

Of course, what is true for our students is true for us as teachers too. You will no doubt have taught lessons where you are surprised to find that your time is up, as indeed are your students. Teaching is a complex and highly skilled profession which is likely to generate episodes of flow on a regular basis. Compared with other ways of earning a living, teaching is also more likely to create a sense of meaning and purpose, which is really the icing on the cake for a flow experience: that you feel your activity to be directed at a noble end which serves a greater good. When teaching is good, it is an extremely fruitful source of opportunities for developing flow for teachers and students alike and if we are in flow, our chances of leading a happy and fulfilled life are greatly enhanced.

Putting it into practice: teaching about flow

- **Notice and reflect**: ask students to pay attention to times during the week when they enter into a state of flow and write about it. Encourage the idea that flow can be found in a variety of areas of life: academic study/games/music/drama and so on. Ask them to pay attention to the conditions that made flow possible and ask them to reflect on how being in flow affected them afterwards. What emotions did it bring about? How did it make them feel about themselves?

- **Inoculation**: how could getting into a state of flow everyday benefit them? What harmful or destructive behaviour might it be able to prevent? Why?

- **Micro-flow**: provide students with a small task that they can become absorbed in during the lesson – some kind of challenge such as finding 20 uses for an empty plastic water bottle, building the highest tower they can out of newspaper, or simply tapping or clapping out a rhythm (perhaps get a student who plays the drums to lead it). Afterwards, ask the students to notice what it felt like to be completely absorbed. Can they think of ways of creating micro-flow situations, especially when it comes to revision or other aspects of learning?

- **Motivation**: ask students to make a list of things that they are intrinsically motivated to do and a list of things that they are extrinsically motivated to do. How do they feel about the intrinsic/autotelic activities and the extrinsic ones? Are there any on the extrinsic list that can be carried across to the intrinsic list? What would need to happen to make that possible?

8 Relationships

Case study: Shaun Dykes

On 27 September 2008, a 17-year-old man named Shaun Dykes took his own life by jumping from the multi-storey car park of the Westfield Centre in Derby. Stories of suicide are not unusual, despite a steady decline in the suicide rate in the UK. However, this story stands out and it received a lot of attention in the press in the weeks after it happened. As Shaun stood on the top of the car park and as two trained police negotiators worked with him for three hours to try to prevent him taking his own life, a crowd of several hundred people gathered in the streets below. This is, again, not unusual. The prospect of death is fascinating to some and this explains why large crowds used to gather at Tyburn gallows in London to watch executions in the eighteenth and nineteenth centuries. What stirred the interest in the media was the small number of people in the crowd below Shaun Dykes who were persuading him to jump, shouting comments such as 'Go on, jump' and 'How far can you bounce?'[131]

The reaction to this story was predictable. The moral majority cried out that we are in a state of moral decline, pointing to the rise in reality television as a numbing influence on our sensibilities and ability to empathize with the suffering of others. Others were horrified by stories of people using mobile phones to video the scenario and lamented the voyeuristic society we now live in, with people sharing every aspect of their lives to as wide a public as they can reach.

This reaction was predictable and also fails to gain perspective on this situation. Crowds of people behave in peculiar ways. People are afforded a sense of anonymity they might not otherwise feel and spurred on by the reactions of others, often do things they might not normally do: anyone who has stood amongst an excited group of football supporters will know this feeling. The reaction also fails to take account of our genuine fascination with things that are out of the ordinary: I defy anyone coming across a situation like this one to turn and walk away, to overcome a deeper urge to know what might happen. I would also be willing to bet that had there been the technology 300 years ago, onlookers would have been just as likely to use it then as now. The reaction also misses the genuine sense of wanting to help that was reportedly felt by many in the crowd and, of course, by the two police officers who spent three hours trying to help Shaun to reconsider his decision.

Nonetheless, stories such as this one cause us to raise questions about the state of our communities and the relationships that comprise them and it demonstrates very clearly what is both profoundly wrong with our communities and what is profoundly right with them.

The importance of relationships

In a report into mental capital and well-being commissioned by the Government Office for Science and published in 2008, connection with the people around you was listed as the first of five 'ways to well-being' and is described as 'a defining characteristic of people who demonstrably function well in the world'.[132] This is borne out by the remarkable story of the town of Roseto in Pennsylvania.

In the late 1880s, a small group of people from the town of Roseto in the province of Foggia in the foothills of the Apennine Mountains travelled to America in search of a better life, which they found. Word soon got back to Roseto and more people followed. By the mid-twentieth century, the Rosetans had built their own town, which they named Roseto as an *homage* and it was a thriving community, with one fascinating feature: it had a fraction of the rates of heart disease and peptic ulcers seen elsewhere in the US – the people seemed only to die of old age. Initially, it was thought that the rustic Italian diet of olive oil and fresh vegetables was the cause, but upon investigation, it was found that cooking was done with lard, pizzas were made from thick dough and covered in sausage and many of the Rosetans were obese. In fact, many of them were chain smokers too. After every possible cause was investigated, Stewart Wolf, the doctor trying to explain the phenomenon, realized the answer:

> In transplanting the culture of southern Italy to the hills of eastern Pennsylvania, the Rosetans had created a powerful, protective social structure capable of insulating them from the pressures of the modern world. The Rosetans were healthy because of where they were from, because of the world they had created for themselves in their tiny little town in the hills.[133]

It was the supportive relationships of a caring community that were inoculating the Rosetans against heart disease and ulcers, two diseases often exacerbated by that very modern malaise: stress. There is more compelling evidence that the behaviour and 'affect' or emotional state of those around us contributes to our own happiness. Nicholas Christakis and James Fowler of the Harvard Medical School have found that having a happy neighbour can increase your own emotional well-being by up to 34 per cent:

> Happiness spreads best at close distances, they found. A happy next-door neighbour ups the odds of personal happiness by 34%, a sibling who lives within 1 mile (1.6 kilometres) by 14% and a friend within half a mile by a whopping 42%. The effect falls off through the network, with friends' happiness boosting the chances of personal happiness by an average of 15% and friends of friends by 10%. 'If you drop one pebble in a pond, it will create ripples out from the pebble,' [Fowler] says. 'That's not what's happening here. You have a whole handful of pebbles and you're throwing them in the pond at once.'[134]

Primed for relationships: mimicry and reciprocity

So, there is very clear evidence that good relationships have benefits for our own health and well-being. As human beings, we are set up biologically to be social and there are some interesting features of the human organism which show how we are physiologically primed for social interaction.

Monkey see, monkey do: mimicry

Humans are not only socially, but biologically primed to live in communities and there are a couple of simple pieces of evidence to back this up. The first piece of evidence is mimicry. Humans naturally attune themselves to the moods and, indeed, biological conditions of the others around them. You will no doubt have had the experience of being in a room of buoyant and cheerful people when suddenly you are joined by someone who is very upset: what do you all do? You temper your buoyant moods to meet their distress. But it goes further than mood. If you look at someone who is sad, your pupils will shrink to match theirs and your temperature will drop to match theirs too.[135]

Even more fascinating than this is the discovery of mirror neurons by Rizzolatti and Gallese in the mid-1990s. Mirror neurons are brain cells that are active when an individual performs an action, or when they observe another individual performing an action and it seems that they might prompt us to imitate what we see. Dr Daniel Glaser, of University College London, conducted a study where he placed experts in two different types of dancing (ballet and capoeira) into an fMRI scanner and played them images of both ballet and capoeira. He found that the part of the brain that controls movement was more active when the dancers saw someone else doing what they could do: in short, they were being prompted by their brains to mimic the actions they saw and recognized.[136]

It seems that part of being human is to be hard-wired to mimic others. But this mimicry is not just confined to copying actions. There is speculation that mirror neurons might lie at the heart of explaining autism: those on the autistic spectrum find it hard to read emotions because their mirror neurons are not activated when they see others in emotional states.[137] Mirror neurons have also been linked to our ability to feel empathy: research shows that the amount of mirror neuron activity measured by an fMRI scanner in an individual corresponds with assessments of their ability to empathize in paper and pencil tests.[138] There is more on empathy and the brain below.

You scratch my back, I'll scratch yours: reciprocity

The second piece of evidence is reciprocity. If another person gives you something, you feel obliged to give them something in return and this impulse is almost impossible to overcome. I recently travelled to Israel and was walking through the crowded streets of the Old City of Jerusalem with my wife and the Israeli family we were staying with. These streets are lined with traders trying to lure tourists to pay more for their goods than they are worth and they are the best salesmen in the world:

they can spot a sucker a mile away and, boy, was I a sucker. I collect t-shirts and I was looking for a nice 'Palestine' t-shirt to complement my Israeli ones. I found a promising looking shop and started to nose around. Pretty soon, the owner arrived. Politically, I am pro-Palestinian rights and the fact that this trader was Palestinian already spelled disaster; the altruist in me wanted to buy something from him. He then told me he had been a teacher and mentioned something about not being able to work anymore because of the Israelis. All I wanted was a £5 t-shirt. I ended up with a necklace for my wife, a t-shirt (one size too small), a nylon Arab head dress (with a stain) and a pen (the free gift). I ended up spending £40. Because he had offered me not only a sob-story, but a free pen, I felt compelled to give him something in return. What was more galling was that my wife *and* Didi, the magnificent Israeli guy we were staying with, *both* offered me exits from the situation, but of course I knew best and I didn't want to damage the relationship I had established with my new friend, the former teacher.

The desire for reciprocity is a strong indication of our desire to exist in groups, a tendency that comes naturally to us. As humans evolved from our primate ancestors, our skull increased in size to accommodate the brain as it grew larger and larger. The larger brain evolved the capacities for social bonds, language and a conception of past and future, as well as the present that most animals live in permanently. It seems that skull (and therefore brain) dimensions are directly related to the number of relationships that we can sustain: the larger the skull, the larger the social network. Humans exist in communities because our brains give us the ability to and it is the relationships that we develop in these communities that, as we saw above, are fundamental to our happiness.

Putting it into practice: teaching about mimicry and reciprocity

- **Mimicry**: ask students to reflect on times when they have found themselves mimicking other people – from yawning to copying their accents.

- **Reflect on reciprocity**: ask students to think about a time when reciprocity has paid off for them – when giving something to someone has helped them to achieve what they wanted to achieve.

- **Christmas reciprocity**: get students to re-enact Robert Cialdini's experiment where he sent Christmas cards to complete strangers. In Cialdini's experiment, many of the recipients sent one back to him, illustrating reciprocity.

- **Tit for tat**: re-enact 'the ultimatum game'. Select a pair of students who don't know each other very well. Blindfold them. Give student A ten £1 coins and say that he can keep them provided that he divides them up somehow between himself and student B and makes them an offer: he can't just keep them all for himself. Once the offer is made, student B has to decide whether or not she accepts the offer. If she refuses, neither of them gets anything. We would expect student A, if he is completely rational, to give just £1 to student B and keep the rest: but he probably won't. About half of all people give half of the money to the other person. We seem to be conditioned to give other people something for nothing in the interests of preserving relationships. It also makes an interesting point about how much money student B might be willing to forego to punish selfishness on the part of student A if he doesn't offer much or anything.[139]

Forming relationships

We find ourselves engaged in a range of relationships in life: family, romantic partners, friends, acquaintances, colleagues and so on. Research shows that those of us who are happiest are those who are supported by good friendships,[140] loving marriage/partnership ('Throughout the Western world, married people of both sexes report more happiness than those never married, divorced or separated'[141]) and a good family.[142] The next section deals with the two types of relationship over which adolescents exert the greatest degree of autonomy: their friendships and romantic relationships.

Friendship

Friendship is one of the most significant sources of well-being available to us. Studies researching the ingredients of a happy life all find that the happiest people have strong friendship networks.[143] The process of forming friendships is one that, initially, we learn from our parents. In Chapter 3, we looked at 'attachment theory', which shows how children learn to relate to others based upon the lead given to them by their parents or primary care-givers. Children who are securely attached are more likely to be able to form meaningful and lasting friendships. When we select people to develop friendships with, we tend to look for people who are similar to us in terms of interests and abilities, because this reinforces our own positive view of ourselves.

In middle childhood, friendships are almost exclusively divided along gender lines and, among boys in particular, relationships tend to be competitive and hierarchical: we should expect to see boys teasing and scrapping with each other as they jostle for position. Girls' friendships tend to be in smaller groups and their play tends to be more co-operative and relationship focused. The friends that children select are very important for finding support and starting 'positive chain reactions' of personal growth; the opposite is also true and children who 'fall in with the wrong crowd' are at risk of engaging in unhealthy behaviour.

Successful friendships are based upon trust and a lack of betrayal, shared experiences, capacity for mutual empathy, appreciation and gratitude, atonement for wrongdoing and forgiveness,[144] all of which are mentioned below.

Putting it into practice: friendship

- **Reflect**: ask students to think about their friendships. What are the ingredients that make them work? How do they think their friendships will change as they get older? How does their understanding of emotions and strengths enhance their understanding of their friendships?

- **Observe**: ask students to pay attention to their friendships for one week and write about them in their journal. Ask them to think about what makes the friendship go well and what makes it struggle. Ask them to think about how their friendships enhance their lives. What do they provide that they don't get elsewhere? How do friendships help them find their strengths or their authenticity?

- *The Prophet*: Khalil Gibran's *The Prophet* contains a section on friendship. Discuss as a class. Does this fit in with their ideas of friendship?

- *Stand By Me*: watch the opening sequences of *Stand By Me*, which contain some excellent examples of the ingredients of friendship. Ask the students to spot them and think about which of those ingredients will be present in those friendships in 10, 20, 30, 40 years' time.

- **Role play**: ask the students to put together a small piece of drama which explores the type of thing we might expect to see in a friendship. Use forum theatre techniques to introduce an adversity for the friends to overcome and use the audience to explore how they might go about overcoming it.

- **Girls and boys**: ask students to think about whether or not there are differences between boy friendships and girl friendships. Put the class into mixed groups and ask them to find out what the differences and similarities are. Ask them to then consider if friendships between boys and girls are different again. Should they expect to behave differently around members of the opposite sex? Are there things they should do more of or less of? How does this fit in with authenticity (Chapter 7)?

Romantic relationships

'Romantic love may not be essential to life, but it may be essential to joy. Life without love would be for many people like a black and white movie – full of events and activities but without the colour that gives it vibrancy and provides a sense of celebration.'[145]

For teenagers, learning how love and relationships work is often a painful process, at a time when they are also undergoing tremendous academic pressures and changing relationships with their families. Love and exclusive long-term partnership is what most people would say is their ultimate aim, but finding 'the one' with whom that is going to be possible is for most of us a long and sometimes arduous journey. Getting romantic relationships right is a lengthy process which involves the development of not only the inter-personal skills of trust, intimacy, empathy, disclosure, sensitivity, compatibility and so on, but also the physical aspect, with all of the social and peer-group expectations that go with it. The process also involves making mistakes and while it might seem, at age 16, that you will be with your current boyfriend or girlfriend for ever, that is very rarely the case any more; of course, this brings with it the need for skills of ending relationships with dignity, dealing with the grief and bereavement felt at the end of a relationship and the ability to put these events into perspective to avoid rumination.

I don't want to dwell too much on this area, as there is already a wealth of materials and resources out there on sex and relationship education. However, research has shed its light on some interesting features of romantic relationships that are worth considering. Primarily, it is important to note that, despite what the press might say, promiscuity during adolescence is *not* the norm.[146] The World Health Organization reported in 2008 that 40 per cent of girls and 35 per cent of boys in the UK had sex below the age of consent.[147] However, it does not give the circumstances: that is, whether or not it was within the confines of a relationship, nor does it explain how frequently young people are having sex. According to the National Office of Statistics, in 2004–5 the vast majority of people aged 16–49 reported having only one sexual partner in the previous 12 months. The greatest proportion of people having no sexual partner in the previous year were aged under 20.[148] It is easy to think that 'they're all at it', when in the majority of cases, they are not.

As for forming relationships that are meaningful, of course, the features of a successful friendship are present in a romantic relationship (trust, empathy and so on). Alan Carr explains that successful and happy couples show respect to each other; that the ratio of positive to negative comments is *at least* 5:1; that they accept differences; they focus conflict on a specific issue (such as taking out the rubbish) rather than criticizing general things ('you're so lazy'), they resolve conflicts and problems in the relationship quickly; and when one partner does something positive, the other explains it as a feature of their personality ('because she's a good person'), rather than chance or the situation ('because it was easy at the time').[149]

Also, as with all other forms of relationships, people engage in them in different ways. The Ancient Greeks had six words to express different types of love: *Eros* – passionate love; *Ludus* – love played as a game for mutual enjoyment, which is short on commitment; *Storge* – friendship and companionship; *Pragma* – practical love, or selecting a partner using methodical or practical criteria; *Mania* – manic love, where the lover desperately wants love, but finds that it is painful; and *Agapé* – unconditional love.[150] Teenagers may very well find that they have experience of a range of these different love styles as they go through life and will need to make decisions about the appropriateness of each in a given situation. A distinction has also been made between passionate love and companionate love. Many teenagers don't get beyond the passionate love stage, where the love is intense, probably largely physical and may become obsessive. It is only over time that the companionate aspect, which is more like deep friendship, can develop so that eventually the companionate and passionate can (hopefully) co-exist in the relationship.

As mentioned above, there is already a wealth of programmes available for teaching about sex and relationships. The best will enable young people to discuss sex and relationships openly and responsibly so that they can develop a relationships vocabulary that they are confident to use. It will provide them with accurate information and provide sources of advice and help. It will also equip them with the skills they need to negotiate what they want in a relationship, rather than what they feel pressured to want and will help to look at any underlying problematic issues of self-image and self-confidence which plague many teenagers and lead them into doing things to gain approval or acceptance. These skills will be developed through discussion initially, but could be later developed through drama and role-playing exercises. Successful, happy and healthy romantic relationships happen when all of the ingredients of well-being are present, so by teaching the skills of well-being and making regular connections with the impact those skills have on relationships, we will be helping students to reflect on how to make their relationships work.

The ingredients of successful relationships

Once we have formed relationships, certain ingredients need to be in place for those relationships and for the communities upon which they are based to flourish:

1. empathy
2. altruism
3. trust
4. forgiveness
5. the ability to resolve conflict
6. common causes and values.

Empathy: the roots of community

I don't know about you, but as I picture the scene of poor Shaun Dykes' last few moments in my mind's eye, I look into the crowd and I can see the faces of students I have taught. Some of them are goading Shaun and some of them are looking away in distress. Two of them are trying their best to help dissuade Shaun from jumping.

It sometimes seems that some children are *naturally* empathetic, while others are callous and only seem to be enjoying themselves when doing something at another's expense. Why is this? Quite simply, some people are given more opportunity and encouragement to develop the skill of empathy than others.

Empathy is the ability to feel another person's emotional state; it is not to be confused with sympathy which is just the ability to put yourself in another person's shoes without a sharing of feelings.[151] Empathy emerges in the first five years of childhood as children have increased opportunity to play with other children. Ability to empathize is usually settled by middle childhood.[152] Communities are dependent upon empathy as we cannot be expected to will the good of those around us if we cannot accurately feel and predict their emotional states. Some interesting research conducted by Professor Tania Singer at the University of Zurich shows that the structure of the brain that deals with our own emotional pain also deals with sensing the emotional pain of others.

In Singer's experiment, she asked a married couple to get inside an fMRI scanner, which can detect patterns of brain activity. Inside the scanner there was a pad on which both the husband and wife placed one of their palms. The pad generated mildly painful electric shocks. In front of the pad was a screen with an arrow indicating to the couple which of them was to receive the electric shock; if the wife was about to experience pain, her husband would know about it and *vice versa*. Singer found that the same part of the brain is active when we feel pain ourselves as when we see the pain of others, especially pain inflicted upon those close to us.

However, there does appear to be a bit of a difference between the sexes when it comes to feeling empathy for people who have wronged us. In another experiment, Professor Singer took groups of male and female volunteers and asked them to play a game with 'confederates': people working for the research team. The confederates either played fairly or unfairly. The volunteers were then placed in an fMRI scanner and the empathy centres in their brains were observed while the people they had just played against received pain. Both the men and the women showed empathic activity in the brain when it was someone who had played fairly with them. For the women, they also experienced empathy when an unfair player was experiencing pain. But for the men, not only did the empathy centres not light up, but the reward centres *did* light up. In other words, the men enjoyed seeing people who had not played fairly with them being 'punished'.[153]

As a result of Singer's (and other) research, we can confidently assert that being able to empathize with the pain of another human being is a cognitive or thinking skill which is activated when particular parts of the brain are used. Unless those parts of the brain are damaged, empathy is something that, given enough opportunities, we can all develop and, as we saw in Chapter 3, because the brain is plastic and new pathways can be created, no one is beyond help. It is Singer's contention that if we can activate the part of the brain concerned with empathy by getting people to the events that have caused them emotional pain (something called *interoception*), it is but a short step to getting them to think about the pain that others feel. She also argues that our ability to empathize must be connected to our brain's learning reward system (see Chapter 2): if we learn that empathizing with others is in fact a deeply rewarding process that can help to strengthen bonds of friendship, as opposed to revenge, which simply widens the divide and increases our own feelings of anger, we will be much more likely to feel empathy than a desire to get our own back.[154]

Predictably, however, there is a significant obstacle to empathy and it is connected to the ego.

I'm right and you're wrong: naive realism

'If I could nominate one candidate for "biggest obstacle to world peace and social harmony," it would be naïve realism.'

Jonathan Haidt

Naïve realism is a term that was coined by Emily Pronin and Lee Ross and it is the belief that our view of the world is *the* correct view and that anyone who disagrees with this view is not just wrong, but somehow inferior to us. As Jonathan Haidt suggests in the quotation above, it is a significant cause of social discord. We see naïve realism everywhere and it is a major cause of strife in communities, if not *the* major cause of strife. My sister is a police officer in rural Gloucestershire and I love catching up with her as she has some extraordinary stories of the conflicts that arise between people. One of her great frustrations is that she finds herself spending a huge amount of time trying to get people to see events as they actually happened, not as they have interpreted them to have happened.

As we all know, humans exist in social groups and this means that we forge relationships with others. But we don't forge relationships with just anyone: as we saw earlier we forge relationships with those who either share our beliefs about the world, or who are useful to us in some way and help to promote our beliefs about the world. This seems incredibly mercenary, but at a basic level, this is true. When I think of all my friends, we all share the same basic worldview and those who are my closest friends are the people with whom I have the most in common. This is not to undermine anything of the joy of real friendship, but we choose certain people as friends and partners for a reason: they don't challenge our view of the world too much.

Unfortunately, this is a mistake in perception of the sort that we saw in Chapter 4:

> the world we live in is not really one made of rocks, trees, and physical objects; it is a world of insults, opportunities, status symbols, betrayals, saints, and sinners. All of these are human creations which, though real in their own way, are not real in the way that rocks and trees are real.[155]

When we look at most of the conflicts that arise between people, they arise because one or more of the parties concerned is simply not willing to let go of *their view* which is probably, in their eyes, *the right, accurate and unbiased* view.

Putting it into practice: empathy

- **From me to you**: put students into pairs. Ask the first student to think of a time in the last week when they have felt a particular emotion and tell the story leading up to it (e.g. feeling pride after winning a match). The second student should listen, reflect the story back to the first student ('so you felt pride when you won') and then think of a time in their own life when they have felt the same or similar emotion and tell the story. The first student should also reflect the emotion. Both students should reflect on how it felt to have been empathized with.

- **Empathy scenarios**: provide students with a series of scenarios where there is some form of conflict (e.g. a teenager wanting to go out to a party and not being allowed) and task them with empathizing with every person in the scenario. They have to see the situation from everyone's point of view and explain their feelings, regardless of who they think is in the right.

- **Back to me**: having looked at some neutral scenarios, ask students to think of an example from their own lives where they have fallen out with someone. Ask them to empathize with the other person, forgetting for the time being who they thought was right. Ask them to reflect on how it feels to empathize with someone, especially if they feel that person was in the wrong.

- **Making connections**: ask students to think of the different domains in life where empathy is of particular importance. Why is it such a vital skill?

Going beyond empathy: altruism and appreciation

Altruism

In 1989, Leslie Brothers from the California Institute of Technology published the results of some research conducted into empathy in Rhesus monkeys. In one experiment, monkeys were taught to fear a particular noise by having it played to them and receiving an electric shock at the same time. The monkeys were then taught to push a lever to turn off the noise, which they now associated with distress. Afterwards, two monkeys who had learned this skill were placed in separate cages, but could see each other's faces via a CCTV link. The first monkey, but not the second, was played the dreaded noise. Each monkey had a lever in its cage that could end the distress of its neighbour. The second monkey seeing the fear on the face of the first monkey via CCTV, pushed the lever to stop their neighbour's suffering: clear evidence of altruism prompted by empathy.[156]

There is very little doubt that humans have brain structures that enable us to feel the pain of another human being and which may very well prime us to act to prevent others from suffering, but it can sometimes feel like encouraging young people to be kind to each other is like trying to push water up hill. As with all things to do with the brain, the ability to empathize has to be practised for it to develop and it has to be connected to the brain's reward centres. In other words, young people have to learn that helping other people is not only in our nature (unless you are the victim of a severe personality disorder), but it also makes us feel good.

Martin Seligman, in collaboration with Ed Diener, conducted a study with 222 college students and they then focused on the happiest 10 per cent to look at the ingredients of their lives. Without fail, one ingredient which came up time and time again was altruism.[157] There is a slight danger of chicken and egg here. It is not entirely clear whether happiness leads to altruism or whether altruism leads to happiness, but there is a definite correlation. As Seligman points out, altruists are less self-focused and it seems that the less selfish we are, the wider the door to positive experiences is opened. The opposite is also true: people who are depressed on average tend to be less altruistic because depression leads sufferers to be more self-focused.

Evidence cited by Sonja Lyubomirsky suggests that being altruistic can lead to overcoming depression. In a study of female Multiple Sclerosis sufferers who were invited to act as mentors for other MS patients it was found that the five women who had acted as mentors and helped other patients reported increased feelings of satisfaction and happiness. Lyubomirsky goes on to argue that performing acts of kindness leads to a 'cascade' of positive social consequences. We feel better about ourselves, which means that other people look upon us positively, which enhances our relationships: they may even help us out when we are in times of need.[158] This is very similar to Barbara Fredrickson's theory of broadening and building with positive emotions (see Chapter 5).

Altruism is also crucial in the formation of trusting relationships. Because we are hard-wired for reciprocity (see above) we tend not to trust people who are very obviously just out for themselves. Altruism is one of the most highly praised virtues in society and can lead to the formation of strong and lasting relationships; we can also expect vilification if we are very clearly out for number one. By performing an altruistic action we can expect others to trust us and enter into relationships with us, as Matt Ridley explains:

> acts of genuine goodness are the price we pay for having moral sentiments – those sentiments being valuable because of the opportunities they open in other circumstances. So when somebody votes . . . tips a waiter in a restaurant she will never revisit, gives an anonymous donation to charity or flies to Rwanda to bathe sick orphans in a refugee camp, she is not, even in the long run being selfish or rational. She is simply prey to sentiments that are designed for another purpose: to elicit trust by demonstrating a capacity for altruism.[159]

Putting it into practice: altruism

- **Random acts of kindness**: ask the students to perform a random act of kindness in between lessons and note how they felt afterwards. It doesn't have to be saving the starving in Africa: just holding a door open for someone or helping someone with a heavy package is a good start. How long does the feeling last compared with other things they do to bring them pleasure (eating chocolate for example)?
- **Free hugs**: find the 'free hugs' video on the internet and play it to the students. What do they think about it? Is giving away a free hug altruism? How might a free hug benefit someone?

Appreciation

Practising random or deliberate acts of kindness is one very good way of making life go well. Another way is to practise the skill of *genuine* and *sincere* appreciation.

Robert Emmons and Michael McCullough have conducted a lot of research into gratitude and appreciation. In one study, they divided volunteers into four groups and asked them to keep a journal of specific things every day. In the first group, volunteers had to write down five things they were grateful for that day. In the second group, volunteers had to write down five things that had caused them hassle during the day. In the third group, volunteers had to write down five things that made them feel better than others during the day and in the last group (the control group), volunteers had to write down any five things from the day.

Rather unsurprisingly, Emmons and McCullough found that people who kept a journal of things for which they were grateful, on a daily basis were more optimistic, were healthier, exercised more, were more benevolent to others and were more likely to achieve their goals.[160]

Martin Seligman encourages his students at the University of Pennsylvania to practise gratitude and appreciation and to reflect upon the impact it has. His favourite form of this is the 'gratitude night'. He asks his students to think of someone who has been extremely important in their life, but whom they have never thanked properly. He asks them write a one-page letter to that person expressing gratitude for whatever it was. Instead of just popping the letter in the post, Professor Seligman asks his students to invite the person in for the 'gratitude night'. His students then deliver and read out the letter in person in front of the rest of the class. Needless to say, these events are often very emotional, but they also produce a lasting feeling of happiness and contentment.[161]

One thing I have found in teaching the practice of keeping a gratitude journal to students is that they often say 'nothing good has happened' or 'Sir, I can't think of anything good'. One reason for this may be that young people are conditioned to think that unless they are personally shaking hands with David Beckham or they have just won a lifetime of free Domino's pizza, that things aren't that good really. This might be because learning to take delight in small things is a taste that we acquire in the same way that we develop a sensitive palate. It is no accident that the practice of reflecting on the little things that go well is called 'savouring': it takes time to learn to enjoy the simple things like spending half an hour with the cat purring on your lap, or an enjoyable conversation with someone you don't normally speak to. It's really important, however, that young people start to acquire this skill early on in life, because the ability to see that life is actually rather good can help to fend off depressive episodes later in life.

Practising this is all well and good, but receiving insincere praise or gratitude can be one of the most infuriating experiences and learning to express praise or gratitude with sincerity is a very important skill to acquire. When we are praised or thanked by a person who does not mean what they say it is extremely de-motivating. We are left feeling more *un*appreciated because it is clear that the person concerned couldn't be bothered to find out what we had really achieved. Empty phrases such as 'thank you *so* much for *everything* you do' belie a lack of real engagement at a personal level and it is frustrating when managers do this to their employees and indeed when teachers express insincere praise to students, who can of course see straight through it.

Putting it into practice: appreciation

- **The gratitude journal**: ask students to keep a gratitude journal every day for at least a week. Ask them to write down three things every day, either that they are grateful for, or that have gone well and explain why they have gone well. Discuss it in lessons. Who found it helpful and why? Who didn't find it helpful and why?

Trust

If you ask young people about friendship they have very clear ideas about the desirable characteristics of a good friend: trust very often comes high up the list alongside honesty, respect and loyalty. And yet we still see young people angry and upset because one of their friends has betrayed them. It seems that the desire to be accepted by one group often ends up competing with the desire to be loyal to another.

Being trustworthy is a complex skill. Fundamentally, it involves having a clear set of values that we do not allow to come into conflict; that way, others know exactly where they stand with us because we are consistent with ourselves. It also involves being self-aware and being a skilled reader of others: we need to know our own motivations and be in control of them and we also need to be able to read the signals which indicate whether or not we can trust another person. Trust also depends upon skills such as empathy and compassion, being a good listener, appreciation of others' strengths and acknowledgement of their shortcomings, knowing when to disclose personal information, knowing how much touch is appropriate and above all seeing every other person as absolutely valuable, not as a means to an end. Trust also involves calculating how at risk we are of betrayal or rejection in a close or intimate relationship: trust develops when the person we are in the relationship with is predictable and dependable.[162]

Teaching trust to children is a fascinating exercise. The important thing about trust is that it is pointless to teach *about* it: the only way to learn to trust others is to learn through doing. You cannot know that you can trust another person unless you give that person an opportunity to be trustworthy. You cannot know how trusting you are until you give yourself the opportunity to be trusting. The classroom provides an excellent test-bed for learning the skills of trust and there are some very simple exercises (described at the end of this section) for helping to do this. One of my favourites is often called 'wind in the willows'. It involves a circle of people with a person standing in the middle. The person in the centre of the circle closes her eyes and allows herself to 'topple' over, keeping her body straight. The ring of people around her catch her as she falls and gently push her back to the upright position.

What you notice when doing this is the vast difference in how trusting some people are compared to others. It is this difference that allows you to explore how a group builds trust. You can ask questions about why the person at the centre allows herself to fall or not to both the person and the group, which allows them to develop skills of self-awareness and awareness of others. For example, one group I was teaching this to recently found it hard not to giggle and make jokes about the person at the centre, who consequently couldn't close his eyes and didn't want to topple very far. The group blamed him for this, but what the children have to learn is that you cannot criticize a person for being untrusting: the group have to accept that they need to do more to be trustworthy to the person who is 'toppling'. You can also explore the nature of your trust in them as a teacher, which may be a fascinating new area for both you and the students to think about: what signals are you giving off that you trust them?

Trust and gossip

Unfortunately, we do not always act in a trustworthy way and the best way to kill off a friendship is to be caught out gossiping about someone behind their back. It may be, however, that the impulse to gossip is harder to overcome than we think. There is an argument that language may have evolved to enable gossip. Before humans had language, social bonds were mainly enforced through grooming: the removal of ticks, lice and mites from each other's fur. Chimpanzees still do this and they live in groups of about 30. Humans tend to live in groups of between 100 and 150: larger groups meant that grooming wasn't a good enough tool for keeping social bonds strong. Once humans had language, however, a lot of information about others in the group could be shared quickly and, according to Robin Dunbar, it may be that language evolved to enable us to gossip and thus play the social game better.[163]

Most people can identify with the conspiratorial delight taken in sharing a tit-bit of controversial information about someone else and in schools this often revolves around the perceived incompetence of the management. It is undeniable that gossip brings people together in the moral disapproval of others, but it also causes communities to fissure into cliques. Trust is the foundation for all human relationships and also for relationships with animals. If children are not able to develop the skills of trusting and being trustworthy, they will find the worlds of friendship, family, romantic relationships, keeping pets and of course the world of work, impossible. Life cannot be lived fully and we cannot flourish if we do not learn how to trust.

Putting it into practice: trust

- **Trust exercises**: there are a number of trust exercises that can be used to help students reflect on what it means to trust another person. You will probably be familiar with the exercise where students work in pairs and they take it in turns to fall backwards while the other student catches them. Another exercise is 'wind in the willows', mentioned earlier. It requires about eight to ten students to participate. One student stands in the centre with eyes closed while the others gather about the student and form a circle. The circle gently hold the person in the centre with their hands and the person in the centre relaxes and allows themself to fall while those about catch the person and return him or her to an upright position. If the person in the centre cannot relax, it is very powerful to discuss why they feel unable to relax. What will it take for that person to trust the group? It is very important with these exercises to set clear rules too: you must emphasize that as soon as you say 'Stop!', the participants are to stop what they are doing immediately. If you feel that the situation is becoming unsafe, you have to stop it. That opens up some interesting avenues for discussing your relationship with the group and whether they had enabled you to trust them.

- **Trust and animals**: a fascinating way of exploring trust, is to look at the way humans have been able to inspire trust in wild animals. If you type 'Christian the lion' into an internet video search engine, you should find the extraordinary story of two young men who bought a lion cub at Harrods in the late 1960s and hand-reared it in London, before releasing it in the wild in Kenya. It is a little sentimental, but the bond of trust between the two men and the lion is very deep and very moving. This could move the group into discussing how we go about building trust with both humans and animals and what the differences might be.

- **Trust signals**: ask the students to think about the trust signals that they give off. What do they do which inspires trust in others and what do they do that makes it difficult for people to trust them? How could they strengthen their trust signals?

- **Role play**: ask the students to come up with a scenario demonstrating being trustworthy or untrustworthy. Get them to pay attention to body language, tone of voice, as well as the things that they do and say.

- ***The Horse Whisperer***: there are some very helpful clips in the film *The Horse Whisperer* which demonstrate how to build trust with both humans and animals. A particularly good section is where the character played by Robert Redford allows the young girl, played by Scarlett Johansson, to drive his truck, as a deliberate way to demonstrate that he trusts her; this allows her the safety to feel that she can open up and talk about the tragic horse-riding accident that had brought her to his farm in the first place.

Forgiveness

We all do things that upset others and at some point everyone will have had to approach another person to ask for their forgiveness. Forgiveness is where the wrong done to you is forgotten: the debt is cancelled, unlike atonement, where the wrongdoer attempts to make up for what they have done. The ability to forgive an act of betrayal, it turns out, is a very important ingredient for the happy life. Primarily, forgiveness can help to strengthen a relationship by removing an obstacle to its optimal functioning: if I have done something to offend you, until you forgive me for that, the offence hangs in the air like an unpleasant odour. Sometimes these grudges can continue for years and certainly, in cultures where vendettas are acted out, unresolved conflicts can take an extraordinary toll.

Forgiveness works in two ways: it benefits not only the person who has a forgiving disposition, but also the person who acknowledges that they have done wrong and seeks to be forgiven. Studies have shown that forgiveness results in greater psychological and physical well-being, greater happiness in marriage, less criminality and better adjustment to loss and bereavement. Also, the ability to forgive reduces one's propensity to stress and anxiety and a study has shown that hostile people who survive heart attacks experience a reduction in heart problems if they learn to be more forgiving.[164]

Resolving conflict

Everybody's life is punctuated by examples of conflict: it is a natural feature of human life. One of the conflicts that I can clearly remember from my own life happened when I was at school. It was not a particularly unpleasant conflict, but for some reason it has stayed with me, and was the first one I thought of when I came to write this part of the book. We had a lovely maths teacher called Mr Pethick. We thought of him as a professor: he was nearly 60, had hair like Einstein and always smelled of pipe smoke. He was also a very good mathematician and he really stretched us. The last question on his homework sheets was always fiendishly difficult and most of us got our parents to do it for us. One Monday morning, one member of the class, Kevin, had clearly not done his homework and he hadn't had the chance to copy the answers like he usually did. Mr Pethick asked for the homework to be handed in. They all came in apart from Kevin's.

'Kevin, where is your homework?'

All of our eyes were on him. We knew that Kevin sometimes found the work hard. We also knew he didn't like being put on the spot. Kevin stared down at his folded arms. We shrank down in our seats.

'Kevin, I won't ask you again, where is your homework?'

Mr Pethick was getting more insistent. We'd never seen him lose his temper and didn't really know what to expect.

'Answer me Kevin! Where is it?! Have you not bothered to do it again?!'

Kevin was going red in the face. He was seething. A couple of people sniggered nervously. That was it. Kevin stood up from his chair and went to storm out of the room, but Mr Pethick was by the door. Kevin must have known that he couldn't get out of this humiliating situation. He was like a cornered animal. We all thought he was going to do the unthinkable: we all thought he was going to hit our teacher.

Mr Pethick opened the door and allowed Kevin to go. We were 15 and Kevin was big for his age. He stood over Mr Pethick, who followed Kevin out as he marched through the doorway into the corridor. When the door was closed behind them, we immediately turned to each other and, in hushed tones, speculated about what would happen. Our minds raced ahead of us. Would Kevin hit him? Would Mr Pethick have a heart attack? Would Kevin get expelled? Should we go outside to intervene? After five minutes, Kevin came back in with red eyes and hunched shoulders and sat back down. The lesson proceeded almost as normal.

Most teachers will know situations like this and it is with good reason that we are told as trainee teachers never to confront a student in front of their peer group. Conflicts get out of hand when the people involved believe that they have lost control and that they are failing to protect whatever they are trying to protect. In this case, Kevin was trying to preserve his reputation. He perceived Mr Pethick's question as a direct attack on his prestige and felt that he had to defend it, rather than admit failure by owning up to not having done his homework. Deep down, Kevin was probably plagued by a fear of being asked to move down a set and was ashamed of this happening to him. As a skilled teacher, Mr Pethick knew this and no doubt apologized to Kevin for confronting him, but also helped him to see a way through the trees. Kevin stayed in the set until we sat our GCSEs.

Fiona Macbeth and Nic Fine are experts in the resolution of conflict using techniques developed in drama. They worked together for a number of years with people who are often most vulnerable from poor resolution of conflict: school refusers, young offenders and other young adults whose poor conflict resolution skills have led to them inhabiting the border territory of being marginalized.

Macbeth and Fine set up an organization called Leap Confronting Conflict[165] which has developed a number of approaches to teaching young people the skills they need to resolve conflict effectively. It is important to note that they do not paint conflict in a negative way. Conflict is, they argue, a natural feature of communities:

> Conflict is not necessarily destructive – in fact it is a vital part of life and growth. Much growth involves pain. Conflict becomes damaging when it is ignored or repressed, or when the only responses to it are to bully, bulldoze or withdraw. Destructive conflict frequently means resourcelessness.[166]

This last point is interesting: Macbeth and Fine describe resorting to violence as being 'resourceless', in other words all of the creative, thinking and intelligent responses cease to be available and there is no other option but to strike out.

Macbeth and Fine's method attempts to provide a series of metaphors for conflict and a safe test bed where young adults can develop an awareness of their own responses to conflict and learn techniques that they can employ when they find themselves in trouble in the real world.

Their work did not start easily. They describe how things went in early workshops: 'We used to describe [the children] as "professional destroyers". The ease and precision with which they could destroy our session, our fragile egos, their schools and communities was impressive.'[167]

It was these early difficulties and the sheer destructive energy that some of the young people displayed, which led Fine and Macbeth to develop the metaphor of 'fire' for conflict. They also realized that words such as 'peacemaker', 'negotiator' and 'mediator' were not really robust enough for use with anger-prone young people. They needed something a bit stronger and settled upon the word 'firefighter'.

Through the use of tableau (creating still images) and role play, participants were able to explore the process of escalating conflict, using the metaphor of fire and were encouraged to explore both the negative consequences of conflict and the positive consequences of conflict, when it is used to effect change. Participants were asked, in the first instance, to think about their 'red rags': the things which caused conflict to begin in the first place. Once we become aware of our 'red rags' we can start to build cognitive defences: we can start to explore the choices we have in those situations, rather than turn into a raging bull in the grip of defensive and aggressive emotions.

The next metaphor used by Macbeth and Fine is of 'hook, line and sinker'. They describe getting embroiled in conflict as being hooked like a fish. This of course implies that there is a person with a rod and some bait and there are often people who know exactly what they have to do to set someone off. The *hook* is the insult or comment delivered with bait to entice us into reaction. The *line* is a metaphor for the reactions that we have, the 'train of thoughts that rush through our mind' and the *sinker* is the emotion we experience, be it anger, fear, shame, guilt or otherwise.

The beauty of this technique is the time that it gives to people. By rehearsing these events over and over again in the safety of an environment where trust has been established, the participants come to realize that rather than leaping across a table to punch someone's lights out in the grip of a full-blown primary emotion, they are able to stop and think, to allow the blood to return to the thinking centres of the brain and regain control of a situation before they do something they regret. Conflict resolution, to use another metaphor, is a time machine.

Macbeth and Fine also describe 'the boxing ring' which is a highly realistic technique for rehearsing very difficult situations in preparation for real life. The 'fighters' go into the ring and play out a series of rounds, with coaching at the end of each round to give them advice on their progress and tips for the next round. The whole fight is overseen by a referee who has absolute authority. Macbeth and Fine relate a very moving example of a young man in Glasgow called Dave Sharp, a repeat offender who was attending an 'alternatives to detention programme' in the hope of breaking the spiral of recidivism. His main fear was returning to crime as his wife had threatened that she would leave with the children if he ever got involved in crime again. Dave entered the ring and 'sparred' with a project worker called Andy who was attempting to test Dave's resolve to its limits. The topic of the fight was Andy's attempt to get Dave to commit one more crime: a seemingly easy job with thousands of pounds in it for everyone. The fight was highly realistic and Andy received tips from his coaches on how to break Dave's resolve. The course organisers knew that there was little point in this training if, once in the real world, Dave was to give in to the first difficult confrontation he faced.[168]

Conflict resolution is exactly the type of testing situation that a well-being programme should aim to provide the skills for. If young people are self-aware, are aware of the impact they have on others, have learned about how to notice and take control of emotions and have a clearly defined set of values (see below), then they should be able to *resolve* conflict positively. These are skills that are reinforced by mindfulness meditation, compassion training and, believe it or not, philosophy. The only hurdle to this is that these skills take time and practice to acquire, but they are skills that are of vital importance, not just to the smooth running of schools, but to society as a whole.

Putting it into practice: conflict resolution

- **Conflict examples**: there are numerous examples of conflict in film and television which can be used and everyone has their favourite. I particularly like 'two angry women', a clip of road rage on the internet: it is a great example of how to unnecessarily provoke conflict just by taking the wrong tone with someone whom you perceive has wronged you. Ask the students how the conflict could have been avoided in the first place, or how it could have been stopped at different stages. Another example containing lots of very tense scenes is Steven Spielberg's first feature film *Duel*, the story of an unsuspecting motorist pursued by a sadistic truck driver. There are some examples of how the driver attempts to resolve the conflict, but each time he does, the stakes are raised forcing him to adopt different tactics.

- **Conflict stills**: start by creating some still images of conflict with the students. Ask them to work in small groups and devise a scene, real or imaginary that exemplifies some kind of conflict. Ask them to present their still image to the group.

- **Red rags**: using Fine and Macbeth's language, ask the students to think about their own 'red rags'. What are the words or actions which make them fly into a rage, or lose their temper or even just sulk and fall out with others?

- **Behind the scenes – empathy**: ask students in small groups to talk about a conflict scenario and create a tableau (still image) of it. Ask individual members of the group to step out of the scene and think about what has brought their character there: why is it that they have become involved in a conflict? Once they have thought about their motivation, ask them to speculate on what their motivation might lead them to do in that situation. The overall aim is to bring out the point that conflicts do not occur in a vacuum: we are all motivated to act in different ways in conflict scenarios by our own past histories.

- **Fanning the flames**: now ask students to think about what fans the flames of conflict. What causes arguments to spiral out of control?

- **The extinguisher**: this is a very important part of the process as it requires the students to think seriously about how to build defences against conflict. Ask them what they can do to stop their negative emotions getting out of control when they are drawn into conflict. Use either the ABC or the self-soothing techniques from Chapter 6, or the empathy techniques from this chapter to help. Students have to find their own way of extinguishing the flames of conflict.

- **The test bed**: ask students to re-enact a recent conflict that they have had. Try to make it as authentic as possible. The emphasis should be on deploying the fire extinguisher to 'put out' the conflict. If needs be, ask students to act as coaches to the people involved in the conflict, to remind them of what their chosen fire extinguishers are. Every student involved should be able to stop the re-enactment if they are uncomfortable by simply raising their hand.

- **Reflect**: ask the students to apply their fire extinguishers between lessons and reflect on how well it went in their journals. Ask them to keep trying and also to try a variety of extinguishers if they need to.

Common causes and values

This section comes with a health warning. In Chapter 4, we looked at the Stanley Milgram experiment where participants were 'duped' into administering what they believed to be electric shocks to strangers up to a maximum of 450 volts. One of the reasons that this experiment was so successful was that those who played the role of 'teacher' were given an ideology to adopt: they believed that what they were doing would result in a greater good (more understanding of learning) despite the pain caused in the short term.

Countless hours of research have gone into the importance of ideologies, common causes and shared beliefs in the perpetration of the worst acts imaginable and they always play a role. You can't just get someone to do something bad: they have to be convinced that, even though there is suffering at first, the consequences will out-weigh the pain – so you just carry on harming and we'll worry about taking any blame.

So the health warning is this: any ideology that unites people is not good *because it unites people*. Ideologies or common causes must be subject to scrutiny using the tools that we explored in Chapter 4. If, at any time, we are denied the opportunity to question the ideology that unites us, alarm bells should be ringing left, right and centre. This is why 'The War Against Terror' is so alarming, as this 'common cause' has enabled governments to rush through some pretty draconian legislation, such as the UK government's (thankfully now failed) attempt to allow 42 days of detention in prison without charge.

Having said that, common causes which are motivated by the good can bring out qualities in humans that we don't otherwise get to see. In a documentary made about the heroes of the terrorist bombings in London on the 7 July 2005, some extraordinary stories were told of spontaneous acts of courage at Edgware Road tube station where people risked their own lives, even though injured themselves, to save the lives of other people.[169] My grandparents frequently told me their stories of how, even while suffering great privations, the defeat of fascism united a whole nation during World War II and prompted people to go to great lengths to help others, people who were very often complete strangers, but to whom they felt connected by the common cause of stopping Hitler.

So when we see great acts of kindness or great acts of protest, we are seeing people who have been driven to change something by a desire to see the values they hold dear being put into action.

Not just this, but our values are of course what prevent us from engaging in destructive behaviour. Why didn't I become a heroin addict? Because I valued life without heroin in it far too highly to even begin to contemplate using it. Why didn't I steal cars and joy-ride as a teenager? Because I had a very clear sense that it was wrong. My values, which were mostly derived from the upbringing my parents gave me, helped me (for the most part) to stay out of trouble. The teaching of values is absolutely central to enabling children to not only avoid all of the harmful things such as substance misuse, promiscuity, poor diet, violent crime and disaffection that we keep reading about in the papers, but it is also essential to helping them to flourish as humans. If young people have a clear and positive value base, they will have a clear sense of their purpose in life and can start to go about fulfilling it.

So what precisely are values? Chris Peterson explains the function of values in society in his book *A Primer in Positive Psychology*. Peterson is most widely renowned for his work in cataloguing values and character strengths across cultures and devising a way of testing this. His Values in Action (VIA) character strengths test is a fascinating test to take.[170] Peterson defines a value as 'an enduring belief that some goals are preferable to others'.[171] Peterson goes on to explain that values perform the following functions:

1. They are expressive. They tell the world and ourselves what is most important about us. The social networking website Facebook has a section where you can join groups that fit in with your beliefs and values. For example, I belong to the groups 'No State Funeral for Thatcher' and

'Agnostic'. There are groups for just about everything and they provide a fascinating window into people's beliefs, values and attitudes.

2. They bring people together.

3. Shared values explain how we ought to behave. For example, schools may value what each student has to say and therefore in lessons only one person is permitted to speak at a time and there may be a student council.

4. Shared values justify punishment of people who breach the values.

5. Values allow group members to judge other groups.

6. Shared values can bring about change: the civil rights movement in the US, or Gandhi's non-violent resistance movement in India are prime examples.[172]

How do we acquire values? According to Peterson, there are various factors at work in the acquisition of values:

- reward and punishment
- modelling of values by others
- being consistent with ourselves
- reflection and self-examination as a result of experience.

The original Star Wars films are a prime example of these in action. As Luke Skywalker learns to become a Jedi knight and fights for the cause of good against the Empire, he acquires a new set of values. He learns the value of perseverance in 'feeling the force' by playing games which hone his light sabre skills by punishing him when he makes a wrong move. He has values modelled to him by Obi-Wan Kenobi, Yoda and Han Solo. He develops integrity by ensuring that his values are internally coherent and don't conflict with each other; for example, his valuing of justice and goodness is not counterbalanced by a valuing of power and influence which he is tempted with by Darth Vader and the Emperor: 'come to the dark side Luke'. Finally, by undergoing trials and tribulations, he re-thinks some of his values; for example, the death of his father makes him value the importance of family and relationships more highly.

We see these forces at work in young people all the time. For many of them, adolescence is a painful period where they have to learn to negotiate their way through the conflict of the values their parents hold dear with the values of their peer group. Initially, our parents' values are the ones most strongly reinforced, but as we develop and acquire more intellectual and moral autonomy, we begin to question those values, or, indeed, the values of society. In the film *East is East*, which is set in Britain in the 1960s, we are shown the consequences of the clash of values between a strict patriarchal Pakistani culture and a more liberal 1960s Western culture. The father in the family moved over to Britain from Pakistan and married an English woman. They had six children together. The eldest son is gay and has been shunned by his father, who is forcing his next two sons into an arranged marriage. It is through this scenario that the clash of values is rendered most starkly: the value of duty to family and religion over the value of freedom of expression and choice.

Adolescence can be a very turbulent time in this respect and young people need to have time not only to explore their values, but also to question them, examine the consequences of holding them and, if needs be, be given the space and support to enable them to change them. So, how do we do this?

Chris Peterson describes the process of 'value self confrontation' which was developed by M. Rokeach in the 1970s. The basic premise behind this work is to confront people with discrepancies in their values, in the hope that they will develop more integrity. Initial experiments were done with US college students in the 1970s when the civil rights movement was at its height. Students were told that their peers rated freedom very highly as a value but rated equality much lower. When the students themselves were tested, their test scores showed much the same pattern. The researcher then made a directed remark such as 'it would seem that college students value freedom much more highly than equality' with the implication that this was an undesirable and contradictory view to hold. In follow-up work, it was found that students exposed to this lastingly changed their values and were more likely to join pro-civil rights organizations.[173]

Putting it into practice: values

- **Images of value**: ask the students to think about all the ways that they express their values – their Facebook groups, the slogans on their t-shirts, the graffiti on their folders and books, the clubs and societies they belong to and so on. What does this tell them about what is important to them? What does it tell others?

- **Critical value**: visit www.essential-education.org and have a look at their 16 guidelines for a happy life, which also double as values. What do the students think of these guidelines? Are they practical? Can they think of people who exemplify them? In what ways do they exemplify them?

- **Value source**: ask the students to think about a person in their life who is responsible for giving them particular values. Ask them to write about what values they have learned from this individual and how those values shape their lives; for example, their grandmother may have taught them to value hard work, which means they put effort into all of their school work.

- **Group values**: ask students to think about what different groups of people value. What does their family value? What does their friendship group value? What does the school value? What does the country value? Do countries as a whole have values? Are there tensions between the different groups they belong to: that is, does one group value something which directly contradicts the values of another group?

- **Values and authenticity**: ask students to write a list of the five things that they value the most in life. How do they uphold those values in their everyday lives? Do they behave consistently with their values? (For example, if they value all life, are they vegetarian?) How can the thinking skills of philosophy help us to be consistent with our values? Can they think of examples of people who are inconsistent with the values they profess to adhere to? How do we feel about people who are inconsistent with their values?

- **Testing values**: ask students to think about how their values might be tested. There are fascinating examples in history of people who, despite threats to their lives, have fought to uphold their values (Martin Luther King, Gandhi, The White Rose movement in Nazi-occupied Germany) and, of course, of others who have not done so: the Holocaust, the genocide in Rwanda and other betrayals. What can students do to withstand the inevitable onslaught their values will take?[174]

9   Modern life is rubbish

The whole of Western civilization is oriented towards history. It believes in historical evolution and in the productivity of time, or in other words – in progress . . . One of the highest forms of praise in the West is to say of something 'It's a new idea.'

   The negative side of the taste for novelty is the vain and frustrating quest for change at any price.

Jean François Revel and Matthieu Ricard[175]

Chapter preview

- Outcome motivation and intrinsic motivation: 'Affluenza'
- Social comparison: keeping up with the Joneses
- Maximizers and satisficers: when good is good enough
- Hedonism and gratification: pleasures versus gratifications
- Delayed gratification
- The culture of busy-ness: stress
- Doing too much and solutions to doing too much
- Technology
- Television

Outcome motivation and intrinsic motivation: 'Affluenza'

Modern life in the West can sometimes seem as Jean François Revel and Matthieu Ricard describe in the quote overleaf: we have become obsessed by progress, change and the avoidance of stagnation or obsolescence. We are fascinated by history, by progress, by improvement and all of us want to leave our mark by doing something that is seen to be distinctive and valuable. But it is not just about achievements, it is about consumption too. We are conspicuous consumers. We like to own and consume things and we like other people to see us owning and consuming. We have all grown up to believe that success as a human being is partially measured by the acquisition of objects. And not just any objects: they have to be the *right* objects. Advertising subtly convinces us that an object does not just perform a function: it is a lifestyle choice which makes a bold statement about who we are. Objects define our identity. Films such as *Fight Club* and books such as *No Logo* by Naomi Klein help us to unpack this culture and partially immunize us against it; but still, at heart, we can't help preferring one brand over another.

I am not opposed to this culture and I like notching up achievements for my CV and having nice things just as much as the next person, but if we blindly allow this culture to consume *us* we have to be aware that there is a cost to our well-being and it can be an unbearable cost for some. Oliver James refers to the tendency to measure happiness by outcomes, external factors and acquisitions as 'Affluenza' and he describes it as a virus:

> Virus motives are more distressing than Virus goals. A motive is the reason we do something; its goal is the outcome we seek as a consequence of doing it. Virus motives are reward and praise, looking for others' approbation in order to feel pleased or disappointed by what we do. Virus goals are money, possessions, good appearance and fame.[176]

For James, the Virus is not *necessarily* bad, but he argues that Virus motivation or Virus goals must be counterbalanced by intrinsic motivation; in other words, when you do something, you ought to do it because it is a good, enjoyable, desirable, engaging thing in and of itself, not because it will achieve something else. Csikszentmihalyi's work on flow, described in Chapter 7, is important here because whilst aiming for and achieving flow, we are more likely to be intrinsically motivated to engage in those activities which cause a sense of enjoyment. Once we become 'Virus motivated', or obsessed by achieving or acquiring fame, possessions or good appearance, we become disconnected from the very things that provide the greatest joy in life: the things that we are good at. They simply become a means to an end.

James describes, through some deeply compelling case studies, the various consequences of Affluenza as stress, depression, substance abuse, eating disorders, a sense of meaninglessness, inability to maintain close relationships and all of the symptoms we associate with deep unhappiness. Why is this? Put very simply, because the 'infected' define their happiness through things external to them; they are constantly chasing the next thing which will bring happiness and feel that their best will never be good enough. Here is just one example:

> Eleanor, aged seventeen, attended a highly competitive all-girl London Comprehensive and got top grades in almost all her GCSEs. Yet she recalls that 'I wasn't pleased when I got my results. All my friends got better than that and I felt terrible.' 'You're such an idiot because you did really well,' interjects her childhood friend, Jessica, sixteen who knows plenty of other similarly high-achieving girls. 'I've a friend who is incredibly stressed out, yet she got ten A-stars in her GCSEs. There's just so much competition between girls in all ways: how you look, the way you dress, how clever you are, everything.[177]

Much of this dis-ease we see in the Western world can be put down to the following causes:

- comparing ourselves too closely with others: 'keeping up with the Joneses'
- focusing on pleasure rather than long-term fulfilment
- not learning to delay gratification.

Social comparison: keeping up with the Joneses

Social comparison is where we compare our status with that of others: this can be in terms of position, reputation or possessions and the comparison is usually between us and those close to us, our 'reference group'. As Alain de Botton writes:

> Our sense of an appropriate limit to anything – for example, to wealth and esteem – is never decided independently. It is arrived at by comparing our condition with that of a reference group, with that of people we consider to be our equals. We will take ourselves to be fortunate only when we have as much as, or a little more than, the people we grow up with, work alongside, have as friends and identify with in the public realm.[178]

One of the main forms of social comparison in the West is through our own income relative to that of others: what is important for happiness is not our absolute level of wealth, but our wealth relative to those around us. In an oft-mentioned study that was conducted by Solnick and Hemenway at Harvard, students were asked if they would prefer to live in a world where they were paid $50,000 and everyone else was paid an average of $25,000 or a second world where they were paid $100,000 and everyone else was paid an average of $250,000. Invariably and in repetitions of this study, people go for the first option.[179] Why? Because we would rather take a cut in pay than *appear* less successful than our peers.

Social comparison can be a curse and it may be a curse of our ancestry. One explanation for this phenomenon is that our forebears thrived when they competed with each other: those who were the most competitive for status in a group achieved it, were able to reproduce and therefore passed on their genes. Richard Layard cites an experiment conducted by Michael McGuire at UCLA, where male vervet monkeys were taken out of their kinship group and placed in a new group. The monkeys' serotonin levels were then measured as an indicator of how happy they were. The results were striking: the higher up the hierarchy the monkey was, the happier he was. Layard argues that the same is true for humans:

> If monkeys enjoy status, so do human beings. We want status not only for what else it makes possible, but also for itself. We hate falling short of others, and we like to excel. We want to entertain other people as well as they entertain us, and we want our children to have the things their friends have. These are not ignoble sentiments of envy; the desire for status is basic to our human nature.[180]

Of course, just because something is 'in our nature' does not mean that we have to act according to it, as Layard argues, 'But now that we have conquered scarcity, we no longer need to be slaves to our nature. Centuries ago we decided to preserve the weak; we can also give everyone a break from the relentless pressure to succeed.'[181] Layard goes on to make the point that 'a society obsessed by status is condemned to that condition'.[182] He argues that while competition can be a useful incentive and motivating force it can also create a mindset of conflict and prevent us from taking opportunities to co-operate when working together would be the better course of action.

A study conducted by Sonja Lyubomirsky adds important weight to this. In the study, participants were asked to unscramble anagrams while sat next to another person (actually a confederate of the researchers), also unscrambling anagrams. In some cases, the confederate would solve the anagrams more quickly than the participant and in others he would solve them more slowly. Lyubomirsky found that people who were happier were not affected by the confederate doing better or worse than them whereas people who were unhappy were affected: their performance increased when the confederate was slower and decreased when he was faster.[183] This has implications for us in education: if we intend to pit students against each other, we must be very sure of their psychological resources before we do so.

It has been said that encouraging children to compete improves their performance and competition is sometimes unskilfully encouraged between students to drive up academic achievement in schools. Comparison and competition among children needs to be very closely regulated. It is de-motivating for any student who is not resilient or who has a fixed mindset to find himself in a lower position than he wants and since schools do not routinely screen for resilience or mindset, they will not know who will suffer as a result of publishing test results or class positions. I would argue that if it either has no effect or hinders performance, all unnecessary comparison and competition should be avoided; in other words, publishing information about students' academic performance *relative to each other* through class position or year position based on exam results, or indeed against any other criteria (such as effort), ought to stop. By encouraging children to compete with each other, they compare themselves against constantly changing criteria which they cannot predict (other people's performance): it is the equivalent of suggesting that people build their house on quicksand. The competition ought to exist between the student and the objective criteria for success set by the school or the exam board; that way, students can move towards those criteria incrementally and monitor their progress effectively.

I would also suggest that a clear distinction is made between competition for academic honours and competition for sporting honours. With academic honours, everyone is able to succeed because there is an objective benchmark to reach which is set by the examinations board or qualification awarding body: there is no need for students to compete with each other. With many sporting honours, there can only ever be one winner and competition, by definition, *has* to exist between participants: this is the nature of sport. However, sport (unless there is an intention to be a professional sportsperson) need not have anything like the implications for future life that academic attainment does. Sport is optional and the level of competition can be chosen by the individual, whereas everyone has to engage in academic work at some level in their life: if competition impedes progress, it should be avoided.

Maximizers and satisficers: when good is good enough

Psychologist Barry Schwartz has paid close attention to the role of comparison in our society and in particular he has looked at the effect that too much choice can have on our levels of happiness. There is no doubt that we live in a world awash with choice: what Schwartz argues is that with the wrong mindset, inability to deal with choice is highly correlated with lower levels of happiness and with depression.

Consumerism depends upon choice for the consumer. The more variety there is, the more autonomous and empowered we believe we are. There isn't just one brand of television with one model, there are many with hundreds of different models: each one with a slightly different set of features. You can't just buy cheese; there are different types, each with different strengths of flavour, grated, sliced or in blocks, low-fat, full-fat, spreadable and so it goes on.[184] Each choice depends upon the weighing up of information in order for us to make a decision. However, Schwartz argues that in fact too much choice can be a bad thing. He suggests that increased choice not only de-motivates us by making it impossible to decide because we suffer from information overload, but it also, he argues, causes some people to suffer.

Schwartz distinguishes between two groups: maximizers and satisficers. A maximizer is a person for whom the best is not good enough. They agonize over every decision they make, almost paralyzed from making a decision by the fear that they might make the wrong choice and regret it for the rest of their lives. Satisficers, on the other hand, do not obsess over the choices they make: they have a clear idea of what they want and are happy with whatever best meets those criteria.

The cost of being a maximizer is high. According to Schwartz, maximizers do not savour positive events as deeply as satisficers and they deal less well with adversity. Maximizers take longer to recover after adversity and they tend to brood or ruminate more than satisficers. Schwartz does point out that the causal relationship is not clear, but there is a correlation between maximization and unhappiness.[185]

There are some suggestions for overcoming the tendency to maximize, and these form part of the teaching ideas at the end of the chapter. However, as with much of the cognitive traps for happiness, of which maximizing is one, it takes time to re-learn how to think through situations which cause unhappiness and this will only come with practice and reflection.

Hedonism and gratification: pleasures versus gratifications

Hedonism is an interest in pursuing pleasure. We get rewarded with a feeling of pleasure when we do something that is perceived to benefit us. The body has a great reward chemical called dopamine and the reward centre of the brain which is most sensitive to reward chemicals such as dopamine and serotonin is called the nucleus accumbens. Monkeys who have sustained damage to the nucleus accumbens are unable to sustain attention for long periods of time as they are unable to experience reward from doing so. It is thought that a poorly functioning reward system is partially responsible for ADHD and the term 'reward deficiency syndrome' has been used to describe people who engage in substance (including alcohol) abuse, smoking, promiscuity and thrill-seeking behaviour in an attempt to artificially stimulate the release of dopamine in the brain and feel reward or pleasure.[186] It seems that some people have a biological set-up which predisposes them towards being pleasure-seekers. It has also been suggested that children process reward differently to adults, meaning that they are more focused on generating short-term pleasures rather than long-term satisfactions.[187] This might explain why many people don't start learning musical instruments or engaging in academic study until adulthood as they simply do not experience the feeling of reward for doing it during adolescence.

There is a catch in the system however and it is called 'habituation', 'adaptation' or the 'hedonic treadmill'. It turns out that we are good at getting used to the things that we predict will make us happy and that we return to our original state of happiness (or unhappiness) pretty quickly. Imagine that you are pinning your hopes of joy on striking it lucky with the lottery in the hope that millions of pounds will solve all your problems. Research conducted by Philip Brickman suggests that within as little as a month, you will, after a blip of joy, be back to normal.[188] The story of Michael Carroll, the self-styled 'King of Chavs', is good evidence for this. Aged 19, Carroll won £9.7 million on the National Lottery, but his life has been a tale of woe ever since: he has been in and out of court, spent some time in prison and his wife and child left him. Writing in the *Guardian* in 2005, Sandra Laville commented that Michael Carroll is proof that 'money doesn't change anything'.[189]

It is not just possessions and material changes that we adapt to: it is changes in appearance and status too. In a documentary made for the BBC in 2007, journalist Louis Theroux took a close look at the effects of cosmetic surgery – even going to the lengths of undergoing a liposuction procedure himself to see what effect it would have.[190] What was most noticeable at the clinics he visited was the number of clients who kept returning to have a little more done. In one clinic, the receptionist, a young mother, charted the surgery that she'd had performed and the surgery she was still planning to have done. She had spent thousands of dollars on 'perfecting' lots of different aspects of her physique from enhancing her bust to removing fat from her legs or midriff – but it still wasn't enough. She was adapting to the results of each surgery and was still desperate for more; she was caught on the hedonic treadmill.

Interestingly, the same principle of adaptation is true for those who encounter great hardship. You would expect a traumatic event to have a significantly negative effect on your feelings of happiness and well-being, but as Daniel Gilbert points out, studies show that after traumatic events, we return to our normal state fairly quickly and can in fact experience enhanced optimism about our future:

> within a couple of weeks even earthquake survivors return to their normal levels of unfounded optimism. Indeed, events that challenge our optimistic beliefs can sometimes make us *more* rather than *less* optimistic. One study found that cancer patients were *more* optimistic about their futures than were their healthy counterparts.[191]

So, as humans, we adapt to changes in our lives, even extraordinary ones, relatively quickly. There are some things that we never really get used to though such as loud and unpredictable noise or widowhood and on the positive side, friendship and sex.[192] By expecting what Oliver James would call 'Virus goals' such as money, fame, good appearance and possessions to bring us lasting happiness, we will be in for a disappointment: we get used to these changes in our lives quickly. Lasting satisfaction comes from the things that constantly cause a release of chemicals such as dopamine and serotonin: friendship and romantic relationships, helping others and exercise – we never get habituated to them.

It is for this reason that Martin Seligman makes the distinction between pleasures and gratifications. He argues that pleasures are those things that are short-lived and which don't require much effort, whereas gratifications are long lasting and require investment of strengths and virtues:

> When we engage in pleasures we are perhaps just consuming. The smell of perfume, the taste of raspberries, and the sensuality of a scalp rub are all high momentary delights but they do not build anything for the future. They are not investments, nothing is accumulated. In contrast, when we are engaged (absorbed in flow), perhaps we are investing, building psychological capital for our future.[193]

Alain de Botton turns to the French philosopher Jean-Jacques Rousseau to make a similar point:

> wealth does not involve having many things. It involves having what we *long* for. Wealth is not an absolute. It is relative to desire. Every time we seek something we

cannot afford, we grow poorer, whatever our resources. And every time we feel satisfied with what we have, we can be counted as rich, however little we may actually own.[194]

Delayed gratification

Modern culture, at least up until the 'credit crunch' of 2008, suggests to us that we don't have to wait for the things that we want in life. Credit has been freely available to enable us to make the big purchases that used to require us to scrupulously save. Internet shopping means that we can buy anything without having to make the arduous and gruelling journey into town and, very often, we don't even have to enter our card details, so it doesn't feel like we are parting with money. Our disposable culture also tells us that if we get bored of our new item, we can just throw it away. A recent advertising slogan in Selfridges & Co. stated 'you want it, you buy it, you forget it'.[195] Very often that delicious anticipation preceding a big purchase is missing and even then, we get used to it and dispose of it.

However, learning to delay the experience of pleasure is a very important skill to acquire. In a study conducted by Walter Mischel in the 1960s at Stanford University, 4-year-old children were given a choice. They could either wait and have two marshmallows when the researcher returned from an errand in 15-minutes' time, or they could give in to desire and have one now, but not a second marshmallow later. The difficult part of the test was that the single, unguarded marshmallow was sitting on a table in front of them and the researcher had left the room. The children believed that no one was watching them: they only had their self-discipline standing between them and the second marshmallow.

What Mischel found upon tracking these 4 year olds until their graduation from high school was that the children who had been able to 'delay gratification' and resist eating the lone marshmallow to gain the reward after the seemingly interminable 15 minutes were:

> as adolescents, more socially competent: personally effective, self-assertive and better able to cope with the frustrations of life. They were less likely to go to pieces, freeze or regress under stress, or become rattled and disorganised when pressured; they embraced challenges and pursued them instead of giving up even in the face of difficulties; they were self-reliant and confident, trustworthy and dependable; and they took initiative and plunged into projects.[196]

The culture of consumerism and choice, of defining ourselves through objects and of deriving pleasure from possessions, status and appearance, can cause a lot of trouble for us if we are not properly equipped. Fortunately, however, there are some simple antidotes and it is essential to equip young people with these strategies to help them to avoid the anomie that can arise from consumerism.

1. Distinguish gratifications from pleasures and do more of the former.
2. Distinguish needs from wants.
3. Learn to consume and dispose ethically.
4. Spend time with people rather than objects.
5. Settle for second best sometimes.
6. Notice habituation.
7. Learn to be critical about advertising.
8. Become task orientated, not goal orientated.
9. Set objective targets rather than subjective comparisons.

Putting it into practice: coping with consumerism

- **Wants and needs**: ask students to do a quick mental scan of their bedrooms. Ask them to draw up two columns and place items that they need in one and items that they acquired because they wanted them in the other. Ask them which is the longer list.

- **A trip to the shops**: encourage students to tag along the next time there is a family trip to the supermarket. Suggest that they take responsibility for choosing five items with no guidance as to brand or price from their parents. Ask them to think about how they make their choice and, also, what their parents' reaction is when they return with the goods. Do they think they are maximizers or satisficers? Ask them to reflect on the experience in their journals.

- **Choice is everything**: construct an exercise where the class is tasked with the simple job of choosing an MP3 player to buy. Split the class in half and divide them into teams of about three to four. Give both teams an imaginary budget. Give team A a 'catalogue' of 20 or 30 MP3 players to choose from (you can find them on a variety of websites), of varying prices, brands, colours and memory capacities. Give team B a 'catalogue' of only four MP3 players. See which team fares best with the task. Afterwards discuss the process. Who found it most difficult? Why? Did they notice anything about maximization/satisfaction?

- **Comparison**: re-enact the Solnick and Hemenway experiment (see above) with your students and see how many of them have been caught in the comparison trap.

- **Compete or co-operate?** A good game to illustrate the importance of collaborating to achieve goals, rather than competing, is called 'see, run, do'. Put together an abstract picture or diagram – it doesn't have to mean anything. Mount the picture on a flipchart. Divide your class into two groups. Give each group some paper and a pen. Each group has to re-create the image on the flipchart without seeing it and having only been given verbal instructions from a 'runner' who is not allowed to use the pen, nor is he or she allowed to take pictures to show them. Give the group a limited amount of time to complete the task. Afterwards, discuss how well they coped. What did they do which enabled them to compete? Was there a leadership struggle? Was there any naive realism (see Chapter 8)? What would they do differently if they had to do the exercise again? Re-run the exercise if you have time.

- **I was happiest when . . .** : give the students this sentence starter and ask them to complete it as many times as they like, with whatever they like. See how many of them write answers that depend upon non-materialistic things such as time with family or being out in nature, and how many of them write responses that depend upon objects or possessions.
- **My life would be better if . . .** : give students this sentence starter and ask them to complete it as many times as they would like, with whatever they like. Given the ideas of habituation and the hedonic treadmill, how many of the responses that they write are likely to *really* bring them happiness?
- **Film**: Pixar's 2008 film *Wall-E* explores many of the problems caused by consumerism.
- **Adbusters**: visit www.adbusters.org. There are a number of images of altered advertisements on the website which are designed to work as 'honest' adverts, particularly for controversial brands or industries. Ask students if they can come up with an 'honest' advert for a particular brand: especially for a product which may exploit the consumer in some way.

The culture of busy-ness: stress

I recently attended a debate where the topic of conversation was the human cost of the huge material affluence that many of us in the developed Western world enjoy. One of the speakers, Ann Pettifor, argued that in the ancient world, goods exchanged had a natural interest or appreciation. For example, if I exchange a laying hen for some seeds, the interest or appreciation of that exchange is right there: the chicken will hopefully lay eggs and the seeds will hopefully bear fruit when planted – there is a return for my exchange. In the modern world, we do not barter like this: we exchange money for goods or services. Money doesn't naturally accumulate interest so in order to make it 'grow' we all have to work harder to increase production to service greater consumption. Her argument therefore is that to service the exponential growth of the value of money we all have to put longer hours in at the mill.[197]

Stress

Because many people are working longer hours, time becomes more precious and our leisure time is squeezed. We find ourselves trying to do too many things in too short a time, either trying to squeeze too much work in to afford more leisure time or trying to achieve as much in our leisure time as we can: ticking off the list of the 1,000 things I have to do before I die. The obvious cost of this is stress. It is estimated that work-related stress costs employers £3.7 billion annually and the loss of about 13 million working days.[198]

This is no different in schools. Many students find that they are spreading themselves very thinly over a vast range of commitments to try to get what they believe, or are led to believe, are the requisite academic and extra-curricular achievements under their belts to get to top universities. Teachers are under increasing pressure to achieve the best results with their students, or offer all of these extra-curricular opportunities for the students. All of this expectation leads to frantically running from one task to the next without a break, or trying to do more than one thing at the same time.

Stress is a word which occurs pretty regularly in the vocabulary of teachers and students, but it often appears in an unexamined way. John Ratey argues that we must differentiate between stress *per se* and chronic or prolonged stress.[199] The former is simply a natural by-product of biological processes, just as wear and tear is a natural consequence of driving your car. Chronic stress occurs when we are stressed for prolonged periods without respite, just as damage occurs to a car that is not serviced or is driven too hard, like my poor old Beetle.

What is most interesting about Ratey's argument is that he suggests that we *need* stress in order to grow and learn and that we possess the natural antidotes to stress: exercise and the company of others. When we encounter a new or difficult situation which requires us to struggle (for example, overcoming illness, climbing a mountain, solving a difficult intellectual problem, resolving an argument) this places demands on various parts of our body, including the brain, and by responding to these demands the various cells needed suffer wear and tear. However, the human body constantly repairs itself and strengthens itself against further stresses, especially in the brain: 'In limited doses [stress] causes brain cells to overcompensate and thus gird themselves against future demands. Neuroscientists call this phenomenon stress inoculation.'[200]

If we protect ourselves from all forms of stress, we will find that cells in the body wither through lack of use. A body that is not stretched and challenged begins to atrophy. The flipside of this is the body which is chronically stressed, or stressed over long periods of time. If we are in a constant state of alert without giving the body a chance to recover and rebuild, we start to do serious damage to ourselves. The body starts to build up a surplus of fat around the abdomen in anticipation of needing fuel which ends up never being used. Over time, this excess of fat can cause blockages in the coronary arteries causing damage to the heart. The finite supply of fuel in the brain is diverted to feeding the alert system, rather than the thinking system, preventing creativity. The memory starts to malfunction, getting in the way of learning. The immune system also takes a beating and we find it difficult to fight off disease.

As mentioned above, the two antidotes to chronic stress are exercise and the company of others. Exercise stimulates the processes in the body that lead to regeneration and strengthening of cells. It also takes your mind off the causes of stress and creates a feeling of mastery and positive emotion which combats the cognitive causes of stress. Being around other people whom you like stimulates the release of serotonin, a chemical creating feelings of well-being, which will help combat stress too.

Doing too much and solutions to doing too much

'I can get a year's work done in nine months, but not in twelve.'

J. P. Morgan

The obvious venue for piling on the different commitments is in the workplace. Under pressure to achieve, we very often try to get several things done at once, with the result that we do more things, but none of them as well as we should. A study conducted by the Institute of Psychiatry helps to explain why this is using the example of 'infomania': the addiction to being permanently in touch by phone or email. It was found that people who leave their email and mobile phones on while trying to focus on completing other tasks lose an average of ten IQ points by being distracted. To put that into context, not sleeping for 36 hours also loses you ten IQ points and smoking cannabis loses you four IQ points.[201]

But we expect to be pressured in the workplace. One place we don't expect to be pressured is in the home. One of the most surprising studies conducted in this area was Daniel Kahneman's work on mothers and their time commitments. Women were asked to list the different things they had done each day and then write about how they felt doing each activity. Surprisingly, it turns out that many of the women did not particularly enjoy looking after their children, or certainly, they *reported* not enjoying it that much. Tal ben Shahar cites this study in his book *Happier*[202] when making the point about being present in everything we do. The explanation given for why these women reported not enjoying spending time with their kids was not that they were bad mothers, but that they were trying to do so much that every time they engaged in one activity, the pressure they were under made them worry about another engagement in the past or the future. They were physically present but mentally absent.

Solutions to doing too much

Tal ben Shahar's suggested antidote to doing too much has two main aspects. The first suggestion is that we simplify and cut out jobs or engagements that we can't sustainably perform. We live in a culture of loading our plates full; ben Shahar argues we should do fewer things more successfully. He refers to 'time affluence' and 'rubbish time'. These are the ideas that we are rich in time to do meaningful things properly and that we also need time to do trivial things like just hanging out. His second suggestion is to build breathing space into each day: literally. In the next chapter I will explain the importance of meditation and the simple technique of attending to the breath that meditation teaches – a very simple and effective technique to practise in between completing and starting jobs. As teachers we should take time between lessons to breathe deeply: even if it is only three deep breaths. Students should be encouraged to stop and be still between doing things.

A fascinating new technique called HeartMath may provide another means of doing this. HeartMath is a form of biofeedback. Biofeedback involves providing a real-time display of some aspect of bodily function and a means of somehow adjusting or optimizing that function. With HeartMath, you clip a heart rate monitor onto your ear or finger. This monitor is connected to a computer which shows you the relationship between your heart-rate variability,[203] your blood pressure and your breathing as a graph on the screen. HeartMath attempts to bring these three things into a state associated with positive emotion and it does this by teaching you to breathe slowly whilst bringing a positive emotion to mind. It may seem too insignificant to do anything, but studies conducted into the effects of HeartMath seem to suggest that it reduces stress, enables people to feel refreshed at the end of a long day and that it may even help to enable students to achieve better results in exams. One school which used the technique in Blackpool saw its GCSE 5 A*–C percentages go from 56 per cent in 2004 to 76 per cent in 2007. HeartMath techniques are being used with executives in firms like Unilever and BP and also with top sports people such as the golfer Ian Woosnam.[204]

Tal ben Shahar also cites research conducted by Lesley Perlow at Harvard, which shows that people who build one or two hours of focused rest time into every day are more creative, more productive and happier. The old adage that less is more really does seem to be true and when we think about this physiologically, of course it is. Our bodies and our minds are simply not designed for sustained and uninterrupted effort without a chance to recover. Stress is good for us, as it helps us to grow and develop, but only when it is balanced out by rest and exercise.

Putting it into practice: coping with busy-ness

- **Stress or *stress*?** Ask students to think about the two types of stressor in their lives. Which help them to grow and which don't help them? What techniques can they employ to deal with unhelpful stress in their lives? Do any of the self-soothing strategies in Chapter 6 work? Do any of the positive action strategies in Chapter 5 work? Do any of the harmony strategies such as exercise, diet or sleep in Chapter 3 work?

- **Audit**: ask students to keep regular track of times that they feel stressed. They should note the cause and also write down what they did to overcome that sense of stress. Who did they ask for help? What active steps did they take to overcome the stress?

- **Schedule**: ask students to make up a schedule of the things that they do during a week and how long they do them for. When they have this information, ask them to decide whether they are doing too much, or indeed, too little. How much of the foundational ingredients of well-being, such as 9 hours of sleep per night, regular exercise and time spent enjoying eating is there? How often do they stretch themselves by learning new information or new skills? How often do they experience flow? How much time do they spend socializing with people who they like? How much time are they passive in front of the television? Ask them to plan to increase or decrease their load so that they are busy and fulfilled, but not burnt out. (By the way, there is no fixed rule for this: they must decide for themselves.)

- **Busy with strengths**: ask students to think about how much of the activity they engage in on a daily basis plays to their strengths. How often do they do what they are good at, or try to develop new strengths? Ask them to plan ways of playing to their strengths on a regular basis.

Technology

I don't know about you, but I have developed a problematic relationship with email. I used to love it and would spend up to two hours each day reading, writing and sending email. The first thing I did each day was to open up Outlook and closing it was the last thing I did before going to bed. I became obsessed with crafting perfect emails and distributing them to exactly the right people. I would solve seemingly intractable problems by sending emails to the appropriate person, awaiting their response with baited breath and feeling triumphant that they had agreed with me, or capitulated. Sometimes they were only in the next room. I used to set silent work for my students in lessons so that I could get on with 'emergency emails'. I used to love the little chime which told me that new mail had arrived: a little flutter of excitement preceded double clicking my mouse – who wanted to contact me now?

But then, like milk left in the sun, our relationship went sour. I would grow frustrated by less skilful users of the medium and occasionally a badly worded email would ruin my whole evening. I would pace around like a frustrated lion when I didn't get an immediate response to a message I had red-flagged as of high importance. I would find myself sending emails late into the night, causing tutting and head-shaking from my wife. Important non-email work just got left as I created new jobs for myself by sending messages to multiple recipients. Then, one day, the email server at work crashed and no one could send or receive email. We started phoning each other instead and, horror of horrors, we even started talking face-to-face. It was as if the sword of Damocles had been lifted. We all realized that we had been held hostage: that we had become slaves to passing around mostly useless and insignificant information.

Despite my epiphany, email still causes me angst. I have now chosen to be incompetent at answering email, but despite this choice I feel guilty that there are emails in my inbox requesting things from me which just go unnoticed and unacknowledged. Sometimes they lie there for weeks. Our culture dictates to us that we must be immediately and permanently contactable and that we must be open to the delivery of new information at all times. This is nonsense.

Now don't get me wrong, I'm not a Luddite: I don't advocate a return to living in yurts, wearing only clothes we have made and living on a simple diet of nuts and seeds and whatever we have grown, foraged or trapped ourselves. I do not believe that 'technology' is evil in the same way that I do not believe that drugs are intrinsically evil. 'Technology' is the product of human ingenuity and when used correctly it can enhance our lives by saving time and energy and can enrich them by providing challenges, information and entertainment.

Technology and attention

In the last two decades there has been an explosion in the amount of information we are bombarded with every day. It is reckoned that in North America, an adult sees on average 3,000 adverts each day – and that's just adverts. Think of all the news stories, text messages, phone calls, emails and various beeps, clicks and whirrs which feed us information about the progress of our washing, our food, our friends and our exercise. In the UK the average person spends a staggering 7 hours and 9 minutes per day using an array of communications devices.[205] We have to question how much of this communication is actually of any value. How many of the texts we receive actually enhance our lives? Unfortunately, the attention system that we use to monitor all of the incoming material evolved to cope with the world as it was 10,000 years ago, meaning many of us are in information overload.

Rodolfo Llinas has likened the brain's attention system to a shop. Imagine yourself walking into a shop. As you walk in, all of the sales assistants are talking to each other; they might have noticed you, but do not acknowledge you. You clear your throat and they all turn around. You indicate that you would like to buy something and suddenly a number of them help you: one with trying the garment on, another one takes your money at the till. The other sales assistants not involved with you carry on about their business. This is a simple analogy where you represent a piece of information coming in to the brain and the shop assistants represent the attention system. If the brain decides that a piece of information is important (you clearing your throat), it pays attention to it and marshals resources to enable action in response.[206]

Like any shop has a finite number of sales assistants, the brain only has a finite amount of attention. Mihaly Csikszentmihalyi suggests that the brain is capable of processing 126 bits of information per second: to put this into context, to understand what another person is saying in conversation, you need to process 40 bits of information per second. To converse with three people simultaneously is possible, but you would have to shut out all other information, such as why they are saying what they are saying, or what clothes they are wearing.[207] If you are engaged in a task and become distracted, you become less efficient at the task. For example, while writing the last paragraph, I heard our cat, Lily, coming up the stairs. Because I like the cat and knew she would want to jump up on my lap, I switched my attention from the paragraph to the cat. She is now on my lap, but I lost the thread of my argument in the last paragraph and had to re-focus my attention. Distractions also come from the somatosensory system (for example, the pain in my shoulders from running yesterday) and, you guessed it, from technology. As we have seen elsewhere, research suggests that having email on while trying to accomplish other tasks reduces your IQ by about ten points. The same will probably be true of mobile phones. But we already know this: we know the feeling of irritation when a friend ducks out of a conversation to answer a phone call or check a text message. We feel as if we do not have their full attention, because we don't.

This is important for young people. Education expects young people to be able to sit for extended periods of time acquiring new skills. The brain will naturally reward us for this when it releases dopamine and we experience a sense of accomplishment. Many technological devices also capitalize on this and the brain releases reward chemicals when we get text messages and emails. Unfortunately, because of the frequency of these messages we are being conditioned to expect rewards more frequently and it may be that we are reducing our own ability to sit still and patiently acquire rewards through effort. Many of life's important skills take time to learn and it is important that the tendency towards more reward more frequently is carefully balanced with activities that take time to complete and that are more satisfying in the end.

Television

Nowhere is the frequent-reward culture more clearly seen than on television. I recently watched the 1982 adaptation of John le Carré's novel *Smiley's People*. It is a perfect example of how television has become easier to watch over the last 25 years. The plot is extremely complex; there are numerous characters and the Cold War secret service strategy of bluff and counterbluff, as if playing chess at a high level, is very difficult to follow in places. The rewards from watching the series seem to come less frequently than when watching modern, rapid-fire programmes, but I would argue that they are much greater. One doesn't often come across television that requires this level of intellectual commitment any more, but it is an example of how television can be an enhancing experience rather than, as we are all too often given to believe, an inherently negative one.

I don't want to spend time rubbishing television and I don't want to suggest that we all throw our televisions away. But we, as with all technology, should be skilful users of it. Television is the number one leisure pursuit in terms of time spent in the UK. According to the National Office of Statistics, the average male aged over 16 spends 2.5 hours per day watching television and listening to the radio or music and the average adult female, 2.25 hours, contrasting with 1.25 hours spent eating and drinking.[208] Another study conducted by Ofcom suggests that people in the north-east of England are the biggest 'telly addicts', watching an average of 4.1 hours of television every day.[209] Other surveys suggest that internet usage is fast overtaking television for some people.

The main problem with watching television is that it uses so little of our brains. As Mihaly Csikszentmihalyi writes:

> The plots and characters of the popular shows are so repetitive that although watching TV requires the processing of visual images, very little else in the way of memory, thinking or volition is required. Not surprisingly, people report some of the lowest levels of concentration, use of skills, clarity of thought, and feelings of potency when watching the television.[210]

As we know, a brain that is not used will start to wither. Leisure activities which stretch us, require the learning of new skills or engage us at a deep intellectual level are vital to a life well-lived. But it's not just that a lot of television does little to stimulate the creation of new brain networks, it can also do harm to us psychologically and at a wider social level. In 1999, the small Himalayan kingdom of Bhutan lifted its ban on television and advertising and opened its airways to an influx of broadcast material. The effect? An almost immediate increase in family break-up, crime and drug taking. In one study, almost a third of Bhutanese parents now preferred watching the telly to talking to their children.[211] In his documentary film *Bowling for Columbine*, Michael Moore explores the culture of violence and gun crime in the US and tries to offer an explanation for the shooting of fellow students at Columbine High School by Dylan Klebold and Eric Harris in 1999. One of the contributing factors, Moore suggests, is the torrent of negative stories on US television networks, particularly on news programmes, which, he argues, contribute towards a climate of fear.

Richard Layard also refers to this distortion of reality on the television and the effect that it has. He argues that children who watch violence on television become more violent in the playground and not just children: after heavyweight prize-fights in the US the murder rate increases by 9 per cent for the next two days. He also suggests that because television presents us with a view of the world that is inaccurate, a world which contains more violence and threat of violence, more acquisitiveness, more sex and more 'beauty', we compare our own world to it and inevitably feel as if we are falling short. On one estimate, Layard points out, watching an extra hour per week of television causes you to spend an extra $4 on 'keeping up with the Joneses'. The more that people watch television, the more they over-estimate the affluence of others in comparison to their own.[212]

Again, this is not a clarion-call to throw away our television, but a reminder that when we do watch it, that we balance our viewing levels against activities that will actually enhance our lives such as exercise and learning new skills and that we become skilful and critical viewers of television, remembering that it does not always depict the world as it actually is and that our experience of the real world must act as a counterbalance to the feelings generated by our viewing.

All in all, I would argue that it is wrong to say 'modern life is rubbish'. As with all of the approaches to increasing our well-being, what is needed is a change in our state of mind, not a revolution in the world outside. As you have hopefully seen already, and as the next chapter will argue more comprehensively, the secrets of a happy life lie within. Our biggest mistake as humans is to believe that happiness is to be found somewhere else.

Putting it into practice: technology and television

- **Audit**: ask your students to make a note of how much time they spend each day using some form of technological device – be it a computer, television, phone, games console or whatever. Ask them to distinguish between uses which they perceive to be constructive or challenging and uses which are passive.

- **Compare**: ask your students to compare the feeling after using a technological device which is either passive (for example, television) or exclusive (for example, texting on a mobile), with the feeling after accomplishing something difficult or challenging, such as learning a new piece of music, helping someone out or doing some exercise.

- **Technology-free**: ask the students to go technology free for one evening. They have to avoid using technological entertainment devices and instead do things which are more social (such as playing games) or more challenging (such as playing music or sport). Ask them to compare technology-free evenings with normal ones. Are they better or worse? Did they find them more or less enjoyable? Why do they think that is? Ask them to compare the rewards they get from technological entertainment rather than self-generated entertainment such as game playing or tree-climbing.

- **Reality TV**: ask students, from an evening's television, to compare the picture of reality they get from the television programmes they watch, with their life as they know it. How much matches up? Are there as many arguments or as much violence? Is everybody as perfect? Does everybody have as much money? A good piece of stimulus to start the discussion off is the documentary *Bowling for Columbine* by Michael Moore, which explores bias in television. Ask students to think about the effect that this has on our view of the outside world. Do any of them feel restricted because of fears/anxieties about the world which may not be accurate?

10 Mindfulness meditation, spirituality and meaning

This final chapter is about the practice of mindfulness meditation and the importance of encouraging spirituality. To do this, I'd like you to imagine what a perfect school environment might be like. What would the teachers be like? What would the students be like? What would the nature of the relationships be like? What would the learning be like?

I think that I could probably hazard a guess at the kind of things that might feature in your perfect school. It would be a place where everyone is compassionate towards each other; a place where people do not feel the need to lose their temper or be just that little bit more aggressive to maintain control in a tense situation. It would be a place where teachers and students do not feel exhausted at the end of each day and where people don't find it more difficult to fight off illness because they are just too tired. It would be a place where people don't bitch, gossip or moan about each other and where people don't let their ego dictate how they interact with the people around them. It would be a place where people can take control of situations and get the best results for everybody. It would be a place where people have time to listen to each other, where people are calm and are not rushing from one thing to the next. It would be a place where people can generate and sustain positive emotional states, where people are focused on what they are doing and where people are creative and energized throughout the day. It would be a place where people are not at the mercy of their desires and where people do not feel the need to endlessly compete and compare with each other; where people co-operate and are all working towards the same goal. Above all, it would be a place where people feel they can take delight in seeing those around them flourish and where people feel as if they are supported in bringing about their own flourishing.

Mindfulness and relationships

Time and time again it becomes clear that the main hurdle to well-being in school communities is negative or faulty relationships – both of people to themselves and of people to others – and time and time again it has become clear to me that the easiest and best solution to this problem, from all of the reading and practice that I've done, is to teach people the simple practice of mindfulness.

In order to explain what mindfulness is, I'd like to tell you a short story. It is about a soldier who had been offered a course in mindfulness meditation to help him come to terms with the feelings of stress and anger that he was experiencing. Over eight weeks of careful meditation, the soldier did indeed feel as if he was able to take increased control over the emotions that he was experiencing and the irrational moments of rage that he used to feel and act out on people were becoming more and more a thing of the past.

One day, the soldier visited the supermarket. He was in a rush. He filled his trolley and took it to the checkout. There was an older lady in the queue in front of him with a baby and she had only one item, but was not in the '10 items or less' queue. The young woman working on the checkout was cooing over the child and she was chatting with the older lady. The soldier could feel his sap rising. This was precisely the kind of situation that made him mad: how could people be so thoughtless when he was in such a rush? Why can't that checkout girl just get on with her job and not chat to *every* customer who comes along? But the mindfulness had taught him to notice and take charge of the anger he felt. He began to realize that he was being taken over by his anger and realized that it was pointless. He didn't need to be in such a rush: the jobs he needed to do could wait for 5 minutes, so why not enjoy watching these people fuss over the baby? He looked at the baby, who at that moment turned around and gave him a beaming smile and a gurgle. The anger he had been feeling moments earlier had been managed so as to make room for the joy of seeing the baby smile at him.

Soon enough the older lady gathered her things, paid and left with the baby and the young woman at the checkout waved them goodbye.

'What a beautiful young baby,' the soldier remarked.

'Yes, he's my son; that was my mother with him.'

The young woman picked up on the slightly quizzical look on the soldier's face and saw that he was in uniform.

'My husband was a soldier too, but he was killed. I'm finding it difficult to make ends meet, so I have to work here every day and my mother looks after my son. He is asleep when I leave in the morning and asleep when I get in at night, so this is the only chance that I get to see him.'

The soldier had been in danger of being dominated by his emotional state and of in turn passing on his unhappiness to others, but the mindfulness allowed him to notice the emotion as it arose and see it for what it was: a mental state that he had complete control over.

If we were to listen in to conversations in schools around the world, we would hear similar stories of people who blow their stack because they *perceive* a direct threat in the world outside them. There are regular stories in the British press of young people injuring or killing others because they *think* that someone else has disrespected them and, in order to maintain face, they have to do something violent or retaliatory about it. Teachers regularly ratchet up their stress levels because they *perceive* that a student or group of students is doing something to deliberately derail *their* lesson. These disproportionate reactions are partly to do with the human emotional system, which we looked at in Chapter 5. The system evolved to help us to work out what is good for us and what is bad for us. Positive emotions draw us towards a person or thing and negative emotions cause us to withdraw from a person or thing. The system is great at moving us out of the way of a speeding bus, but not so good at helping us to deal with threats to the ego. If a bus is bearing down on us, we need to get out of the way fast and the unconscious brain helps us to do this. If someone acts in a way that we *perceive* to be an attack on our personality, we need to think before we act because the unconscious brain might cause us to punch or strike out first: the now infamous story of Britain's former deputy prime minister, John Prescott, punching a member of the public who threw an egg at him is a case of the primitive brain taking over operations before the thinking brain could respond.

The other aspect to the story of the soldier is the problem of being in a rush and believing that everything and everyone else has to help us to achieve our goal. Anything which gets in the way is deliberately conspiring against us; the person standing at the photocopier making booklets 4 minutes before your lesson starts is deliberately standing in the way of *you* copying those worksheets for *your* students. The previous chapter explored the idea that modern Western society is often pressured and rushed and that we find ourselves charging from one thing to the next under constant pressure to maximize our productivity. This culture of achievement and production, if not properly balanced out, leads to stress, and this is the world that we are preparing our young people for. England has the most examined children in the world and we are constantly looking for ways to test, check and modify their academic performance. They feel the pressure to get the best qualifications *and* have their career path mapped out at the age of 17. Work life is non-stop and so is leisure life. How many of us choose to bombard ourselves with sensory stimulus during our leisure time through TV, film, video games, music and the radio? We always have to be doing, planning the next opportunity to do or thinking about things that we have done.

What is mindfulness?

Mindfulness is about creating a refuge from being at the mercy of our emotional states and a refuge from the culture of endless doing. It is about making a space for us to step back and examine who we are outside of the hustle and bustle of life, rather like a dry-dock is a space to examine a ship outside of the constant movement of the sea. Jon Kabat-Zinn defines mindfulness as 'openhearted, moment to moment, non-judgmental awareness'.[213] It is the act of being mindful of our minds, drawing our attention to how our minds act and react to the various situations that come our way each day. So often we react without thinking and find ourselves regretting what we have done upon reflection later. Practising mindfulness enables us to develop the skill of noticing our reactions *as they arise* and of being able to see many of them for what they are: creations of the ego. Jack Kornfield describes it as follows:

> Mindfulness is attention. It is a non-judging and respectful awareness. Unfortunately, much of the time we don't attend in this way. Instead, we continually react, judging whether we like, dislike, or can ignore what is happening. We evaluate ourselves and others with a stream of expectations, commentary and criticism.[214]

Mindfulness also encourages us to stay in the present moment. Minds do a wonderful job of digging around in the past and of casting themselves off into the future, but don't spend as much time in the present. Test yourself. How many times has your mind wandered off as you have been reading this chapter so far?

Mindfulness teaches us to simply draw our attention to what we are doing right now and to then notice the thoughts that arise in our minds as they arise.

Our mind's constant flitting about can be a source of anxiety. Thich Nhat Hanh, a Buddhist monk who has published some wonderful books on mindfulness, points out that our mistake is to believe that happiness lies somewhere in the future or in the past, or in a past that we feel we should have had. The aim of mindfulness is to show us that happiness in fact lies in the present moment and, indeed, it cannot lie anywhere else. If we cannot experience happiness in the present moment, we are making happiness conditional on the fulfilment of other criteria and conditions that are unpredictable.

> If you cannot find joy in peace in these very moments of sitting, then the future will only flow by as a river flows by, you will not be able to hold it back, you will be incapable of living the future when it has become the present. Joy and peace are the joy and peace possible in this very hour of sitting. If you cannot find it here, you won't find it anywhere. Don't chase after your thoughts as a shadow follows its object. Don't run after your thoughts. Find joy and peace in this very moment.[215]

Mindfulness is at once simple and difficult. The simple aim of mindfulness is to draw our attention to the present moment and pay attention to what we are doing in the present moment. Mindfulness has tended to use the breath as a focus for the attention, although mindfulness is just the action of paying attention, so can be practised whilst breathing, sitting, walking or doing the dishes.[216] The difficulty comes from maintaining that focus and you may find that in a 10-minute sitting, you have to draw your attention back to your breathing many times. However, simply to notice that the mind has wandered is to practise mindfulness. Some people find this boring, or they feel guilty for stopping. Some people say that they can't do this as they have very active minds. These tend to be the kind of people who are looking for happiness elsewhere than in the present moment and as Thich Nhat Hanh says, if you can't find it here, you won't find it anywhere.

Mindfulness in schools

I have been teaching mindfulness for 10 minutes at the start of every well-being lesson for the last three years and had been teaching it as part of Religious Studies for several years before that. In the informal surveying that I have done of the students' attitudes to their well-being lessons, one thing consistently comes out on top as the favourite thing that they have learned: mindfulness. Many of them use it to reduce stress; others use it before sporting, musical or dramatic performances to enhance their focus; others use it just because they enjoy the sense of peace and tranquillity that it brings.

Contrary to popular belief, young people love to practise this. Many of the people that I tell about teaching mindfulness automatically assume that young people would see this as esoteric: something a bit weird and wacky and use it as an opportunity to mess around. In the first few attempts, there might be some silliness, but this arises just because they are doing something new: how often do we ask children to do nothing but concentrate on their breathing? Also, some young people, when asked to close their eyes in a room full of peers, are genuinely afraid that the joke is on them and that when they open their eyes again, everyone will be laughing at them. None of the acting up is malicious, it is exactly as you would expect from people confronted with something alien. The more opportunity you give the students to see that this is safe and hugely enjoyable, the more comfortable and more competent they will get at it. Mindfulness also depends for its success upon the spirit in which it is introduced: if you take it seriously, but also give your students the room to discuss how they got on with it, they will take it seriously too and see the difficulty in settling to stillness not as deliberate or wilful disobedience, but as a genuine difficulty to settle to a new skill.

Just to give you an idea, here are a couple of comments from my students about mindfulness which I received as a result of an informal survey about well-being classes in general.

Overall, what have you enjoyed the most about your well-being lessons?

'The meditation, because I found that it really did calm me down for the week.'
Euan, aged 16.

What has been the most useful thing that you have learned in a well-being lesson?

'To meditate and how to find harmony with yourself in this busy world.'
Alexandra, aged 16.

'Overall the meditation has helped most; it really calms you down in a school day where everything is too hectic. In the house cultural evening 20 minutes before I was performing on guitar I took myself away and meditated and just thought about the piece I was playing and everything was very clear and calm, and I was really focused.'
James, aged 15.

'My favourite well-being lesson was when we learnt how to meditate because that told me how to calm down, that is what I enjoyed most, it is also the most useful thing that I have learnt. Thank you for giving them to us, they have really helped me.'

Matthew, aged 15.

The benefits of mindfulness

Mindfulness meditation has been of interest to psychologists for some time and as a result, since 1980 nearly a thousand studies have been done into its effectiveness and many more are being done right now.[217] The results of these studies show five clear benefits to be had from practising mindfulness:

1. reduced stress
2. increased awareness of and control over emotional states: emotional management
3. happiness
4. improved immune system function
5. improved thinking.

Reduced stress

'. . . there is now abundant evidence that meditation techniques are perhaps the most powerful means that humans have – besides opiates and other people – of inducing relaxation and positive emotion.'[218]

The practice of mindfulness has been associated with reduction in stress for many years. In 1979, Jon Kabat-Zinn established a Mindfulness Based Stress Reduction (MBSR) clinic at the University of Massachusetts Medical Centre. MBSR is now standard practice in over 200 medical centres across the US and is also widespread in other countries including the UK.[219] As Kabat-Zinn writes:

Thirty years ago it was virtually inconceivable that meditation and yoga would find any legitimate role, no less widespread acceptance, in academic medical centres and hospitals. Now it is considered normal. Increasingly, mindfulness programs are being offered for medical students and for hospital staff.[220]

Over the last 30 years, numerous studies have been conducted into the effects of mindfulness practice on stress and anxiety. In one study conducted by Miller, Fletcher and Kabat-Zinn, published in 1993, some patients with severe anxiety were given a course of mindfulness as treatment and were followed for three years. After the mindfulness training, of the 18 who participated, eight had no further treatment for those three years and 12 of them reported that mindfulness practice was very important in their lives three years after the initial training.[221]

But MBSR is not just effective in the treatment of serious anxiety disorders: it is extremely effective in reducing those niggling causes of stress in everyday life. As mentioned above, stress and anxiety can be caused by our mind's tendency to dart about from past to future and focus on regrets or fears. It is also caused by our mind's tendency to distort our perception of reality. By focusing on being in the present and paying attention non-judgementally, we can combat some of the *cognitive* causes of stress. By paying attention to judgements that we make as they arise, we can see that they are just illusions created by our mind: the judgements being made by the soldier about the cashier and her two visitors were just in his mind, they did not correspond to reality. As soon as he realized this, he was freed from the stress that they were causing him to experience.

The benefits do not stop there. As Ruth Baer has explained, because mindfulness does not attempt to solve a specific problem, but is simply the action of paying attention to whatever arises in the mind, this results in an attitude of mind which enables acceptance rather than a striving to change. Many of the stresses that we experience are due to a sense of dissatisfaction with life and a feeling that we need to change things which cannot or do not need to be changed. She also explains that mindfulness increases our awareness of ourselves, so that we become more attuned to anxieties *as they arise* or even *before they arise*.[222] It is this awareness that can help us to stop stress taking hold of us.

Emotional management

Another benefit of mindfulness, which is related to stress, is its role in bringing about positive emotional states. As we saw in Chapter 5, positive emotions encourage us to move towards something and negative emotions cause us to withdraw from it: approach and avoidance. It has been discovered, by using brain-monitoring equipment, that when mindfulness is practised, there is more activity in the left side of the pre-frontal cortex (just behind the left eye), which is the part of the brain associated with positive emotional activity and there is a corresponding reduction in activity in the right pre-frontal cortex (just behind the right eye), the part of the brain associated with negative emotional activity.[223] These positive emotional states are vital for enhancing our ability to be creative and, needless to say, vital in helping to create and cement good, healthy relationships.

Why is this? Much of the time we are driven by our emotional states. If you think about any given day and the emotions that you experienced, they usually arise by themselves in response to things that happen in your mind or in the world outside you. Not only this, but we are accompanied throughout the day by our mind's running commentary and judgement on events in our lives. Mindfulness teaches us to notice our emotions as they arise, to question why that emotion has arisen and to decide whether or not that emotion is useful. Emotions are not facts: they are reactions to our *perception* of the world. We no more have to be governed by our emotions than we have to be governed by the price of cod in Azerbaijan.

> When mindfulness is focused upon the process of thinking, an entirely different dimension of existence becomes visible. We see how our ridiculous, repetitive thought stream continually constructs our limited sense of self, with judgments, defenses [sic], ambitions and compensations. When they are unexamined, we believe them. But if someone were to follow us close by and repeatedly whisper to us our own thoughts, we would quickly become bored with their words. If they continued, we would be dismayed by their constant criticisms and fears, then angry that they wouldn't ever shut up. Finally we might simply conclude that they were crazy. Yet we do this to ourselves![224]

What is interesting about the effect of mindfulness is that in talking to people who practise it, they feel as if time is extended: before mindfulness, they felt as if they had to feel, think and act quickly; mindfulness allows them to take longer over feeling, thinking and acting.

Meditation may not of itself cause positive emotion, but it can lead us to understand what causes positive emotional states in us and give us the ability to bring them about more often. It can also help us to take charge of negative emotions as they arise, make use of them and then let them dissolve once they have served their purpose.

Compassion

Another main focus of much meditative practice is the development of feelings of compassion towards all beings. A large barrier to happiness is our mind's wonderful ability to turn into ogres people whom we think have done something against us (for example, the checkout girl or the person at the photocopier at 8.56 a.m.). We let our imaginations run riot by developing feelings of real antagonism. Obviously, this tendency causes us to experience negative emotions when thinking about or seeing certain people and, over a long time, this isn't healthy as it is a source of stress. By meditating on feeling compassion for all people, we can overcome these negative emotional states.

This is backed up by research done by Professor Tania Singer at the University of Zurich. Using an fMRI scanner, Professor Singer has not only discovered the part of the brain activated when we feel compassion, but she has observed that it is much more active in experienced meditators.[225]

Happiness

It has long been known that people who experience more positive emotion show more activity in the left pre-frontal cortex of the brain and people who show more negative emotion, show more activity in the right pre-frontal cortex of the brain. In yet another study involving placing Buddhist monks into fMRI scanners, it was discovered that monks who had practised meditation for a number of years showed states of positive emotion (happiness) that were literally off the scale. It turns out that focusing on the development of compassion dramatically increases our ability to see the world positively. What's more, practising meditation can help people to decrease their left pre-frontal activity and increase right pre-frontal activity, so much so that techniques of combating depression have been developed (called MBCT) which have shown remarkable results.[226]

Improved immune system

Why is it that the end of a busy term of teaching always seems to bring two or three days laid up in bed with some nasty lurgy or other? Stress is a lovely example of how the body and the mind are intricately woven together and it seems that thinking has an impact upon our health. When we are anxious, our body over-produces a chemical called CGRP (calcitonin gene-related peptide). CGRP coats cells called Lanerghan's cells whose job it is to deliver unwanted cells to the body's lymphocytes where they can be dispatched. When the Lanerghan's cells are coated with CGRP, they cannot do their job properly and thus the immune system stops fending off disease effectively.[227] There is a clear connection between physiological and mental stress and the reduced functioning of the immune system.

It seems that there may be an answer to this from mindfulness. Jon Kabat-Zinn, in a now classic study, has shown quite clearly that mindfulness practice can improve the functioning of the immune system. He took a group of people working at a biotechnology company in Madison, Wisconsin in the United States and gave them eight weeks of mindfulness training alongside a control group who received no such training. At the end of the study, all the participants were injected with a flu vaccine to see how their immune systems would respond. All of the members of the meditation group, depending on how much meditation they had performed, exhibited *improved* immune response to the flu vaccine. The study also showed that there was a direct relationship between the improvement in immune system function and improvement in activity in the left-hand side of the pre-frontal cortex: the more positive emotion that was shown, the stronger the immune system.[228]

Improved thinking

In 2006, *Time* magazine reported on a study conducted by Sara Lazar at Massachusetts General Hospital which found that daily mindfulness practice thickened the part of the brain's cortex responsible for attention, decision making and memory. The study also found that mindfulness practice may help to slow the thinning of this part of the brain which occurs as part of the aging process.[229]

Mindfulness may also be able to increase attention span: one of the holy grails of increasing academic achievement. In an article published in *The Times*, studies done on experienced meditators showed that there was greater activity in the brain circuits associated with paying attention and that this ability was not dulled even when distracting noises were played nearby. Richard Davidson, a professor of psychology and psychiatry at the Wisconsin School of Medicine and Public Health was quoted in the article as saying: 'Attention can be trained in a way that is not that different to how physical exercise changes the body.'[230]

There is other evidence that practising meditation can help the learning process. The brain is always active and the constant firing of neurons in brain activity is called noise. When the brain's attention is directed at something specific that it has to process, the neurons fire in an organized and synchronized way and process the incoming information. When we are anxious, afraid or stressed, the random neuronal firings increase and the brain becomes less able to process information: it is a bit like a radio that is out of tune and can't pick up the signal. This process is explained by John Ratey in his book, *The User's Guide to the Brain*:

> This is what can happen when highly anxious people take tests. The heightened activity drives up the mental noise, so much so that people may literally see less of their environment, as though the brain space usually open for perception is busy with the internal noise . . . If the brain is busy trying to filter uncomfortable and frustrating noise, worries or other concerns, there is less 'brain stuff' available for perceiving.[231]

When we practise the breathing techniques used in meditation, our body becomes calm and a signal is sent to the brain via the vagus nerve to inform the brain that it is safe and happy. This can quell the excess random noise created by neurons becoming over-excited and enable the brain to be focused, perceptive and concentrated: the ingredients needed for learning. Meditation can also pave the way for positive emotions.

Summary

If it is possible for meditators to train their minds to make their destructive emotions vanish, certain practical elements of that meditation training could be valuably incorporated into the education of children and help adults achieve better quality of life. If such meditation techniques are valid and address the deepest mechanisms of the human mind, their value is universal and they don't have to be labelled Buddhist . . . If happiness and emotional balance are skills, we cannot underestimate the power of the transformation of the mind and must give due importance to the profound methods that allow us to become better human beings.[232]

As Matthieu Ricard argues here, the practice of mindfulness may well be the most important skill that can be introduced into a school setting and, as he points out, they are universal skills that do not have to be labelled Buddhist. The benefits of meditation are enormous and have been demonstrated and measured extensively through research conducted by respected scientists and published in peer-reviewed journals. The skills brought by mindfulness are skills that are needed for life as they underpin all of our interactions with ourselves and with other people.

Mindfulness is simple and cheap to introduce. It is possible to be trained in mindfulness practice easily and there are many centres which offer excellent opportunities to learn how to do it.[233] There are also some excellent books which describe practice and explain the benefits in more detail. The three that I would recommend the most highly are:

- *The Miracle of Mindfulness* by Thich Nhat Hanh
- *Coming to our Senses* by Jon Kabat-Zinn
- *The Wise Heart* by Jack Kornfield.

All three contain some great ideas on exactly how to practise meditation and the Kabat-Zinn and Kornfield books also give very detailed explanations of the benefits of meditation.

Putting it into practice: mindfulness meditation

In its simplest form, mindfulness simply involves drawing the attention to one object of focus: breathing is often the most straightforward as it is a resource you can count on all of your students possessing. In the early stages 5–10 minutes might be the most that you can achieve and I would recommend attending training before providing longer periods of mindfulness. A 5-minute session might look something like this:

- Ask your students to sit upright on a chair (posture for mindfulness should be dignified), with both feet flat on the floor and hands somewhere comfortable in the lap.

- Ask students to bring their attention into the space of the classroom they are in and then into the space that their body occupies. Ask them to cast their mind over their body and release or relax any areas of tension that they may have.

- As they sit, ask them to bring their attention to the natural rhythm of their breathing: follow the breath in and out, up and down and close or half-close the eyes. Tell them that they may find their attention wandering. Assure them that this is natural and is what minds do; simply becoming aware that the mind has wandered is to practise mindfulness. Ask them to focus on the journey that the air makes as it enters the body: feel its coolness on the nostrils as it passes inwards; feel the lungs expand and fill with air; feel the pause at the top of the breath and then feel the warmth of the air as it is released from the lungs back through the nostrils. Ask them to become aware of the sensation of sitting and breathing.

- After a few minutes, let the group know that in a few moments you are going to ask them to bring their attention back to the room and then ask them to slowly relax their attention and open their eyes.

- **Reflect**: after the first few occasions that you practise meditation, it is worth asking students to spend 2 or 3 minutes writing about how the meditation went. What did they feel? Was there any part that they found difficult? How much better did it go this time than last time?

- **Experiment**: ask students to experiment with 5–10 minutes of meditation each day and write about each time they did it. Ask them to notice any changes that occur, or any differences or benefits that they notice: that is, do they feel less stressed or better able to concentrate?

- **Other meditations**: take your class outside and do some walking meditation. Ask the students to focus on every aspect of taking a step, from the moment the foot touches the ground, through to the moment it leaves it again. Ask them to do this in silence and try to keep the attention focused on walking to the exclusion of everything else. Alternatively, ask the students to meditate on other sensory information such as touch, sight or hearing: get them to concentrate their attention solely on information from those senses.

Spirituality

In this next section of the chapter, I would like to look at the importance of spirituality as a component of well-being. Spirituality might at first glance appear to be an odd inclusion or, for some, a down right controversial one, but I think that it is important for us to recognize the huge importance that having a spiritual aspect to one's life can have for leading a happy and fulfilled human existence.

Research into the ingredients of a happy life indicates that those who have a religious faith report higher levels of happiness than those who do not.[234] This of course should come as no surprise. Religion provides a very clear sense of individual meaning and purpose in life and a feeling that the universe itself has ultimate meaning; it actively encourages the practise of altruism, another key ingredient of a life well-lived; it offers a clear and generally unambiguous set of guidelines to live by and it provides both a strong and supportive community *and* security in the face of suffering and death by giving supernatural assurances about things such as God and heaven. Most importantly though, religious belief connects us to something greater than ourselves, something transcendent and it is this capacity for religion to carry us beyond ourselves, to dissolve the illusory barrier between subject and object, between the self and the other, which can enable those who belong to it to experience feelings of happiness seemingly unattainable by other, more mundane means.

But there are two very large caveats to this. Firstly, there are clearly people who are religious or who belong to a religion who are deeply *unhappy*. History and current affairs are littered with examples of people whose adherence to religion has turned them into bigoted and angry zealots whose sole purpose in life seems to be to root out and persecute unbelievers (the Christian Church has a particularly murky past in this regard), or for whom adherence to religion has led to their persecution (the Jonestown massacre in 1978). Secondly, there are numerous examples of people who are not religious in any obvious way, but who lead good and profoundly happy lives.

Spirituality and religiosity

I think that there are important distinctions to be made between spirituality, religion and religiosity and I would like to tell you a story to help to illustrate this distinction.

I have a distant relative who is a religious bigot. I think that most of us probably do. I only ever seem to see this man at important family gatherings and the story I am about to tell you happened on the day of my grandmother's funeral.

It was a beautiful summer's day and before we left my grandparents' house in Worthing for the cremation and memorial service, the family gathered there for drinks. My family is almost exclusively Christian; my uncle is high up in the ministry of the Methodist church and my parents are both heavily involved in their respective church communities. The bigoted relative is really no exception. Upon hearing that I had just completed my first year of a theology degree, he came to find me to chew the fat. Given my family's religious proclivities, he probably assumed that he was on safe and friendly territory and when he found out about my studies he probably expected me to be destined to follow my uncle into the ministry. However, religiously speaking I am a little bit of a black sheep: despite my Christian upbringing and confirmation as a Roman Catholic, I am agnostic, which means that I am open to the *possibility* of God's existence, but I just don't think that it can be proved one way or the other, nor do I believe that there is one exclusive route to God.

We chatted at the fireplace in the front room and the conversation found its way onto the topic of religion quite quickly. It turned out that this relative had a degree in theology (I think it was the kind you send away for) and he told me about the youth work he was doing. He told me about the youth camp he had recently been helping at and he informed me of his incredulity at the rock bands who played there:

'Don't they know that God doesn't like rock music?'

I nearly choked on my canapé. God doesn't like rock music?? I was only a first year and had yet to discover the majesty of Thomas Aquinas' explanation of the fundamental unknowability of God, but intuitively I knew that my relative was having a laugh. I had often entertained the idea that if God had a body, he would enjoy playing 'In the Light' by Led Zeppelin, or 'Kashmir' perhaps. I searched the relative's face for a glimmer of a wry smile, a twinkle in his eye, some sign that he did not genuinely believe what he had just said. There was none.

The conversation went on and headed inexorably towards the thorny issue of the creation. I should have known better, but I couldn't help myself. Having done some basic biblical study and knowing that the relative had a degree in theology, I thought that I would be saying nothing controversial by challenging the literal truth of the creation story in the Bible; surely, I thought to myself, no one can *really* believe that this 3,000-year-old story is the indisputable truth of how our universe came to be?

The relative did.

And what's more, on the day of my grandmother's funeral my bigoted relative told me that I was going to hell for challenging the truth of the Bible.

He was exhibiting the more unpleasant side of religiosity. His concern at that moment in time was for the *rightness* or *wrongness* of certain statements or ideas and to make it perfectly clear to me that he had access to the *right* answers and that I did not and, what's more, that there are supernatural consequences for believing in the wrong answers. I have seen people go to extraordinary lengths to try to preserve *rightness*. I once heard a very bright PhD student argue that contrary to the evidence from modern palaeontology, the agents of Satan had buried dinosaur bones in the earth to lead us away from the truth of the creation story in the Bible. There are people in the world who will take up arms to prove that their version of the truth is the right version of the truth and I think that it is fair to say that once this has happened, we are no longer dealing with religion in its truest sense and we are certainly not dealing with spirituality; we are dealing with fragile egos that have invested more energy in *being right* than they have in reflecting on the spiritual side of existence.[235]

The foundations of spirituality

In his book *Spiritual Evolution*, George Vaillant attempts to explain why the human being evolved a capacity for spirituality. His thesis is based upon the idea that there are really two aspects to spirituality: the part that is more emotional and instinctive and which is to be found in the operations of the brain's limbic system and the part that is most associated with language and definitions which is to be found in the 'thinking' part of the brain, the neo-cortex. For Vaillant, spirituality is at its best when there exists a strong relationship between the positive emotions provided by the limbic system and the thinking provided by the neo-cortex. When the cortical aspect is too dominant, the resulting religiosity goes against the evolutionary purpose of spirituality to bind people together through positive emotion and meaning. In other words, people become too obsessed with being right (cortical) and not concerned enough with fostering positive emotions and relationships (limbic).

Vaillant also discusses spiritual development and discusses Michael Commons' idea of 'post-formal operations':

> Post-formal operations involve appreciation of irony and paradox. By paradox I mean learning to trust a universe in which the uncertainty principle is a basic axiom of quantum physics, in which good and evil can exist side by side, in which innocent children die from bubonic plague, and in which to keep something you have to give it away. As in quantum mechanics, certainty is an impossibility. Only faith and trust remain.[236]

Vaillant goes on to mention the research of Kenneth Kendler which found that 'as adults become older, their religious "conservatism" (their literal belief in the Bible and in a belief that God rewards and punishes) weakened and they became more spiritually inclusive. In other words, with maturity, the patriarchal model of pleasing God *only* if you meet *His* expectations gave way to a more maternal spirituality of forgiveness and unconditional love'.[237]

What is spirituality?

Spirituality is quite different to a petty concern over correctness, which seems more like a gang turf war or a playground fight over whose dad is bigger than serious religious debate; and religion, when informed by spiritual practice, is quite different too.

Spirituality is openness to the transcendent elements of human existence and it appears that, biologically speaking, we are set up for experiences of the transcendent. There are areas of the brain which, when stimulated in particular ways, give rise to extremely profound feelings which are often referred to as religious experience. Research shows that these areas of the brain can be stimulated by psycho-active drugs such as LSD and psilocybin[238] or by regular, repetitive movements or speech patterns[239] and during these experiences we can lose a sense of the self and feel a profound connection with the universe or, indeed, we can feel united with the divine. Whether or not these experiences are caused by God is a different question, but it is clear that these experiences are authentically human.

Research conducted by Jonathan Haidt suggests that there is an emotional state which he calls 'elevation' and this is the sense of joy or deep gratification we feel when we witness acts of moral beauty. You have probably experienced the sensation when you hear a story of enormous self-sacrifice: you feel a sort of fluttering, warm or pleasant sensation in the chest, perhaps a welling-up of tears and an overall feeling of calm and contentment. When we see acts of moral beauty, a physical reaction is stimulated: we are moved. Interestingly, one of Haidt's research assistants wanted to measure the release of oxytocin, the body's bonding chemical, during elevation experiences and discovered that one way to do this was to measure the release of breast milk in lactating women, as one of the functions of oxytocin is to stimulate the release of breast milk. In a wonderful-sounding experiment, 45 lactating women were gathered into a lab, were asked to insert a nursing pad into their bras and were then played moving clips from the Oprah Winfrey show. Afterwards, the researchers weighed the nursing pads and found that nearly half of the mothers had either produced breast milk or breast-fed their babies as a result of watching the clip.[240] Acts of moral beauty can stimulate not only a physical reaction, but also an emotional and cognitive one: they stimulate our desire to form bonds with other human beings.

Nature can also stimulate these feelings within us: feelings that there is something greater than us, something for us to stand in awe and wonder at. As I write this, my wife is pregnant with our first child. As an avowed agnostic, I do not believe in 'the miracle of birth', but I do, however, stand in awe of what nature does. When we went for our first scan at 13 weeks and I saw our child moving around in my wife's belly, I was overcome and could not stop the tears from streaming down my face. Similarly, just being in the natural world and observing its beauty and complexity can generate a feeling that we are standing in the face of something magnificent that is truly greater than us.

These feelings may turn into religious devotion or practice, or, indeed, religious devotion or practice may produce these feelings but in order to avoid religiosity becoming pernicious and divisive, our beliefs, religious or otherwise should be held in place by a sense of awe and wonder, openness to mystery, willingness to accept wisdom from other sources of authority, delight in beauty and, above all, a desire to do good.

Spirituality and the child

An appreciation of the spiritual side to life is very clearly part of being human. If we accept the premise that education should be about enabling our young people to acquire the skills to live full human lives, then spirituality should form part of their educational experience. But schools find this difficult for a number of reasons.

Primarily I think there is the worry that this kind of thing just can't be taught. Spirituality appears an unwieldy and nebulous concept that cannot be broken down into manageable chunks or lesson plans. I would agree that spirituality cannot be taught. You cannot teach someone to be spiritual in the same way that you can teach them to be proficient at French grammar. Grammar does not need to be experienced in order for it to be right: it is right in and of itself and has certain principles that are instructed and then followed. Spirituality is just not like this. You can give students a couple of pointers as to what spirituality is (or indeed, what it is not) but from then on, you can only really provide opportunities for them to experience it. For someone to see the value of spirituality in their lives they have to experience the emotional and cognitive states associated with it and see their benefits, and, believe it or not, it isn't that difficult.

At the school where I teach, we have been experimenting with the teaching of spirituality to our 13–14 year olds. We take a broad approach to it and teach the students that spirituality is made up of three basic components: awareness of something greater than ourselves and the interconnectedness of all things; religious devotion; ethical and moral awareness. One of the lessons involves going for a silent walk. I start the lesson by playing a short video clip that inspires wonder at nature (the last one I used was one on the Aurora Borealis). We then go for a walk around the school grounds in silence and I ask the students to take their time and notice things of beauty. I just sit and watch them. Last year, I was teaching the top set and they are academically talented kids who learn both Latin and Greek as well as two foreign languages and the other normal programme of subjects. When I told them they were going for a walk, some of them sneered. How could this be a proper lesson? We then went out and pretty soon they were studying plants and flowers with intensity, climbing trees, listening to birds singing – all in silence. They were lost in what they were doing and experiencing a sense of wonder at the natural world. They skipped back to the classroom and couldn't wait to talk about what they had experienced and about the feelings that they'd had. Their homeworks reflecting on the lesson were the best of the year.

There may also be the feeling that children are not cognitively ready for spirituality. David Hay and Rebecca Nye, in their study of the spirituality of children argue that this is simply not the case and that children, from a very young age, have a language of spirituality. In interviewing a large number of children about spirituality they discovered that children do indeed have a spiritual aspect to their thinking (which Hay and Nye call 'relational consciousness') and that there is evidence that children are becoming culturally conditioned to feel uncomfortable about discussing spiritual experiences:

> Few children had actually shared their spirituality with others, and the negative consequences . . . were their imagined predictions of how they would feel if they spoke of it. More worryingly, whilst aware of their own experience, they often admitted that they would be unlikely to speak kindly to others who had the temerity to speak publicly about these matters. Some explained their reluctance as due to an anxiety about not being believed or taken seriously; a few had direct experience of this.[241]

In other words, many children don't talk about spirituality for fear of being ridiculed for being weird.

Secondly, I think there is a fear of treading on toes and this is not unfounded. At my first ever parents' evening as a Religious Studies teacher, I nervously awaited the arrival of the parents of my class of 11–12 year olds. The position of responsibility that I held was still new and daunting for me. My star pupil arrived with her mother. She was a great student who was really outperforming her peers and I was looking forward to passing on my praise in front of her mother, especially on her work on Sikhism, which showed real empathy and insight. All was going well and the student beamed as I explained how well she was doing. Her mother seemed quite stern-faced however, and I wondered whether I was doing enough, so I upped the praise ante a little bit. The mother still had a very serious expression on her face, so I decided to see if she had any questions.

'Yes Mr Morris, I do have one question.'

I wondered what it could be.

'I know that you have to do it because the government requires you to, but why do you insist on teaching my daughter about all these *other* religions [other than Christianity]? Don't they know that they're wrong?'

Luckily my head of department, who was at the next table, had been listening and stepped in with a much more diplomatic answer than I could have mustered at the time. I was floored.

There are parents who are, like my relative, obsessed with the notion of one way or the other being *the right way*. This will always be the case. Religion is a controversial issue for many people. However, the cost of giving in to these types of critique, I think, is greater. I read in the paper that Richard Dawkins, the prominent atheist, has announced a research project into the effect of teaching fairy tales to the young. He is concerned that 'bringing children up to believe in spells and wizards' is anti-scientific and may have a 'pernicious effect' on the intellectual development of the young. He has added that calling a child a Muslim child or a Christian child is a form of child abuse 'because a young child is too young to know what its views are about the cosmos or morality', furthermore 'it is evil to describe a child as a Muslim child or a Christian child'.[242]

Dawkins may have a point that in certain cases, labelling children as belonging to a certain religious community, if not done skilfully, can lead to a closing down of doors of exploration. But if we follow everything that Dawkins says and stop teaching religion (and fairy tales) in schools and, indeed, stop teaching theology at university, we are missing the point and we get mired in a tawdry battle over who is right – and life is not just about being right. The Bible makes historical mistakes; this is a fact, but that does not mean that we should discard it altogether, because many of the forms of literature we find in it teach us new ways of thinking and also teach us wider lessons about the human condition. If we deny children the opportunity to experience the wonder of spiritual experiences because we believe that in doing so openly we are condemning them to the eternal fire or by doing so at all we are making them weak-minded, we are also denying them a fundamental part of being human.

Putting it into practice: spirituality

As is hopefully clear, it is the thesis of this chapter that spirituality cannot and should not be prescribed for people. Spirituality is a natural capacity that we all possess to varying degrees and that, ultimately, we have to awaken ourselves through our own choices and practice. The teaching of spirituality should make clear its importance and suggest and provide opportunities for experiencing that huge variety of ways that spirituality might be encountered and expressed.

- **Spirituality through stillness**: practise stillness exercises with your class, perhaps some form of meditation and ask them to reflect on what they notice in that stillness.
- **Spirituality through altruism**: explore examples of great acts of kindness and ask the students to explore how those acts may have affected the spirituality of those responsible for them. There are great examples in film such as Gandhi and Oskar Schindler. Get the students to practise acts of kindness and compassion and reflect on whether it connects them with a sense of greater meaning and purpose.
- **Spirituality through nature**: explore how the experience of being out in nature can make us feel connected to something greater than ourselves. Take your class out for a silent walk and ask each member of the group to pay close attention to all the natural or living things they

encounter. Clips of David Attenborough that have been posted on the internet are often an excellent resource for stimulating awe and wonder at nature.

- **Spirituality and meaning**: examine how identifying with a cause or a passion in life can generate feelings of spirituality by belonging to a movement which is greater than the individual. Examine the pitfalls of identifying with groups which may have sinister aims.

- **Spirituality through creativity**: examine some of the great works of art and think about how they have been the result of spiritual inspiration. Explore how being creative can spark spiritual states and help us to forget mundane cares.

- **Spirituality through flow**: look at how being totally absorbed in an activity can produce reverie and spiritual awareness. A particularly good example of this is 'Parkour' or 'Freerunning' created by a group of Parisian teenagers in the 1990s; not only is it an extremely demanding physical discipline, but it has a philosophical and spiritual underpinning too.[243]

- **Spirituality through others**: examine how religious leaders and prophets have arisen. In what way do they inspire spirituality in those who become their followers? How can we distinguish between the genuinely spiritual and the fraudulent prophet such as Jim Jones or David Koresh?

Well-being and meaning

In 1945, after being liberated from the horrors of the Holocaust and its aftermath, the young Austrian psychologist Viktor Frankl wrote his extraordinary book *Man's Search for Meaning* over a nine-day period. What is even more extraordinary than the speed with which he wrote is that much of the manuscript had been written before his incarceration in Auschwitz and other concentration camps. When Frankl was imprisoned, he was stripped of his clothes and belongings, one of which was his book:

> I tried to take one of the old prisoners into my confidence. Approaching him furtively, I pointed to the roll of paper in the inner pocket of my coat and said, 'Look, this is the manuscript of a scientific book. I know what you will say; that I should be grateful to escape with my life, that it should be all I can expect of fate. But I cannot help myself. I must keep the manuscript at all costs; it contains my life's work. Do you understand that?'[244]

The manuscript was taken from him. Part of Frankl's drive to survive, part of what gave his existence in the concentration camps meaning and purpose, was the preservation of his manuscript in his mind. His manuscript was about a new form of therapy, 'Logotherapy', which argues that man's search for meaning is the primary motivation in life. Frankl's book is brilliant because he used the experiences he had in the Holocaust at the hands of brutal SS guards and equally brutal fellow inmates to show that even in the direst circumstances and even when other conditions of well-being are absent, we are driven to establish meaning for our own lives.

> What was really needed was a fundamental change in our attitude toward life. We had to learn ourselves and, furthermore, we had to teach the despairing men, that *it did not really matter what we expected from life, but rather what life expected from us.* We needed to stop asking about the meaning of life, and instead to think of ourselves as those who were being questioned by life – daily and hourly. Our answer must consist, not in talk and meditation, but in right action and right conduct. Life ultimately means taking the responsibility to find the right answer to its problems and to fulfil the tasks which it constantly sets for each individual. These tasks and therefore the meaning of life, differ from man to man, from moment to moment. Thus it is impossible to define the meaning of life in a general way . . . No man and no destiny can be compared with any other man or any other destiny.[245]

In the film *This is England* we a follow the life of an 11-year-old boy called Shaun over the course of a summer as he falls in with an older group of skinheads. It is 1983 and Shaun's father had been killed in the Falklands conflict. Shaun's mother does not have much money and he finds himself being bullied at school for his appearance and for the death of his father. Once he joins the older group he finds acceptance and respect and his life seems to have value and meaning.

Things start to become unsavoury with the return from prison of a violent and racist member of the group, who rapidly starts to encourage the group to join the National Front and participate in racist attacks. What is most disturbing about this film is its depiction of the ease with which young people can be drawn into violent and abusive behaviour if they do not have a strong value base and sense of meaning in their lives. The writer and director draw skilful lines between characters in the film who have yet to form their values and sense of purpose and those who have already done so. For those characters for whom there is a void, the ideology of racism and the camaraderie of a neo-Nazi organization fill that void, and this includes Shaun. It is not until one of his friends is beaten nearly to death by the group's leader that Shaun realizes that he has fallen into a pattern of behaviour that conflicts with his values and his sense of meaning and purpose: something referred to as cognitive dissonance.

Ultimately, the teaching of well-being is aiming to equip young people for situations just like this: where they find themselves faced with a decision between patterns of behaviour that will enable them to find meaning and purpose in life or that will result in them doing harm to themselves and others. The teaching of well-being is aimed at helping young people to create *for themselves* the conditions of life that will make them thrive and flourish and once we start to thrive and flourish we can start to ask deep and vital questions about the nature of our own existence and have a sound set of foundations to build our answers on.

The discovery of meaning and purpose is the summation of everything else in this book and in this sense we are returned to Aristotle whom we encountered in the first chapter. Aristotle argued that humans flourish and discover their purpose by practising the practical and intellectual virtues. Modern research supports Aristotle's view. If we establish harmony between the different physical, emotional and intellectual aspects of ourselves, we will reduce the likelihood of physical and mental illness. If we pay attention to our emotional states and learn to regulate them, we can establish lasting individual contentment and lasting contentment in our relationships with others. If we develop the cognitive skills of resilience and optimism, we can learn to challenge the unhelpful beliefs that lead to depression and antagonism. If we learn what our strengths and the strengths of others are, we can create more positive encounters in our daily interactions as we employ our own strengths and appreciate the strengths of others in action. If we think critically about trends in Western consumer society, we can make informed choices about the extent to which we allow acquisitiveness, comparison, materialism and busy-ness to dominate our lives and avoid many of the modern Western dis-eases. And if we practise philosophy, we can ask more fundamental questions about the ideologies we see around us and, unlike Shaun, spot the thinking errors that are present in extremist ideology and avoid getting swept along by them in the first place.

It is time that education took notice of the research in this field and realized that we can teach children the skills that can help them avoid the precipice that Shaun found himself standing over. There is a vacuum in education that is stretched open by the emphasis on academic learning and measured outcomes and this vacuum is what makes it hard for many children to realize their own value and to discover their own sense of meaning in life. Academic learning is a tiny aspect of the range of skills we must acquire as humans in order to flourish and find meaning and many of these skills of flourishing and of meaning can only be acquired by practising them and reflecting upon them, not just by learning about them. The teaching of well-being helps to close the vacuum and complete what is missing from education and it can transform the experience young people have of education and the experience that educators have of young people.

Appendix 1: A well-being curriculum – the spider's web

This final section of the book is designed to give you an idea of what a curriculum in well-being might look like. I have kept this deliberately brief and non-prescriptive as schools have different levels of resources available to introduce this sort of material. Lesson length, timetable allocation, teachers given over for delivery: all of these are variable. It is also important that individual schools tailor a bespoke well-being course to the specific needs of their communities and, for this reason, the structure has been kept loose.

The curriculum model that I recommend for teaching well-being is called the 'spider's web' and like a lot of ideas in the book, it doubles as a metaphor.

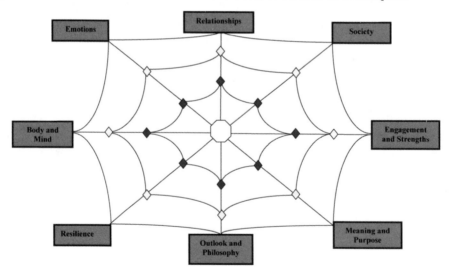

The eight boxes around the edge of the web correspond to the eight chapters in this book, which deal in detail with content and teaching ideas: Chapters 3 to 10. If you imagine your course starting at the centre of the web, as the students build knowledge and skills, they slowly move out to the edge of the web. The diamonds represent lessons or learning opportunities and the amount of time you have available to you to teach well-being will dictate how many of those diamonds there are.

The reason that I have chosen a spider's web as a model for building a well-being curriculum is that just as the whole of a spider's web is affected when a tasty insect lands on it for the spider to eat, almost all of the topics that you could teach in well-being will have resonances somewhere else in the course. The reason for this, as no doubt you will have already realized, is that the teaching of well-being relates *directly* to life as it is lived and life does not divide neatly into categories and sub-divisions: it is a web of connections and inter-related experiences.

Deciding how to populate the diamonds will depend on your preferred teaching style. They could be populated with topics, as you have encountered them in the book. For example, the relationships strand could be populated as follows:

- the benefits of relationships
- the biological basis for relationships
- family
- friendship
- romantic relationships
- empathy
- altruism
- trust
- forgiveness
- conflict resolution
- common causes and values.

The delivery of this strand could take place over consecutive weeks, or over the space of several years.

An alternative way of populating the diamonds would be to use particular scenarios that the students encounter to drive the material that you cover. For example, 'managing stress' could be a topic that would draw on different elements of the web from body and mind, to resilience.

It would also be possible to build a hybrid of both, where you start with the delivery of particular content in the early stages and then apply that content to scenarios and get your students to rehearse the different skills they have acquired by reflecting on how to apply them to scenarios that they may very well encounter.

At the school where I have introduced a well-being course, the particular demands of the independent boarding environment and the particular provision I have been given have shaped the course that we have developed. Our students arrive aged 13 and the majority of them board. For that first year, they have 30 minutes of well-being per week and that course is taught by their pastoral tutors. We have identified the specific needs of that year group to be resilience, emotional intelligence, recognition and development of strengths and work on values, because in the early stages of joining the school, many of them have to get used to living with others, working out group influences and managing increased academic pressures.

In the subsequent two year groups, students are allocated 60 minutes per fortnight for well-being. Because of this, lessons have to be taught as 'one-offs' because all momentum is lost between seeing the students. The course is taught by seven teachers, all of whom chose to teach it and who have a passion for the subject. This is important because it helps to raise the profile of the subject in the eyes of the students as it is well-taught and they enjoy their lessons. The majority of them teach more than one group too, which means that they can try lesson ideas out more than once and hone their skills, rather than waiting 12 months to teach a lesson again. The course covers what was missed in the first year and also re-visits and expands upon the first-year content.

All students over the three year groups are expected to keep a well-being journal: they are set reflective exercises each week to consolidate what they have learned and test out interventions that they have been taught. Over the years that the course has been in place, the students have become more used to writing in their journals and whereas initially journal work tended not to be completed, students now enjoy the opportunity to reflect on their ongoing well-being work and the effect it has on their lives.

Appendix 2: Further reading and useful websites

Before I draw the book to a close, I would like to suggest some sources of information for help in devising a curriculum on well-being. As teachers, we often spend many years developing our expertise in our chosen academic discipline and continue to read around our subjects long after finishing formal education. Why should it be any different with this aspect of education? Why do we so often let it just boil down to common sense? There are some excellent books available on this topic and here are six of them.

The Happiness Hypothesis: Jonathan Haidt

The aim of *The Happiness Hypothesis* is to tie the modern discipline of Positive Psychology in with ancient wisdom. What is remarkable is that everything that is being said now with the backing of empirical results derived from experimental psychology was presaged by people such as the Buddha, Aristotle, Jesus of Nazareth and Shakespeare. The book is brilliant. It gives a deep insight into what it *really* means to be human and contains a large number of descriptions of fascinating experiments that have been conducted into human behaviour over the last 50 years or so.

Authentic Happiness: Martin Seligman

Professor Martin Seligman of the University of Pennsylvania is arguably the reason that this book is being written. In the mid-1990s, he assumed the presidency of the American Psychological Association and told them that they had been getting it all wrong for the last 100 years: they had been focusing on what breaks humans and causes them misery, rather than what helps them to flourish. The 'Positive Psychology' that resulted has produced some fascinating research and much of it is either specifically designed for schools, or can be used in them. *Authentic Happiness* gives some very clear practical advice on what we need to do to live fuller lives and avoid the seemingly pandemic depression and angst. The website that accompanies the book also has some excellent free resources that can be used for teaching: www.authentichappiness.org and for a more in-depth treatment of resilience, have a look at *The Resilience Factor* by Karen Reivich and Andrew Shatté.

Emotional Intelligence: Daniel Goleman

If there is a manifesto for this kind of teaching, Daniel Goleman's book is it. It is the book that everyone should read as it makes it absolutely clear how important and fundamental an understanding of the function of emotion is to overcoming so many of those inter-personal hurdles that make life difficult. In fact, it is Goleman's assertion that 'emotional intelligence' may just be the most important skill that a human can develop if they wish to lead a successful life. All teachers should read this book and all children should be exposed to the ideas that Goleman explores; indeed, the UK Social and Emotional Aspects of Learning (SEAL) programme takes quite a lot of its inspiration from Goleman's work.

Stumbling upon Happiness: Daniel Gilbert

Many of the very best books in this field (such as Haidt's) arise out of a mixture of philosophy and psychology and Daniel Gilbert's book is no exception. He takes us on a fascinating journey which shows us all of the little foibles we have as humans and all of the cognitive or thinking barriers we place in front of happiness, often just in order to preserve our ego. This book is brilliantly written, funny and accessible and is littered with examples of things you could do with a class to show them some of the tricks our minds play on us.

The User's Guide to the Brain: John Ratey

You will find as you go through this book that I make quite frequent references to the findings of neuroscience: the science of the brain. One of the key ingredients of well-being is self-awareness and self-understanding and one of the great mysteries of being human has always been the functioning of the pile of grey matter sitting inside our skulls. Not so any more. Scientists have made great advances in the study of the function of the brain and, what's more, authors such as John Ratey make this material accessible to people like me who have had no formal scientific training since school. This book is truly excellent and full of fascinating information about how the brain works and its effects upon our behaviour.

Flow: Mihaly Csikszentmihalyi (pron. cheeks-sent-me-high)

Flow is one of those books that make you completely re-think the way that you see the world. Csikszentmihalyi's research is into the fascinating phenomenon of 'flow', which is where our ability in a given area and our concentration perfectly coincide on a task and we lose track of time. A lot of people refer to this as 'being in the zone'. This book may have very profound implications for education: if we could tap into flow states for all children, schools would be *very* different places, as so many of our problems arise out of boredom or frustration and this book spells out the solution. *Flow* is expansive and its content and the implications thereof reach into every aspect of life.

The Tao of Pooh: Benjamin Hoff

One of the most important steps along the route to thinking seriously about well-being is to re-focus our attention away from some of the less than healthy obsessions that modern Western culture would have us pursue. There are a number of books that can help to do this: Oliver James' *Affluenza* is one, Matthieu Ricard's book *Happiness* is another and Thich Nhat Hanh's *The Miracle of Mindfulness* still another. I have picked Benjamin Hoff's book out, because it is wonderfully clear and simple: it is the kind of book that can be read in a couple of days, but that you will keep going back to. It is also the kind of book that children could read. The book discusses the ancient Chinese religion of Taoism (pron. *d*aoism) using the character of Winnie the Pooh, who demonstrates many of the qualities of Taoist wisdom. This book is hugely instructive in realizing the need to restore balance in life and also the great damage that can be done to us and our relationships by the unchecked ego.

Internet resources

www.authentichappiness.org: this website contains a number of the questionnaires and tests recommended for analysing personal levels of happiness and well-being, which can be taken there for free. It also contains links to a wide range of information on positive psychology.

www.casel.org: this website is dedicated to social and emotional aspects of learning within schools and has access to a wide range of resources and teaching ideas.

www.centreforconfidence.co.uk: the Centre for Confidence is based in the UK and campaigns to raise public awareness of much of the research in Positive Psychology and well-being that has practical applications in social settings. It is a very useful source of information.

www.thriving.org: Thriving was set up to gather information about projects that are designed to help people to flourish. As a result it contains information about a very wide range of initiatives and contains some inspirational ideas for use in a range of settings.

Endnotes

Notes to Chapter 1: Learning to train elephant riders

1. Jonathan Haidt, *The Happiness Hypothesis*, p. 22.
2. Matthieu Ricard and Jean-François Revel, *The Monk and the Philosopher*, p. 332.
3. In 2007, 25 per cent of 11–15 year olds reported the use of any illegal drug, with the greatest proportion of that figure arising from cannabis use. This is the figure for use, not addiction. In 2007, 5 per cent of pupils reported taking drugs at least once a month; 1 per cent reported taking drugs on most days (source: www.ic.nhs.uk, accessed 29 December 2008). In 2007, 20 per cent of 11–15 year olds reported drinking alcohol in the previous week. The average consumption for those who consume alcohol within that age group fluctuates around the 12.7 units per week mark: about six pints of beer, or a bottle and a half of wine. Some 46 per cent of pupils reported never having consumed alcohol (source: www.ic.nhs.uk, accessed 29 December 2008). All of the figures for drug consumption of any sort amongst teenagers show a decline up to 2007.
4. It is important that schools devise their own well-being courses, which suit the particular circumstances of the staff and children, and indeed the practical provision such as curriculum allocation. Schools are made up of individual mixes of students with their own needs and some schools have particular issues that need to be addressed in more depth than others and for that reason, a well-being curriculum has to be bespoke.
5. See for example *Gamesters' Handbook* by Donna Brandes and Howard Phillips or *101 Games for Groups* by Maxie Ashton and Lana Varga.
6. Two very good books for this are *Opening Skinner's Box* by Lauren Slater and *The Happiness Hypothesis* by Jonathan Haidt.
7. See Jonathan Haidt, *The Happiness Hypothesis*, pp. 147–9.
8. For example, 'Rehab', from her album *Back to Black* is a good place to start.
9. For example, the VIA strengths test at www.authentichappiness.org and a fascinating test of our inbuilt prejudices at www.projectimplicit.org.
10. For example, the satisfaction with life scale developed by Ed Diener *et al.*
11. Alan Carr's *Positive Psychology* is particularly helpful in giving a list of measures available.
12. The VIA can be found at www.authentichappiness.org.

[13] Foresight Mental Capital and Well-being Project. Final Project report. The Government Office for Science. 2008, p. 131.

[14] Taken from a lecture given at Wellington College, Berkshire, UK, 11 November 2008.

[15] Oliver James, *Affluenza*, p. 182.

Notes to Chapter 2: Happiness

[16] Matthieu Ricard and Jean-François Revel, *The Monk and the Philosopher*, p. 30.

[17] Richard Schoch, *The Secrets of Happiness*, p. 1.

[18] Jonathan Haidt, *The Happiness Hypothesis*, p. 32.

Notes to Chapter 3: Learning to unite elephant and rider: caring for the human body

[19] Andrew Curran, *The Little Book of Big Stuff About the Brain*, p. 7.

[20] For more detailed information on dietary advice, see *They Are What You Feed Them* by Alex Richardson.

[21] 'Healthy lifestyle raises beneficial enzyme: study' by Will Dunham. Published at www.in.reuters.com, 16 September 2008, accessed 29 December 2008.

[22] Alex Richardson, *They Are What You Feed Them*, p. 81.

[23] John Ratey, *Spark*, pp. 32–3.

[24] Alex Richardson, *They Are What You Feed Them*, p. 395.

[25] Reported in the *New York Times*, 28 October 2007.

[26] John Ratey, *A User's Guide to the Brain*, p. 189.

[27] *Ibid.*, p. 192.

[28] Research conducted by Crowne Plaza Hotels and the Edinburgh Sleep Centre and published in December 2007. Source: www.ameinfo.com, accessed 28 December 2008.

[29] Nick Baylis, *Learning from Wonderful Lives*, p. 230.

[30] 'Pet therapy "helps schizophrenia"', www.news.bbc.co.uk, 15 January 2005, accessed 28 December 2008.

[31] Iris Murdoch, *The Sovereignty of Good*, p. 82.

32 Jonathan Swift, *Gulliver's Travels*, p. 156.

33 *Ibid.*, p. 160.

34 John Ratey, *A User's Guide to the Brain*, p. 118.

35 Foresight Mental Capital and Well-being Project. Final Project report. The Government Office for Science. 2008, p. 118.

36 *Ibid.*, p. 125.

37 *Ibid.*, p. 57.

38 Cited in *Stumbling on Happiness* by Daniel Gilbert. Six months after the study, 30 per cent of the low control group had died, compared with 15 per cent of the high control group.

39 Two books with excellent and detailed chapters on the process of learning from a neurological perspective are John Ratey's *A User's Guide to the Brain* and Andrew Curran's *The Little Book of Big Stuff About the Brain*.

40 John Ratey, *A User's Guide to the Brain*, p. 206.

41 *Ibid.*, p. 191.

42 Malcolm Gladwell, *Outliers*, Chapter 9.

43 For more on this, see Chapter 6 of *The Happiness Hypothesis* by Jonathan Haidt.

44 Note from transcript from the keynote seminar of the all-party parliamentary group on scientific research in learning and education held on the 23 October 2007.

Notes to Chapter 4: Philosophy and well-being

45 Transcribed from 'Jon Ronson on . . . states of mind' broadcast 18 September 2008 on BBC Radio 4.

46 *Ibid.*

47 Source: Wikipedia. Accessed September 2008.

48 Guy Claxton, *What's the Point of School?*, p. xi.

49 Aristotle, *The Nicomachean Ethics*, Book 1.

50 Bertrand Russell, *The Conquest of Happiness*, Chapter 10.

51 Martin Seligman, *Authentic Happiness*, Chapter 14.

52 Daniel Gilbert, *Stumbling on Happiness*, p. 162.

53 The best book for exploring this in more depth is *Stumbling on Happiness* by Daniel Gilbert.

54 More information at www.derrenbrown.co.uk/news/messiah.

55 Cited in Daniel Gilbert, *Stumbling on Happiness*, p. 164.

[56] Visit www.sapere.net or www.thephilosophyshop.co.uk for ideas on how to teach philosophy.

[57] Two of the best books on the tools needed by philosophers are *Bad Thoughts, A Guide to Clear Thinking* by Jamie Whyte and *Thinking from A to Z* by Nigel Warburton.

[58] There is an excellent online resource for exploring the assumptions we make (and prejudices we have). It is an online test which explores how we make decisions along racial, gender and age lines. The test is very interesting to take and the results are fascinating. It is at https://implicit.harvard.edu/implicit.

[59] For more detailed philosophical problems, have a look at *The Philosophy Gym* by Stephen Law or '*Can a Robot Be Human?* by Peter Cave.

[60] Lauren Slater, *Opening Skinner's Box*, p. 35.

[61] *Ibid.*, p. 60.

[62] A. C. Grayling, *The Choice of Hercules*, p. 172.

Notes to Chapter 5: Emotions

[63] This is argued by Paul Ekman in *Emotions Revealed*.

[64] Matthieu Ricard, *Happiness: A Guide to Developing Life's Most Important Skill*, p. 110.

[65] For example, Tal ben Shahar tells the story of how Buddhist monks with a lifetime of meditative practice can overcome the startle response that causes us to blink or flinch, something that not even some of the most experienced army snipers can do.

[66] This section is a necessary simplification. For more detailed descriptions of brain function in relation to the emotions, read *Emotional Intelligence* by Daniel Goleman, Chapters 1 and 2 and *Descartes' Error* by Antonio Damasio, Chapter 7.

[67] Daniel Goleman, *Emotional Intelligence*, p. 16.

[68] Affective style is the tendency we have towards particular temperaments, in part set by genetics. Jerome Kagan suggests that there are at least four basic temperaments: timid, bold, upbeat and melancholy (Daniel Goleman, *Emotional Intelligence*, Chapter 14). It is important to stress that 'affective style' is only partially set by genetics (discovered through the study of identical twins separated at birth) and that the brain and our temperament remains plastic to change throughout our lives.

[69] Jonathan Haidt explains this with customary clarity on pp. 115–17 of *The Happiness Hypothesis*. It is important to stress that 'affective style' is only partially set by genetics (discovered through the study of identical twins separated at birth)

and that the brain remains plastic to change throughout our lives. As Goleman puts it 'temperament is not destiny'.

70 Winnicott and Bowlby, cited in Goleman, p. 57.

71 Alan Carr, *Positive Psychology*, p. 124.

72 Jonathan Haidt, *The Happiness Hypothesis*, p. 118.

73 Of course there are some cases where this may not be so. Children on the autistic spectrum may have difficulties interpreting emotional cues or expressing emotional states. There are also cases where surgery or brain damage results in a loss of emotional ability, particularly where the damage is to the pre-frontal cortices.

74 Antonio Damasio, *Descartes' Error*, p. 133.

75 Alan Carr, *Positive Psychology*, p. 124.

76 Antonio Damasio writes about the 'as if' emotional circuitry. It seems that there is a circuit in the brain that enables us to imagine an emotional state without fully feeling it. This may be at the root of empathic ability. See *Descartes' Error*, p. 155.

77 Matthieu Ricard, *Happiness*, p. 131.

78 Adapted from Averill (1997), Larsen and Diener (1992) and Loehr and Schwartz (2003).

79 Daniel Goleman, *Emotional Intelligence*, p. 85.

80 Sonja Lyubomirsky, *The How of Happiness*, p. 271.

81 More detail, including the research that underpins these interventions can be found in *Emotional Intelligence*, Chapter 5.

82 Jonathan Haidt, *The Happiness Hypothesis*, p. 197.

83 For a full assessment of the impact of pre-frontal cortex damage, see Chapters 1 to 4 of *Descartes' Error*.

84 Sonja Lyubomirsky, *The How of Happiness*, p. 262.

85 Alan Carr, *Positive Psychology*, pp. 268–9.

86 Daniel Goleman, *Working With Emotional Intelligence*, p. 3.

87 Daniel Goleman, *Emotional Intelligence*, p. 115.

88 *Ibid.*, p. 116.

89 'Open' body language = eye contact frequently made and held; smiling or other facial expressions of warmth and acceptance; nothing covering the face (e.g. hair); limbs not crossed defensively over body: legs uncrossed, hands in lap. 'Closed' body language = eye contact avoided; facial expressions such as scowls or frowns worn; face covered by hands/hair; limbs crossed defensively.

Notes to Chapter 6: Resilience

[90] 'Optimism' by Carver and Scheier in *The Handbook of Positive Psychology* by Snyder and Lopez (eds).

[91] Martin Seligman, lecture delivered 10 September 2008 at Wellington College, Berkshire, UK.

[92] Carver and Scheier, *The Handbook of Positive Psychology*, p. 235.

[93] Peterson, Maier and Seligman, *Learned Helplessness*, pp. 20–25.

[94] Martin Seligman, *The Optimistic Child*, p. 129.

[95] Martin Seligman, lecture delivered 10 September 2008 at Wellington College, Berkshire, UK.

[96] For instance, *An Unquiet Mind*, Kay Redfield-Jamison's moving account of her own experience of bi-polar disorder makes it very clear that taking the drug lithium saved her life.

[97] Martin Seligman, *The Optimistic Child*, pp. 52–7.

[98] Quoted in *The Wise Heart*, by Jack Kornfield, p. 299.

[99] Alan Carr, *Positive Psychology*, p. 220.

[100] Martin Seligman's books *The Optimistic Child* and *Authentic Happiness* contain detailed explanations of the different types of exercise that you might like to practise with young people to develop optimism. You should also consult *The Resilience Factor* by Karen Reivich and Andrew Shatté. In the UK, Hertfordshire, South Tyneside and Manchester LEAs have been implementing Seligman's optimism programme in their secondary schools since September 2007, with great success. The evaluation of the impact was published in January 2009. It is numbered DCSF-RR094 and can be found at www.dcsf.gov.uk.

[101] *Ibid.*, p. 211.

[102] *Ibid.*

[103] *Ibid.*, p. 212.

[104] Jonathan Haidt, *The Happiness Hypothesis*, p. 140.

[105] *Ibid.*, p. 144.

Notes to Chapter 7: Strengths and flow

[106] Malcolm Gladwell, *Outliers*, extract published in the *Guardian* newspaper, 15 November 2008.

[107] Benjamin Bloom, quoted in *Mindset* by Carol Dweck, p. 65.

[108] Carol Dweck, *Mindset*, p. 59.

109 Chris Peterson, *A Primer in Positive Psychology*, pp. 198–205.

110 Carol Dweck, *Mindset*, p. 66.

111 John Ratey, *The User's Guide to the Brain*, p. 17.

112 Chris Peterson, *A Primer in Positive Psychology*, p. 198.

113 Alex Linley, *Average to A+*, p. 73.

114 Mihaly Csikszentmihalyi, *Flow*, p. 191.

115 Found at www.authentichappiness.org, along with other excellent tests.

116 Susan Harter, 'Authenticity', in *Handbook of Positive Psychology*, Snyder and Lopez (eds), p. 382.

117 *Ibid.*, p. 383.

118 *Ibid.*, p. 385.

119 *Ibid.*

120 *Ibid.*, p. 387.

121 Mihaly Csikszentmihalyi, *Flow*, p. 54.

122 *Ibid.*, p. 49.

123 *Ibid.*, pp. 208–10.

124 *Ibid.*, p. 88.

125 Alan Carr, *Positive Psychology*, p. 47.

126 *Ibid.*

127 *Ibid.*

128 Csikszentmihalyi, *Flow*, p. 99.

129 *Ibid.*, Chapter 6.

130 *Ibid.*, p. 149.

Notes to Chapter 8: Relationships

131 Reported at www.mirror.co.uk, accessed 4 October 2008.

132 Foresight Mental Capital and Well-being Project. Final Project report. The Government Office for Science. 2008, pp. 62–6.

133 Malcolm Gladwell, *Outliers*, p. 9.

134 'Happiness Spreads Like the Plague', Ewen Callaway, www.newscientist.com, accessed 11 December 2008.

135 Tania Singer, 'Happiness and its Causes' conference presentation, 9 October 2008. See also *Emotional Intelligence* by Daniel Goleman, p. 104 which describes Robert Levenson's research into married couples' physiological responses to each other's suffering.

136 http://www.pbs.org/wgbh/nova/sciencenow/3204/01-monkey.html; accessed 11 November 2008.

[137] This has been called into question by research conducted by Ilan Dinstein at New York University. *New Scientist*, 5 November 2008.

[138] George Vaillant, *Spiritual Evolution*, p. 154.

[139] The original experiment, designed in 1982 by Guth, Schmittberger and Schwarze, is described by Jonathan Haidt on p. 51 of *The Happiness Hypothesis*.

[140] David Watson, 'The Disposition to Experience Pleasurable Emotional States', in Snyder and Lopez (eds), *The Handbook of Positive Psychology*, p. 113.

[141] Myers and Diener (1995) quoted in 'Love' by Susan Hendrick and Clyde Hendrick in Snyder and Lopez (eds), *The Handbook of Positive Psychology*, p. 478.

[142] Ann Masten and Marie-Gabrielle Reed, 'Resilience in Development', in Snyder and Lopez (eds), *The Handbook of Positive Psychology*, p. 82.

[143] For example Argyle 2001, 2000, Diener and Seligman 2002, cited in Alan Carr, *Positive Psychology*, p. 23.

[144] Alan Carr, *Positive Psychology*, pp. 251–7 and 268–70.

[145] Susan Hendrick and Clyde Hendrick, 'Love', p. 472.

[146] Alan Carr, *Positive Psychology*, p. 270.

[147] Aislinn Simpson, 'Britain has worst underage sex rates', www.telegraph.co.uk, 7 January 2008, accessed 12 December 2008.

[148] 'Sexual Partners', www.statistics.gov.uk, accessed 12 December 2008.

[149] Alan Carr, *Positive Psychology*, pp. 259–60.

[150] Hendrick and Hendrick, 'Love', p. 475.

[151] Daniel Goleman, *Emotional Intelligence*, pp. 98–9.

[152] Alan Carr, *Positive Psychology*, p. 268.

[153] Singer *et al.* (2006), 'Empathic neural responses are modulated by the perceived fairness of others', *Nature*, 239(26).

[154] Tania Singer, *ibid.*

[155] Jonathan Haidt, *The Happiness Hypothesis*, p. 76.

[156] Described in *Emotional Intelligence*, p. 103.

[157] Martin Seligman, *Authentic Happiness*, p. 43.

[158] Sonja Lyubomirsky, *The How of Happiness*, pp. 130–32.

[159] Matt Ridley, *The Origins of Virtue*, p. 137.

[160] Robert Emmons and Charles Shelton, 'Gratitude and the Science of Positive Psychology', in Snyder and Lopez (eds), *The Handbook of Positive Psychology*, pp. 466–7.

[161] Martin Seligman, *Authentic Happiness*, p. 74.

[162] Alan Carr, *Positive Psychology*, p. 253.

[163] Discussed in *The Happiness Hypothesis*, p. 53.

[164] Alan Carr, *Positive Psychology*, pp. 255–6.

[165] www.leaplinx.com.

[166] Fiona Macbeth and Nic Fine, *Playing With Fire: Creative Conflict Resolution for Young Adults*, p. 3.

[167] Nic Fine and Fiona Macbeth, 'Playing With Fire. The Creative Use of Conflict', in Mariann Liebmann (ed.), *Arts Approaches to Conflict*, p. 37.

[168] The full description of this can be found in Nic Fine and Fiona Macbeth, 'Playing With Fire. The Creative Use of Conflict', in Mariann Liebmann (ed.), *Arts Approaches to Conflict*, pp. 55–65.

[169] *The Angels of Edgware Road* screened on Channel 4 in 2008.

[170] It can be found at www.authentichappiness.org and is free to take.

[171] Christopher Peterson, *A Primer in Positive Psychology*, p. 170.

[172] *Ibid.*, pp. 169–70.

[173] *Ibid.*, p. 186.

[174] Philip Zimbardo has come up with a number of guidelines for resisting evil situations that can cause us to abandon our values and do things we later regret. They can be found in Chapter 16 of his book *The Lucifer Effect* or on his website: www.lucifereffect.org, by clicking on the 'resisting influence' tab.

Notes to Chapter 9: Modern life is rubbish

[175] From *The Monk and the Philosopher*, pp. 306–7.

[176] Oliver James, *Affluenza*, p. 105.

[177] *Ibid.*, p. 180.

[178] Alain de Botton, *Status Anxiety*, pp. 45–6.

[179] Quoted in Richard Layard, *Happiness: Lessons from a New Science*, p. 41.

[180] *Ibid.*, p. 150.

[181] *Ibid.*, p. 162.

[182] *Ibid.*

[183] Barry Schwartz, *The Paradox of Choice*, p. 195.

[184] There is a nice resource to illustrate this. One of the deleted scenes from the Borat film depicts Borat, the dishevelled journalist from Kazakhstan visiting an American supermarket, where he is confronted with two refrigerator units full of different types of cheese.

[185] Barry Schwartz, *The Paradox of Choice*, Chapter 4.

[186] John Ratey, *The User's Guide to the Brain*, Chapter 3.

[187] Foresight Mental Capital and Well-being Project. Final Project report. The Government Office for Science. 2008, p. 57.

[188] Tal ben Shahar, *Happier*, p. 68.

[189] 'King of the Chavs – the neighbour from hell or a polite and popular charity

worker?' by Sandra Laville, published at www.guardian.co.uk, accessed 28 November 2008.

[190] Louis Theroux: 'Under the knife', broadcast in autumn 2007 on BBC2.

[191] Daniel Gilbert, *Stumbling on Happiness*, p. 18.

[192] Richard Layard, *Happiness: Lessons from a New Science*, p. 49.

[193] Martin Seligman, *Authentic Happiness*, p. 116.

[194] Alain de Botton, *Status Anxiety*, p. 62.

[195] 'Catch of the day: Is the Selfridges joke on us?' by Mark Hooper, published at www.guardian.co.uk, accessed 28 November 2008.

[196] Daniel Goleman, *Emotional Intelligence*, pp. 81–2.

[197] Ann Pettifor, campaigns director of Operation Noah. Debate held 9 October 2008 at the 'Happiness and its Causes' conference.

[198] Foresight Mental Capital and Well-being Project, p. 82.

[199] John Ratey, *Spark: The Revolutionary New Science of Exercise and the Brain*, Chapter 3.

[200] *Ibid.*, p. 61.

[201] ' "Infomania" worse than marijuana', www.news.bbc.co.uk, published 22 April 2005, accessed 14 December 2008.

[202] Tal ben Shahar, *Happier*, p. 152.

[203] Heart rate variability (HRV) is the moment to moment difference in the gap between heart beats. The heart does not beat in a regular way, like a metronome. As our body reacts to stimulus in the world outside, our heart beat changes: even at rest. Low variability in heart rate is quite a good predictor of poor chances of recovery after a heart attack, whereas high heart rate variability is an indicator of stress.

[204] 'A Cure for Stress?', published in the *Independent* on 28 May 2006. Accessed 12 November 2008.

[205] Source: www.ofcom.org.uk, accessed 1 December 2008.

[206] John Ratey, *The User's Guide to the Brain*, p. 112.

[207] Mihaly Csikszentmihalyi, *Flow*, p. 29.

[208] Source www.statistics.gov.uk, accessed 1 December 2008.

[209] Source www.which.co.uk, accessed 1 December 2008.

[210] Mihaly Csikszentmihalyi, *Flow*, p. 30.

[211] Richard Layard, *Happiness: Lessons from a New Science*, pp. 78–9.

[212] *Ibid.*, pp. 87–90.

Notes to Chapter 10: Mindfulness meditation, spirituality and meaning

213 Jon Kabat-Zinn, *Coming to Our Senses*, p. 24.

214 Jack Kornfield, *The Wise Heart*, p. 96.

215 Thich Nhat Hanh, *The Miracle of Mindfulness*, p. 36.

216 There is a lovely passage about this on p. 3 of *The Miracle of Mindfulness*.

217 For example, the Institute of Well-Being at the University Cambridge is currently (in 2008) conducting studies into the impact of teaching mindfulness in schools.

218 George Vaillant, *Spiritual Evolution*, p. 38.

219 For more information, go to www.mbsr.co.uk.

220 Jon Kabat-Zinn, *Coming to Our Senses*, p. 35.

221 'Three Year Follow-Up and Clinical Implications of a Mindfulness-Based Meditation Stress Reduction Intervention in the Treatment of Anxiety Disorders', Miller, Fletcher and Kabat-Zinn (1993). www.web.archive.org.

222 Ruth Baer (2003), 'Mindfulness Training as a Clinical Intervention: A Conceptual and Empirical Review', *American Psychological Association Journal*, www.web.archive.org.

223 Jon Kabat-Zinn, *Coming to Our Senses*, p. 372.

224 Jack Kornfield, *The Wise Heart*, p. 139.

225 Paper delivered at 'Happiness and its Causes' conference, 9 October 2008.

226 The Buddhist monk Matthieu Ricard discusses this in detail in Chapter 16 of his book *Happiness*.

227 Antonio Damasio, *Descartes' Error*, p. 120.

228 Jon Kabat-Zinn, *Coming to Our Senses*, pp. 368–75. The full peer-reviewed study was published in *Psychosomatic Medicine*, 65 (2003), pp. 564–70.

229 Lisa Takeuchi-Cullen, 'How to Get Smarter: One Breath at a Time', *Time*, 10 January 2006.

230 'Meditation Can Alter Brain Structure', Barbara Lantin, *The Times*, 14 March 2008.

231 John Ratey, *The User's Guide to the Brain*, pp. 61–2.

232 Matthieu Ricard, *Happiness: A Guide to Developing Life's Most Important Skill*, p. 201.

233 For example, in the UK, Bangor University Centre for Mindfulness Practice and Research, London Insight Meditation and Gaia House all provide excellent opportunities for training and retreats.

234 'Positive Affectivity' by David Watson, in Snyder and Lopez (eds), *The Handbook of Positive Psychology*, pp. 113–14.

[235] For an excellent study of religious extremism in Christianity, Islam and Judaism, have a look at *The Battle for God* by Karen Armstrong.

[236] George Vaillant, *Spiritual Evolution*, p. 63.

[237] *Ibid.*, p. 74.

[238] For example, Walter Pahnke's 1962 experiment at Boston University, discussed in *Religious Experience*, by Peter Cole, pp. 97–8.

[239] The research of neuroscientist Andrew Newberg seems to back this up. Jonathan Haidt discusses this in more detail in Chapter 10 of *The Happiness Hypothesis*.

[240] Jonathan Haidt, *The Happiness Hypothesis*, pp. 197–8.

[241] David Hay and Rebecca Nye, *The Spirit of the Child*, p. 127.

[242] *Daily Telegraph*, 25 October 2008.

[243] The discipline is best exemplified in the British television documentary, 'Jump London', first broadcast on Channel 4 in September 2003.

[244] Viktor Frankl, *Man's Search for Meaning*, p. 27.

[245] *Ibid.*, p. 85.

Bibliography

Aristotle (1955), *The Nicomachean Ethics*, London: Penguin.

Armstrong, K. (2004), *The Battle for God*, London: HarperCollins.

Ashton, M. and Varga, L. (2000), *101 Games for Groups*, Adelaide: Hyde Park Press.

Baylis, N. (2005), *Learning From Wonderful Lives*, Cambridge: Cambridge Well-Being Books.

ben Shahar, T. (2007), *Happier*, New York: McGraw-Hill.

Brandes, D. and Phillips, H. (1990), *The Gamester's Handbook*, Cheltenham: Stanley Thornes.

Carr, A. (2004), *Positive Psychology*, Hove: Routledge.

Cave, P. (2007), *Can a Robot be Human?* Oxford: Oneworld.

Claxton, G. (2008), *What's the Point of School?* Oxford: Oneworld.

Cole, P. (2005), *Religious Experience*, London: Hodder Muray.

Csikszentmihalyi, M. (2002), *Flow*, London: Random House.

Curran, A. (2008), *The Little Book of Big Stuff About the Brain*, Carmarthen: Crown House.

Dahl, R. (1974), *Fantastic Mr Fox*, London: Puffin.

Damasio, A. (2006), *Descartes' Error*, London: Vintage.

de Botton, A. (2005), *Status Anxiety*, London: Penguin.

Dweck, C. (2008), *Mindset*, New York: Ballantine Books.

Ekman, P. (2003), *Emotions Revealed*, London: Weidenfeld and Nicolson.

Fine, N. and Macbeth, F. (1996), 'Playing With Fire: The Creative Use of Conflict', in M. Liebmann (ed.), *Arts Approaches to Conflict*, London: Jessica Kingsley Publishers.

Foresight Mental Capital and Wellbeing Project (2008), Final Project, London: Government Office for Science.

Frankl, V. (2004), *Man's Search for Meaning*, London: Rider.

Gerhardt, S. (2004), *Why Love Matters*, Hove: Routledge.

Gilbert, D. (2007), *Stumbling on Happiness*, London: Harper Perennial.

Gladwell, M. (2008), *Outliers*, London: Penguin.

Goleman, D. (1996), *Emotional Intelligence*, London: Bloomsbury.

Goleman, D. (1998), *Working with Emotional Intelligence*, London: Bloomsbury.

Grayling, A. C. (2007), *The Choice of Hercules*, London: Weidenfeld and Nicolson.

Hadot, P. (1995), *Philosophy as a Way of Life*, Oxford: Blackwell.

Haidt, J. (2006), *The Happiness Hypothesis*, London: Random House.

Hay, D. and Nye, R. (2006), *The Spirit of the Child*, London: Jessica Kingsley Publishers.

Hoff, B. (1982), *The Tao of Pooh*, London: Methuen.

James, O. (2007), *Affluenza*, London: Random House.

Kabat-Zinn, J. (2005), *Coming To Our Senses*, New York: Hyperion.

Kornfield, J. (2008), *The Wise Heart*, London: Random House.

Law, S. (2003), *The Philosophy Gym*, London: Headline.

Layard, R. (2005), *Happiness: Lessons from a New Science*, London: Penguin.

Linley, A. (2008), *Average to A+*, Coventry: CAPP Press.

Lyubomirsky, S. (2007), *The How of Happiness*, London: Sphere.

Macbeth, F. and Fine, N. (1992), *Playing With Fire: Creative Conflict Resolution for Young Adults*, Leicester: Youth Works Press.

Murdoch, A. and Oldershaw, D-L. (2008), *16 Guidelines for a Happy Life, the basics*, London: Essential Education.

Murdoch, I. (2001), *The Sovereignty of Good*, Abingdon: Routledge.

Peterson, C. (2006), *A Primer in Positive Psychology*, New York: Oxford University Press.

Peterson, C., Maier, S. and Seligman, M. (1993), *Learned Helplessness, A Theory for the Age of Personal Control*, New York: Oxford University Press.

Ratey, J. (2001), *A User's Guide to the Brain*, New York: Random House.

Ratey, J. (2008), *Spark*, New York: Little, Brown and Company.

Redfield Jamison, K. (1997), *An Unquiet Mind*, London: Pan Macmillan.

Reivich, K. and Shatté, A. (2002), *The Resilience Factor*, New York, Broadway Books.

Revel, J.-F. and Ricard, M. (1998), *The Monk and the Philosopher*, New York: Schocken.

Ricard, M. (2006), *Happiness, A Guide to Developing Life's Most Important Skill*, New York: Little, Brown and Company.

Richardson, A. (2006), *They Are What You Feed Them*, London: HarperCollins.

Ridley, M. (1997), *The Origins of Virtue*, London: Penguin.

Russell, B. (1993), *The Conquest of Happiness*, Abingdon: Routledge.

Schoch, R. (2006), *The Secrets of Happiness*, London: Profile.

Schwartz, B. (2005), *The Paradox of Choice*, New York: HarperCollins.

Seligman, M. (2003), *Authentic Happiness*, London: Nicholas Brealey.

Seligman, M., Reivich, K., Jaycox, L. and Gillham, J. (1996), *The Optimistic Child*, New York: Harper Perennial.

Slater, L. (2004), *Opening Skinner's Box*, London: Bloomsbury.

Snyder, C. and Lopez, S (eds) (2005), *The Handbook of Positive Psychology*, Oxford: Oxford University Press.

Swift, J. (1971), *Gulliver's Travels*, Oxford: Oxford University Press.

Thich Nhat Hanh (1991), *The Miracle of Mindfulness*, London: Rider.

Vaillant, G. (2008), *Spiritual Evolution*, New York: Broadway.

Warburton, N. (1996), *Thinking from A to Z*, Abingdon: Routledge.

Whyte, J. (2003), *Bad Thoughts, A Guide to Clear Thinking*, London: Corvo Books.

Zimbardo, P. (2007), *The Lucifer Effect, How Good People Turn Evil*, London: Random House.

Index